Weaving *Te Whāriki*

Aotearoa New Zealand's Early Childhood
Curriculum Framework in Theory and Practice

3RD EDITION

Edited by Alexandra C. Gunn and Joce Nuttall

NZCER PRESS

Wellington 2019

NZCER PRESS

New Zealand Council for Educational Research
PO Box 3237
Wellington
New Zealand

www.nzcer.org.nz

© Authors, 2019

ISBN: 978-1-98-854280-5

No part of the publication may be copied, stored, or communicated in any form by any means (paper or digital), including recording or storing in an electronic retrieval system without the written permission of the publisher.
Education institutions that hold a current licence with Copyright Licensing New Zealand may copy from this book in strict accordance with the terms of the CLNZ Licence.

A catalogue record for this book is available from the National Library of New Zealand.

Designed by Re:brand

Contents

ABOUT THE AUTHORS	vii
INTRODUCTION *Alexandra C. Gunn and Joce Nuttall*	1
PART 1: THE DEVELOPMENT OF *TE WHĀRIKI*	5

CHAPTER 1
Te Whāriki, 2017: A refreshed rallying point for the early childhood sector in
Aotearoa New Zealand 7
Sarah Te One and Jane Ewens

Introduction	7
The rationale for refreshing the 1996 edition of *Te Whāriki*	8
The process for the refresh and consultation	14
Conclusion	17

CHAPTER 2
Tōku Rangatiratanga nā te Mana Mātauranga: "Knowledge and Power Set Me Free ..."   25
Tilly Te Koingo, Lady Reedy

Their horizon, my heritage	26
A tangata whenua perspective of early learning	28
For some, indoctrination took place before they were born ...	29
But what about today?	32
Dimensions of the learner	36
Ngā Taumata Whakahirahira	37
Conclusion	39
Te Whāriki: The Explanations	40

CHAPTER 3
Te hōhonutanga o *Te Whāriki*: Developing a deeper understanding of *Te Whāriki*   45
Lesley Rameka and Brenda Soutar

Introduction	45
Te Tiriti o Waitangi	47
Kaupapa Māori theory	48
Whakataukī	49
Te reo Māori	50
Tikanga Māori	52
Challenges and potential	53

CHAPTER 4
Reconceptualising professional learning as knotworking: Actualising the transformative potential of *Te Whāriki* — 57
Maria Cooper, Helen Hedges, and Joanna Williamson

Introduction	57
The transformative potential of *Te Whāriki*	58
Implementing *Te Whāriki*: A complex issue	59
Theory and pedagogy	61
Professional learning and development: History and research findings	62
A CHAT reconceptualisation of PLD: Negotiated knotworking	65
Creating a knotworking culture	66
Conclusion	68

PART 2: *TE WHĀRIKI* IN PRACTICE — 71

CHAPTER 5
Frayed and fragmented: *Te Whāriki* unwoven — 73
Jenny Ritchie and Mere Skerrett

Introduction	73
Te Whāriki and Te Tiriti o Waitangi: Two versions, differing outcomes	74
(Mis)understandings of Te Tiriti o Waitangi	79
Demographic challenges	81
Responding to the crisis of the Anthropocene and the challenge of meeting the SDGs	83
Implications for teacher education and the Ministry of Education	85
Conclusion	86

CHAPTER 6
Towards an authentic implementation of Teu Le Va and Talanoa as Pacific cultural paradigms in early childhood education in Aotearoa New Zealand — 91
Diane Mara

Introduction	91
Analysis of *Te Whāriki* and Pasifika ECE in Aotearoa New Zealand	92
Tapasā: A framework for Pacific professional cultural competence	95
A small-scale study with early childhood kaiako: Culturally responsive pedagogy focused on Pasifika models and approaches	97
Gathering of evidence phase	99
Analysing the evidence using Pacific frameworks	99
Conclusion	102
Acknowledgements	103

CHAPTER 7
The paradox of age for the infants and toddlers of *Te Whāriki* — 105
E. Jayne White

Introduction	105
Contemplating the paradox of age	107
Reconciliation of the paradox for infants and toddlers in *Te Whāriki*	114

CHAPTER 8
Moving *Te Whāriki* from rhetoric to reality for disabled children and their whānau in early childhood education   119
Bernadette Macartney

Introduction	119
Barriers in the education of disabled learners in Aotearoa New Zealand	120
Sociocultural interpretations of disability and diversity	122
Te Whāriki and ableism	124
Discourses and approaches to diversity within *Te Whāriki*	125
Conclusion	129

CHAPTER 9
***Te Whāriki*, possibility thinking and Learning Stories: Tracking the progress**   135
Margaret Carr, Wendy Lee, Karen Ramsey, Kim Parkinson, Nadine Priebs, and Vera Brown

Introduction	135
PART ONE: Learning "how to learn": knowledge, skills, attitudes and dispositions that support lifelong learning	136
PART TWO: They need to learn "how to learn" so that they can engage with new contexts, opportunities and challenges with optimism and resourcefulness	139
PART THREE: *Te Whāriki* emphasises the development of knowledge, skills, attitudes, and dispositions that support lifelong learning	139
Task 1: Dictating Stories and Making Books	140
Task 2: Mosaic Work	143
Task 3: Lunch Preparation	144
Tracking the learning progress: A conclusion	145

CHAPTER 10
Click, drag, drop, resize, omit: An activity theory view of how technology is mediating the production of learning in early childhood education   149
Alexandra C. Gunn and Danneille Reeves

Viewing teachers' assessment work through activity theory	150
The context of teachers' assessment work in Aotearoa New Zealand at this time	151
Inputting information and working with and through software to construct stories about learning	152
Constructing learning with images and text	156

CHAPTER 11
Back to the future: Curriculum and the pedagogue in the age of Communities of Learning | Kāhui Ako   163
Andrew Gibbons and Sandy Farquhar

Introduction	163
Theorising curriculum	166
Te Whāriki and *The New Zealand Curriculum*	167
Curriculum coherence and transitions	170
Communities of Learning and curriculum dialogue	171
Concluding thoughts	174

PART 3: *TE WHĀRIKI* IN INTERNATIONAL CONTEXTS — 179

CHAPTER 12
Re-reading and re-activating *Te Whāriki* through a posthuman childhood studies lens — 181
Marek Tesar and Sonja Arndt

Introduction	181
Childhood studies as a point of departure	183
Te Whāriki's child and people, places, and things	186
Re-activating *Te Whāriki*'s child through a posthuman childhood studies lens	188
Concluding comments: Perpetually re-activating *Te Whāriki*	192

CHAPTER 13
The theoretical foundations of *Te Whāriki* and the *Early Years Learning Framework*: Enduring and living or capturing fossilised practices? — 195
Marilyn Fleer

Introduction	195
Methodological note	197
A static document within a dynamic research context	198
Curriculum longevity or has it passed its use-by date?	199
Theoretical genealogy	199
Theoretical plurality made visible or covertly embedded?	202
Theoretical plurality in early childhood curriculum in Australia	205
Conclusion	208

CHAPTER 14
***Te Whāriki* and the Nordic model: Comments on *Te Whāriki* from a Norwegian and Danish perspective** — 213
Stig Broström

Introduction	213
Implementation of Nordic curricula for early years education and care	214
Te Whāriki seen in the light of a Nordic educational perspective	223
Conclusion	225

CHAPTER 15
Early childhood curriculum policy texts in England and Aotearoa New Zealand: A rhetorical analysis — 231
Elizabeth Wood and Joce Nuttall

Rhetorical analysis	232
Rhetorical features of the *Early Years Foundation Stage*	233
Rhetorical features of *Te Whāriki*	238
Te Whāriki, the *EYFS*, and the rhetoric of early years reform	241

INDEX — 245

About the authors

Sonja Arndt is a lecturer in the Melbourne Graduate School of Education at the University of Melbourne. She has been involved in early childhood education in Aotearoa New Zealand and internationally for 30 years as a teacher, researcher, and lecturer. Sonja is a co-editor of the book series titled *Children: Global posthumanist perspectives and materialist theories*, and her teaching, research, and scholarship focus on global and intercultural studies, intersecting childhood studies, early childhood education, and philosophy in/of education.

Stig Broström holds a PhD in early childhood education. He is Professor Emeritus in early childhood education at Danish School of Education, Aarhus University. His main areas of research are based in cultural historical theory related to preschool, transition to school, the first years in school, curriculum theory, science and sustainability, children's play, narrative and aesthetic learning, and social competence and friendship.

Vera Brown was a 4-year-old at Roskill South Kindergarten during the collection of data for Chapter 9. The Learning Stories in that chapter were from her portfolio. Vera and her mother have given permission for these stories to be published.

Margaret Carr is Professor of Education and a co-Director of the Early Years Research Centre at the University of Waikato. She was a co-author with Helen May, Tilly Reedy, and Tamati Reedy of the 1996 *Te Whāriki* curriculum, and has worked on a number of research projects alongside teachers in early childhood centres. Margaret's topics and publications include work on narrative assessments, learning 'in the making', literacy and narrative in the early years, young children visiting museums, and creative capacity building.

Maria Cooper is a Senior Lecturer at the Faculty of Education and Social Work at the University of Auckland. Her research and teaching interests include teachers' collective leadership, early years curriculum, infant and toddler pedagogy, and cultural diversity in ECE.

Jane Ewens is the Programme Manager Education at Toi Ohomai Institute of Technology. She has recently completed a PhD focused on early childhood teacher beliefs about what it takes to be a good early childhood teacher. Her research interests include teacher education and early childhood teaching.

Sandy Farquhar is a Senior Lecturer in the Faculty of Education and Social Work at the University of Auckland. Her research and teaching focuses on critical issues in curriculum, policy, and teacher professionalism. Her current research is around teachers' work, identity, and wellbeing.

Laureate Professor **Marilyn Fleer** holds the Foundation Chair of Early Childhood Education and Development at Monash University, Australia. She was awarded the 2018 Kathleen Fitzpatrick Laureate Fellowship by the Australian Research Council and was a former President of the International Society of Cultural-historical Activity Research (ISCAR). Additionally, she holds the positions of honorary Research Fellow in the Department of Education, University of Oxford, and a Professor II position in the KINDKnow Centre, Western Norway University of Applied Sciences.

Andrew Gibbons is an Associate Professor at the School of Education, Auckland University of Technology. His research engages with the philosophy of early childhood education, with a particular focus on the possibilities and limitations of early childhood education policy.

Alexandra Gunn is Associate Professor of Education at the University of Otago College of Education. An early childhood teacher by profession, Alex teaches and conducts research into many aspects of early childhood education, including curriculum, assessment, teachers' beliefs, and practice.

Helen Hedges is Professor of Early Childhood Education in the Faculty of Education and Social Work at the University of Auckland. Helen's research programme explores children's and teachers' interests, knowledge, and learning in the contexts of early childhood education and teacher education.

Wendy Lee is the Director of the Educational Leadership Project, a professional learning provider for the early childhood education sector New Zealand. Formerly she was a teacher, lecturer, and researcher. Over the past two decades she has been involved in leading professional learning projects focused on *Te Whāriki*. Wendy was an author for the book *Understanding the* Te Whāriki *Approach* and has co-authored two books on Learning Stories with Margaret Carr.

Bernadette Macartney is an early childhood teacher, teacher educator, writer, and disability rights activist. She is the mum of a young disabled person. Her doctoral research explored the presence and effects of deficit discourses in early childhood education on young disabled children and their families. Her writing also explores *Te Whāriki* as a framework for critical thinking to guide and sustain inclusive teaching, communities, and environments.

Diane Mara is a Pacific consultant working across the education, health, and social services sectors on community-focused projects. Dr Mara is currently a member of the Ministry of Social Development Pacific Steering Group developing the newly launched Pacific Prosperity Plan. She is also a member of the Oranga Tamariki Pacific Panel advising the agency on working with Pacific children, youth, and families. Diane is a member of the Hawke's Bay District Health Board Consumer Council and contributed to the team that recently completed the board's Disability Strategy. Dr Mara continues her work with IHC on the national Member Council and as Chair of the Napier Family Centre Board.

Joce Nuttall is a Research Professor in the Institute for Learning Sciences and Teacher Education in the Faculty of Education at Australian Catholic University. Joce's research interests are in early childhood policy, workforce, and the continuing professional development of early childhood teachers.

Kim Parkinson is a teacher at Roskill South Kindergarten. Kim has been part of the Roskill South teaching team for 13 years and has been involved in internal and external research projects. She has co-presented at workshops and conferences, and has contributed Learning Stories to other early childhood publications. Kim's pedagogical practice aims to deeply embed the principles of *Te Whāriki*.

Nadine Priebs is a teacher at Roskill South Kindergarten. Nadine has been part of the Roskill South teaching team for 8 years and during this time has been involved in internal and external research projects. Nadine's pedagogical practice aims to deeply embed the principles of *Te Whāriki*. She has co-presented at workshops and conferences, and has contributed Learning Stories to other early childhood publications.

Lesley Rameka is a Senior Research Fellow at the Wilf Malcom Institute of Educational Research in the Faculty of Education at the University of Waikato. Lesley has worked in early childhood education for over thirty years, beginning her journey in Te Kōhanga Reo and working in a number of professional development and tertiary education providers over her career.

Karen Ramsey was the Lead Researcher of the 3-year action research project undertaken as a Centre of Innovation at Roskill South Kindergarten, where she has been Head Teacher since 1997. She has presented at several national and international conferences, and authored and co-authored a number of early childhood papers and articles. Karen's pedagogical practice aims to deeply embed the principles of *Te Whāriki*.

Lady Tilly Reedy (Ngāti Porou), with her husband Sir Tamat Reedy, spearheaded the development of the 1996 publication of *Te Whāriki* in its Māori form. Together they were instrumental in the development of early childhood Māori-language immersion education in Aotearoa New Zealand through the Te Kōhanga Reo National Trust.

Danneille Reeves is an early childhood kaiako (teacher) who works with children and families in community-based early childhood education in Ōtepoti I Dunedin. Danneille is committed to ongoing professional learning, and is keen to develop ideas and practices through collaborative research.

Jenny Ritchie is an Associate Professor in Te Puna Akopai, the School of Education at Te Herenga Waka Victoria University of Wellington, New Zealand. Her research and teaching focuses on social, cultural, and ecological justice in early childhood care and education.

Mere Skerrett is a Senior Lecturer in early years teacher education in the School of Education, Victoria University, and is Co-President of the *New Zealand Association for Research in Education (NZARE)*. Her research interests focus on Indigenous languages, early years learning with a focus on decolonising pedagogies, Indigenous epistemologies, bilingualism/biliteracy, and language/s acquisition.

Brenda Soutar is a founding member and leader of Mana Tamariki, a Māori immersion educational setting for infants through to the end of high school. She was Lead Researcher for the Mana Tamariki Centres of Innovation project, Associate Investigator for a Marsden Fund Research Project collaboration with the University of Waikato, and a member of the *Te Whāriki* update writing team in 2017.

Sarah Te One works for Tātai Aho Rau CORE Education as a facilitator and researcher currently involved with projects about children's wellbeing in primary and secondary schools, and innovative practices with teachers working with children newly entering school. Sarah has been part of a team designing hui (gatherings), webinars, and resources to support awareness about, and engagement with, *Te Whāriki* 2017. Sarah is a passionate advocate for children's rights in all her work.

Marek Tesar is Associate Professor of Childhood Studies and Early Childhood Education, and Associate Dean International, in the Faculty of Education and Social Work at the University of Auckland. His scholarship focuses on childhoods and their connection with educational philosophy, policy, pedagogy, methodology, and curriculum. His work draws on his background as a qualified teacher as well as his extensive knowledge of international education systems.

About the authors

E. Jayne White has spent most of her professional life working with *Te Whariki* as an ECE teacher and scholar in Aotearoa New Zealand. Jayne is President of the Association for Visual Pedagogies and Co-Editor of *Video Journal of Education and Pedagogy*, reflecting her life-long interest in the potential of video in education to revision pedagogies and philosophies, particularly with infants and toddlers. In her current role as Professorial Lead of RMIT University's Pedagogies of Possibility Lab (PoPLab), she is working to promote this potential across all aspects of the life span and disciplines.

Joanna Williamson is studying for her PhD in early childhood education at the University of Auckland. She has taught across secondary, early childhood, and tertiary settings, and owns two early childhood centres that have received high quality reviews. Her research interests include curriculum and pedagogy, early language and literacy, and concept mediation.

Elizabeth Wood is Professor of Education in the School of Education at the University of Sheffield, specialising in critical perspectives on early childhood education. Her research and teaching focus on learning, pedagogy and curriculum, play and learning, critical policy analysis, and teachers' knowledge and practices.

Introduction

Alexandra C. Gunn
University of Otago College of Education, Dunedin, New Zealand

Joce Nuttall
Institute for Learning Sciences and Teacher Education, Faculty of Education and Arts,
Australian Catholic University, Melbourne, Australia

Aotearoa New Zealand's early childhood curriculum framework, *Te Whāriki* (Ministry of Education, 1996) was recognised internationally as an innovative and far-sighted early childhood curriculum policy text on its first publication. In 2017 the New Zealand Ministry of Education released a 'refreshed' version of the 1996 framework, which aimed to both underscore and strengthen the principles upon which *Te Whāriki* was based, and to update its content and advice about quality teaching and learning in early childhood education in the 21st century.

This volume brings together chapters that revise and update scholarship from earlier editions of *Weaving Te Whāriki* (Nuttall, 2003, 2013), as well as adding new chapters. As a collection, the chapters respond to the 2017 version of *Te Whāriki*, as well as demonstrating the extent of the framework's influence since it was first released in its draft form in 1993. Although originally intended as a scholarly curriculum studies volume (as is the case with this 3rd edition), the first and second editions of *Weaving Te Whāriki* have also become essential texts for undergraduate and postgraduate early childhood education students. Additionally, many early childhood services and organisations make *Weaving Te Whāriki* available as part of their staff library, and the earlier editions have been widely cited by international scholars in their considerations of curriculum policy texts around the world. The chapters in this edition present a mix of empirical work conducted in field settings, empirical work grounded in document analysis, and commentaries on cultural and historical features of curriculum and curriculum implementation, including curriculum policy development in Aotearoa New Zealand and elsewhere—Denmark, Norway, Australia, and England.

The volume is divided thematically into three sections. Part 1 (Chapters 1 to 4) reflects on the initial development of *Te Whāriki* and its enduring influence. This section includes a new chapter about the role of *Te Whāriki* in supporting teachers to identify 'what matters' in early childhood curriculum provision, and a new chapter on *Te Whāriki*, enduring effects of colonisation, and obligations to Te Tiriti o Waitangi (Aotearoa New Zealand's founding treaty). Part 2 (Chapters 5 to 11) examines *Te Whāriki* in practice contexts including work in Pasifika communities, with infants and toddlers, and children with disabilities and their families. This section includes a new chapter on assessment in early childhood settings and includes reconsideration of notions of progress and the context of learning and its influence. It also brings critical voices into discussions over the framework's implementation, and its potential for challenging educational inequity and injustices in the education system more generally. Part 3 (Chapters 12 to 15) considers *Te Whāriki* in the context of international trends in early childhood curriculum policy development. It includes a new chapter on *Te Whāriki* from the perspective of recent international work on the new sociology of childhood.

As well as these three section themes, the volume offers several conceptual themes that resonate across chapters. These include the growing emphasis on 'children's voice' in curriculum construction, assessment, and evaluation; and recognition of children's efforts with teachers to create meaningful curriculum and learning for all. Questions of power sharing, whose curriculum is being enacted, and kaiako's responsibilities in supporting and recognising children's agency feature here. The collection urges kaiako to recognise children's rights and participation as social actors, to be active in their lives and communities, and be central to quality early childhood education practice and curriculum implementation.

A second conceptual theme concerns re-engagement with theoretical influences in and on *Te Whāriki*. Taking a lead from the framework's content regarding underpinning theories and approaches, writers in this volume frequently urge kaiako to read, think, and practice beyond the principally developmental and socio-culturally-based interpretations of *Te Whāriki* that have previously dominated. In an effort to actualise relevant and culturally-sustaining early childhood education, the writers convey an urgency over the pursuit of ever more inclusive, socially just, and responsive early childhood education practice. Theory is positioned as central to shaping and expanding practice, and the introduction of post-foundational and new sociology of childhood ideas is a welcome addition in this volume.

A third conceptual theme woven through *Weaving Te Whāriki*'s third edition concerns the authors' systematic and close critiques of the framework's text and associated policy settings to support implementation. The textual analyses provide an acute sense of both the fragility of the framework, in that its words and images can

Introduction

and should be read multiply, and its mobility, in that such re-readings continually open possibilities for new insights, conversations, and experiences of how early childhood education policy and practice might continue to evolve. This delving deeper into the texts of *Te Whāriki* includes discussions of the whakataukī included in the framework, questions over uses, and, as writers here have argued in some cases, the misuse of particular terms and ideas (for example, the use of the word "additional" in reference to children with disabilities), and the positioning of Te Tiriti o Waitangi and its English language translation as documents of equivalent status. A strength of this volume is that these critiques can be read here alongside considerations of policy settings for effective implementation, provoking new and continuing conversations for thinking about, and working with, the framework.

We trust students of early childhood education, practitioners, policymakers, and academics alike will be challenged and stimulated by the new and renewed chapters in this edition.

PART 1

The development of *Te Whāriki*

CHAPTER 1

Te Whāriki, 2017: A refreshed rallying point for the early childhood sector in Aotearoa New Zealand

Sarah Te One and Jane Ewens

Introduction

Te Whāriki (Ministry of Education, 1996) has been "refreshed". Since it burst onto the scene in 1996, locally and globally, its conceptual, non-prescriptive framework has become a rallying point for Aotearoa New Zealand's early childhood sector and one which set it apart from other curricular developments of the time (Nuttall, 2013; May & Carr, 2016). Most significantly, the concept of a whāriki, a woven mat, where theory, culture, and practice were interwoven, was located in te ao Māori—the Māori world. The ideological, educational and cultural agendas of that time led to the emergence of an idea that was, prior to the late 1980s, almost anathema to early childhood education: national curriculum guidelines. In a ground-breaking, innovative process, the curriculum guidelines were founded on an Indigenous conceptual framework, which incorporated Māori and Western principles of learning and teaching alongside views of children as rights holders—citizens in a democratic society reflecting very "Kiwi" values about childhood in a country with a great backyard.[1] This chapter describes the background context to the refresh, and considers some of the local and global influences on children, childhoods, and curriculum on the revision, including an account of the rationale and process for the update.

---

1 For an historical account of the original version of *Te Whāriki*, see the previous editions of this book (Nuttall, 2003; 2013) notably Chapters 1 and 2. See also May & Carr (2016), pp. 316–326.

The rationale for refreshing the 1996 edition of *Te Whāriki*

A range of factors contributed to the rationale for updating, reviewing, and refreshing the 1996 edition of *Te Whāriki*. Since the 1990s, significantly more—and younger— children have been enrolled in and attending early learning services (Ministry of Education, 2017b). Long-term plans to ensure educational success for Māori as Māori became part of the policy landscape (Ministry of Education, 2013; Education Council, n.d.) and revisions of *The New Zealand Curriculum* (Ministry of Education, 2007) included explicit links to *Te Marautanga o Aotearoa* (Ministry of Education, 2008) and Te Aho Mātua[2]—the curriculum frameworks for Māori immersion and Kura Kaupapa Māori. International and national reviews highlighted concerns about the current system's response to equity in relation to the long tail of underachievement (Action for Children and Youth Aotearoa, 2015; Office of the Children's Commissioner, 2018; Office of the Children's Commissioner & Oranga Tamariki, 2019; UN Committee on the Rights of the Child, 2016). Also, since the 2000s the demographic profile (in Auckland especially) had diversified, presenting its own set of challenges, with over 120 different languages now recorded as spoken in Aotearoa New Zealand. Furthermore, by 2017 the digital age had well and truly arrived for children and adults. Learning Stories (Carr, 2001) are now accessible online and many early years services use Facebook as a way to communicate with whānau. A rumbling backdrop to these issues was global consciousness about the impact of climate change and the importance of sustainable futures. The issues were summarised by the Ministry of Education and CORE Education (2017) for the sector as:

- higher participation in ECE
- younger children in ECE for longer
- Māori medium pathways
- ethnic and cultural diversity
- digital tools—children and adults
- global consciousness and environmental sustainability
- changes in theory and practice
- a systems challenge for equity and excellence.

Lists, however, are deceptively simple and, on closer inspection, each bullet point represents a contested space between aspiration, policy, and practice. In the next sections, we discuss the backdrop to the refresh, and the emerging global and local critique of the 2017 version of *Te Whāriki*.

---

2 See https://www.educationcounts.govt.nz/publications/91416/105966/79522/te-aho-matua

1: *Te Whāriki*, 2017: A refreshed rallying point for the early childhood sector in Aotearoa New Zealand

Backdrop to the refresh: Wicked problems facing children

Since the 1984 Labour Government adopted neoliberal economic policies in an attempt to reignite a stagnant economy and confront growing inequality, a discourse of vulnerability has emerged in social and educational policy in Aotearoa New Zealand about child wellbeing (Kelsey, 1997; Boston & Holland, 1987). An almost uncritical belief in the ability of the market to redress growing disparity led to a restructure of the public sector, including education administration and provision (Boston & Chapple, 2014; Rashbrooke, 2013). The public sector was decimated, unemployment increased, and whole communities were impacted negatively (Rashbrooke, 2013).

The effects of these policies were dramatic, polarising, and long-lasting, especially for children (see Boston & Chapple, 2014; Nairn, Higgins, & Sligo, 2012). Aotearoa New Zealand's ratings for overall child wellbeing and educational achievement have been slipping on the world stage (see Chzhen, Gromada, Gwyther, Cuesta, & Bruckauf, 2018). High rates of child abuse, a housing crisis, poverty, and concerns about inequality—so-called "wicked problems" (Cribb, Lane, Penny, van Delden & Irwin, 2011)—underpin an unprecedented interest in the critical importance of the early years of a child's life (Grimmond, 2011; Morton et al, 2015; Poulton, 2012). Māori children, Pacific children, refugee children, and children with disabilities are more likely to experience hardship than their Pākehā peers (Action for Children and Youth Aotearoa, 2015; Duncanson et al. 2017; Morton et al., 2017).

The relatively low participation rate in ECE for these target groups has been well documented (see, for example, Action for Children and Youth Aotearoa, 2015; Mitchell, 2017; Morton et al., 2017; UN Committee on the Rights of the Child, 2016). Based on research that demonstrates participation in early education of good quality can result in positive social and educational outcomes, the National-led coalition Government from 2009 to 2018 proposed a targeted funding system for early childhood services as a solution (see Mitchell, Meagher-Lundberg, Arndt, & Kara, 2016). But in a "robbing Peter to pay Paul" scenario, the injection of funds to increase participation targeting vulnerable children was undermined somewhat by removing the funding incentive to employ fully-trained and registered teachers.

So, despite a focus on child-centred policy, rigorous analyses of increases in budgets for the early childhood education sector under the National-led coalition indicated that these did not compensate for previous cutbacks and only included basic funding for the increased numbers of children participating (Child Poverty Action Group, 2014). In other words, while the government's $1b investment in early education looked impressive, after taking inflation and increased child numbers into account, funding was less than it had been in 2008. Increases between 2011 and 2015 were still lower than the recommended 1% of GDP (Action for Children and Youth Aotearoa, 2015).

In summary, issues such as hunger, lack of heating, homelessness, and poor health were seriously disruptive to a significant number of children in Aotearoa New Zealand in both the short and long-term (Office of the Children's Commissioner & Oranga Tamariki, 2019). Targeting participation rates in early learning services as a way to improve life course outcomes was not matched by an equivalent investment in known structural quality indicators such as teacher–child ratios and qualified, registered teachers, or even good pay and work conditions. This gave rise to concerns about the quality of services. Inequitable delivery of culturally appropriate, responsive ECE services to Māori and Pacific families also remains an issue of concern (UN Committee on the Rights of the Child, 2016; Office of the Children's Commissioner, 2018; Ritchie, 2018; Skerrett, 2018). Children with disabilities have their access to early childhood education restricted if they do not have specialist support workers funded and in place (Action for Children and Youth Aotearoa, 2016a, 2016b).

Underlying concerns and emerging critique of *Te Whāriki* (1996)

> We love *Te Whāriki*, we do *Te Whāriki*, and we teach courses on *Te Whāriki*. But to what extent are we really engaging with *Te Whāriki*, exploring *Te Whāriki*, debating *Te Whāriki*, confronting *Te Whāriki*, and confronting ourselves? (May, 2017, p. 5)

Curriculum documents are political instruments and serve to reinforce and promote the status quo. They are not educationally neutral. As early as 1996, and again in 2008, Cullen (1996, 2008) identified tensions between theoretical understandings and practice arising from *Te Whāriki*, something Helen May (2007, cited in Ritchie, 2018) described as an ongoing issue for teachers. Since then, many have noted the recent accumulation of critical evaluations of *Te Whāriki* (see, for example, Alvestad, Duncan, & Berge, 2009; Dalli, 2011; McLachlan, 2018; Te One, 2013). These range from pedagogical, pragmatic concerns about a disconnect between aims and content—where teachers used *Te Whāriki* to justify existing practices—to concerns that the transformational potential of *Te Whāriki*'s aspirations towards a socially just society remain unrealised (see Duhn, 2006; Farquhar, 2010; May, 2009). Dalli (2011) was one of many to observe that, despite widespread acceptance at the time, possibly tinged with relief, the 1996 version of the curriculum did not explicate aims, objectives, and measurable outcomes for learning. However, this did not "future proof" the early childhood sector against schoolification (May, 2002, cited in Gunn & Gasson, 2016). The threat of standardised measures of assessment emerged again in 2010 with the introduction of National Standards in literacy and numeracy (Gunn & Gasson, 2016). The trickle-down effect of these could be seen in early childhood service advertisements promoting special numeracy and literacy programmes as preparation for school and, as such, potentially narrowing the intent of *Te Whāriki* as an open-ended framework for learning possibilities (Alcock &

Haggerty, 2013). *Te Whāriki*'s child-centred pedagogy, with its rights-based framework (Te One, 2009), was "neither a guaranteed outcome in day-to-day practice, nor necessarily an unproblematic one" (Dalli, 2011, p. 3).

From the early 2000s, numerous Education Review Office (ERO) publications (for example, 2009, 2011, 2012, 2013, 2016) revealed "mounting evidence that the early childhood sector was struggling with implementation" (McLachlan, 2018, p. 46). More work to support effective implementation of self-review was also needed to realise the full potential of *Te Whāriki* (Education Review Office, 2009). In attending to children's social and emotional competence, 45% of services were highly effective, and the remaining 55% ranged from mostly effective (38%), through somewhat effective (14%) to ineffective (3%) (Education Review Office, 2011). The ERO (2015) review of curriculum for infants and toddlers "showed that centres with 100% qualified staff were included in the list of 'least responsive' services" (McLachlan, 2018, p. 46).

Equally concerning was an ERO review of partnership with Māori whānau in 2012 which noted that, while 78% of services had built positive relationships with whānau, only 10% had built the "effective and culturally responsive partnerships" required for meaningful dialogue and exchange (Education Review Office, 2012, p. 9). *Te Whāriki*'s status as an international "first", which gave primacy to the image of an empowered Māori child with a rich, meaningful, and relevant cultural repertoire, was contradicted by discourses that class Māori tamariki (children) as "at risk and under privileged" (May, 2009, p. 300). Dalli (personal communication, July, 2012) noted that the aim of a truly bicultural curriculum remains "a distant lodestar".

Jenny Ritchie is one scholar who has consistently raised concerns that "the non-prescriptive nature of the document allowed teachers to 'do *Te Whāriki*' without addressing bicultural aspirations" (Ritchie, 2018, p. 10, citing Ritchie, 2003). Maintaining the integrity of bicultural practices remains a challenge and, as ERO (2013) noted, despite many services including Te Tiriti o Waitangi in their philosophy statements, "often bicultural practice meant the use of basic te reo, some waiata in the programme, resources such as puzzles that depicted aspects of te ao Māori and posters and photographs that reflected aspects of Māori culture" (Education Review Office, 2013, p. 13). Ritchie (2018) comments that "moving beyond such tokenism remains a challenge for many teachers and programmes" (p. 10). Adding to the challenge and cited as a reason for reviewing *Te Whāriki* was a rapidly changing demographic:

> Over the last two decades New Zealand has become one of a small number of culturally and linguistically super diverse countries (Spoonley & Bedford 2012). Superdiversity indicates a level of cultural complexity surpassing anything previously experienced. New Zealand is now home to 160 languages, with multiethnic depth forecasted to deepen even further (Statistics New Zealand, 2011).
>
> (Royal Society of New Zealand, 2013, p. 1)

These matters did not go unnoticed by the sector, with the Early Childhood Taskforce (2011) recommending that the implementation of *Te Whāriki* be evaluated. The Advisory Group on Early Learning's report (Ministry of Education, 2015), took this even further, recommending an update because:
1. childhoods had changed since the early 1990s
2. interpreting, implementing and adhering to Kaupapa Māori and Te Tiriti o Waitangi had been subject to "drift"
3. Pasifika content, omitted in 1996, should be reinstated, particularly to support language learning
4. links between *The New Zealand Curriculum / Te Marautanga o Aotearoa* and *Te Aho Matua* required updating
5. implementing curriculum for children with special educational needs across the early years required updating (Ministry of Education, 2015, p. 15).

Matters related to *Te Whāriki* were no longer straightforward. Compounding concerns about the efficacy of *Te Whāriki* was a comprehensive ERO synthesis of its national reviews (Education Review Office, 2016). It noted:

> The depth and richness of *Te Whāriki* is internationally recognised, however, the holistic and interpretive nature of this curriculum document is both its strength and a challenge. ERO's evaluations signal the need for increased support for the early childhood sector to work with the full intent of *Te Whāriki* as part of their curriculum design and implementation. (Education Review Office, 2016, p. 44)

The synthesis identified numerous features of effective practice required to implement *Te Whāriki*, and concluded that: "Strong pedagogical leadership, curriculum knowledge and collaborative learning partnerships play a critical role in how well early learning services promote positive outcomes for all children" (Education Review Office, 2016, p. 45). None of these were new issues but, collected together in one document, and on the back of the Advisory Group's recommendations (Ministry of Education, 2015), they influenced the inevitable review of *Te Whāriki*.

Future focus: Global considerations influencing curriculum design

As noted at the beginning of the chapter, *Te Whāriki* was acclaimed internationally and showcased as one of the world's top five curriculum models (OECD, 2004). However, challenges also emerged from OECD reporting on early childhood education in Aotearoa New Zealand (Taguma, Litjens, & Makowiecki, 2012), with reporting suggesting that implementation of *Te Whāriki* could be strengthened by learning from other countries' approaches to:
- strengthening parental involvement in curriculum design or implementation;
- reflecting on children's agency (rights) and child-initiated play; and

- further improving the communication and leadership skills of staff for effective implementation. (p. 25)

Interestingly, a year later, in an OECD national hui in Aotearoa New Zealand (May & Carr, 2016), the open-ended principles to support mana mokopuna (children's agency) were publicly affirmed but the issues surrounding effective engagement remained on the table. Since then, ERO reports have commented, to varying degrees, on the importance of all three bullet points raised by the OECD report (Taguma, Litjens, & Makowiecki, 2012) and this has been reflected in professional development foci in the roll-out of the refreshed *Te Whāriki* (Ministry of Education, 2017a) where strengthening parent/whānau and community involvement in designing local curriculum has been a theme, alongside the importance of leadership to establish environments that support child-initiated play (Education Review Office, 2018).

In late 2016, the OECD was proposing to trial an international assessment of early learning. Dubbed the "preschool PISA" (Moss et al., 2016) concerns were raised which struck at the heart of curriculum development. Citing Malaguzzi, the authors argued that education is "first and foremost, a political practice, and policy is the product of politics" (Moss et al., p. 346). In a strong argument against a 'technocratic' tool, the writers mounted a case for a curriculum located in sociocultural contexts. They asked:

What is the image (or social construction) of the child?

What are the purposes of early childhood education?

What are the fundamental values of early childhood education?

(Moss et al., p. 346)

In Aotearoa New Zealand, leading scholars in the early childhood education sector actively rejected New Zealand's participation in the proposed trial (Carr, Mitchell, & Rameka, 2016), claiming that the philosophical premise of the OECD's planned programme undermined the intention of *Te Whāriki*.

Further international influences on what a curriculum should be can be found in the United Nations Sustainable Development Goals 2030,[3] which raise questions to inform curriculum design and implementation by asking:

What is possible?

What is probable?

What is desirable?

When we consider these goals and questions in light of the future, a gap appears between the education provided and the education needed (Bolstad & Gilbert, 2012).

---

3   https://sustainabledevelopment.un.org/sdgs

To close or bridge that gap means thinking about how children learn and how teachers teach: this has direct relevance to curriculum design. Smith (2013) argued the need to shift curriculum design from a transmission approach towards co-constructing working theories, "creating and using knowledge ... in the context of people coming together and collaborating to solve problems" (p. 10).

The report of the Advisory Group on Early Learning also referred to 21st century learning principles and, while not explored in any depth, mentions several times the importance of taking a system-wide approach to changes in the early education sector (Ministry of Education, 2015). Interestingly, at the same time, leadership scholars were commenting along similar lines. Gilbert (2015), Wenmoth (2015), and others comment that system-wide change should be networked, collaborative, and relevant to the social and cultural milieu—ideas that resonate with the themes of future-focused learning. The 2016 ERO review also observed that "If everyone in the education system works together, we can improve outcomes for our children and set them on pathways as confident and successful lifelong learners" (Education Review Office, 2016, p. 45).

Therefore, the Advisory Group recommended in its report (Ministry of Education, 2015) that *Te Whāriki* be updated, digitised, and that a comprehensive policy of professional learning and development be offered to give effect to growing concerns that the transformative potential of *Te Whāriki* remained unrealised.

The process for the refresh and consultation

The culmination of the concerns described so far led the Ministry of Education, in mid-2016, to publish a Request for Quote (RFQ) seeking three to five writers to update the English/bicultural version of *Te Whāriki*. Their role would be to update the context, curriculum implementation, and links to the curricula for school and kura sections. The Ministry sought to address significant variability in the understanding, use, and interpretation of *Te Whāriki* in early childhood settings and limited understanding of the links between *Te Whāriki* and *The New Zealand Curriculum* and *Te Marautanga o Aotearoa*. These were the issues the review aimed to address. In addition, the selected writers would be asked to review the document's learning outcomes.

What eventuated was a much more substantive review than seemed to be indicated in the initial RFQ. To aid our understanding of the refresh process, we requested comment from two writers, the Ministry of Education, and a small number of practitioners involved in the first round of Ministry contracted professional development. Their comments are woven into this section. Claire McLachlan, one of the writers, explains the apparent growth in the scope of the review:

1: Te Whāriki, 2017: A refreshed rallying point for the early childhood sector in Aotearoa New Zealand

> We weren't allowed to touch the gazetted parts of the curriculum so we didn't touch the principles, goals and strands and, basically, we looked at everything else. You couldn't update one bit without looking at everything ... Because the whole document had to talk to each other, there were parts that you couldn't leave untouched. (C. McLachlan, personal communication, October, 2018)

To address the issues raised in the RFQ, the writers' group was required to be a mix of academics and practitioners.[4] Nancy Bell, Director Early Learning at the Ministry of Education and the person responsible for implementing the review, explained:

> [We needed] to retain the bicultural approach that underpinned the development of the original document ... [so we appointed] writers who could strengthen the bicultural framing and content of the language, examples and implementation advice with a focus on identity, language and culture, and on inclusion of all children. (N. Bell, personal communication, October 2018)

Helen May, Margaret Carr, and Tamati and Tilly Reedy, the original writers, were invited to be kaitiaki (caretakers) of the process and to ensure the spirit of *Te Whāriki* remained intact. The kaitiaki role was a first for the Ministry of Education and recognised the value of *Te Whāriki* as a taonga, while demonstrating high-level respect for the Te Tiriti o Waitangi principle to protect such taonga. Strategically, this provided much relief for those concerned to avoid the introduction of a top-down standards-based approach into early childhood education.

The turnaround time for this project was incredibly tight. The writers first met in August 2016 and a draft for consultation with the sector was completed by November 2016.

> Everybody worked hard ... That big rush to get everything ready and done for it to go out in November—that was tight. (C. McLachlan, personal communication, October, 2018)

Even the Ministry would have preferred a longer lead in time:

> It would have been good to have had a longer time frame from the start of the project—this would have allowed us to 'slow down to speed up' in the early stages. (N. Bell, personal communication, October 2018)

The draft was released in November 2016 for a 6-week public consultation period, ending on 16 December, 2016. The consultation process included 36 hui held across the country and an online survey. Individual and group submissions were also invited. The hui were attended by over 1,400 people, and there were almost 800

---

4   The personnel were Dr Helen Hedges (The University of Auckland), Professor Claire McLachlan, Associate Professor Sally Peters and Dr Lesley Rameka (University of Waikato), Brenda Soutar (Te Kōhanga Reo o Mana Tamariki) and Lealofi Kupa (Whānau Manaaki). In addition, Keri Pewhairangi was nominated by Te Kōhanga Reo National Trust to work as the liaison between the English and Māori versions.

surveys and submissions completed online. In addition, 26 substantive submissions were received via email (Ministry of Education, 2017a).

As expected, consultation feedback on the proposed changes to *Te Whāriki* was mixed and ranged from supportive to significantly critical. This variability raised some issues for the writers but care was taken by all concerned to try and represent as many perspectives in the sector as possible:

> It was ultimately an iterative and collaborative process where the writers and Ministry worked carefully with stakeholders to understand their views and find ways to reflect these in the document. At times this was challenging but ultimately very satisfying as there was a sense of consensus being achieved across a very diverse landscape. (N. Bell, personal communication, October 2018)

Significant concern was raised by the sector about the tight deadlines for both development and feedback, and the time of year chosen for consultation, particularly in relation to the subsequently limited opportunities for teaching teams to get together to discuss and debate the changes. Despite the tight timeframes, the early childhood and teacher education sectors mobilised quickly and the writers received significant feedback, both in quantity and quality. Some of those who did not provide feedback also made a decision based on the politics of the day. As one kaiako explained:

> I didn't contribute to consultation because I didn't feel that it was a good use of my time as the political climate did not seem conducive to major/visionary changes. (M. Bachmann, personal communication, October 2018)

While many bemoaned the difference between this consultation process and the lengthy process used in the development of *Te Whāriki* prior to 1996, the Ministry of Education was pleased with the response from the sector.

> We were very pleased with the quantity and quality of the feedback received. It told us *Te Whāriki* really matters to the sector and that we had more work to do. The specificity of commentary was very helpful in making the changes needed in the final document. (N. Bell, personal communication, October, 2018)

All feedback was read and considered, and a comprehensive summary was published on the Ministry of Education's website.[5] The main themes to emerge from the consultation on the draft revision were:
- learning outcomes, specifically the reduction, prominence, and focus
- how learning outcomes would impact assessment practices
- inclusiveness, including bicultural, multicultural, children with additional needs and the focus on infants and toddlers

---

5 The feedback was originally published on www.education.govt.nz but has since been moved to the newly developed website intended to support the implementation of *Te Whāriki*: www.tewhariki.tki.org.nz

- broadening of educational theories
- the use of the term 'kaiako'
- the level of guidance and implementation support for services
- the layout and design.

(Ministry of Education, 2017a).

To help make sense of the feedback, the Ministry of Education appointed a small number of subject-matter experts to provide advice—particularly around infants and toddlers, the inclusion of children with additional learning needs, and assessment. The consultation document was significantly restructured as a result but still represented the thinking and ideas of the writers, while at the same time responding to many of the issues raised:

> It's not like it disappeared into the Ministry and morphed into something else. I think the sector should feel heard. (C. McLachlan, personal communication, October, 2018)

Incorporating feedback is always a matter of compromise and there were some losses for the writers. Helen Hedges (2017) bemoaned the lack of footnotes. Similarly, Claire McLachlan commented on the referencing:

> The biggest problem with the first curriculum was that there were no references[6] [in the final publication]. It's the same problem with this one. There was a reference list constructed but it didn't make it in. As a researcher, I think you should be able to identify where the ideas came from. (C McLachlan, personal communication, October 2018)

While the commentary in this chapter gives some insights into the processes and complexities of the review, they are partial and subjective, and therefore only tell part of the story. Their underpinning theme, however, is one of consultation and compromise; the review, while a step in the right direction, has perhaps not achieved all that was dreamed.

Conclusion

When first released in 1996 as the official curriculum for early childhood education in Aotearoa New Zealand, *Te Whāriki* gained widespread acceptance throughout the early childhood sector. At that time both sides of the political spectrum used the economic crisis of the late 1980s as a rationale for restructuring and reforming public education and that impacted early childhood education provision (see Kelsey, 1997). What was initially only going to be a reform of the nation's educational administration extended into curriculum and assessment (see Te One, 2013). The 2017 review of *Te*

---

6   A draft version of *Te Whāriki* was released in 1993 and included an extensive reference list. Between 1993 and its final release, there was an extensive period of consultation with the sector.

Whāriki was to be expected—after over 20 years with no change but a plethora of reports and reviews, commentaries and research, it was time. The relevance of the 1996 *Te Whāriki* was not in question, but, as when it was first released, there were enduring concerns about how effectively its aspirations, principles, and strands were being implemented.

The socioeconomic, cultural, and educational context of Aotearoa New Zealand changed significantly between 1996 and 2017, and the early years sector had experienced loss, gain, and then loss again. At the same time, the demographic profile of Aotearoa New Zealand had become 'super diverse', inequalities had worsened, and child wellbeing statistics—including educational achievement—were trending down, especially for children of Māori and Pacific origins. The original version of *Te Whāriki* reflected the idea that curricula need to be culturally and nationally appropriate. Internationally this notion has been widely recognised and supported, and *Te Whāriki* 2017 will likely remain a model curriculum because of the way it foregrounds Te Tiriti o Waitangi obligations, articulates a children's rights approach, and emphasises a local curriculum that includes mana whenua, community, whānau, and family as partners in learning.

The early childhood education sector has been subjected to dramatic policy changes since *Te Whāriki* (Ministry of Education, 1996) was first released (Mitchell, 2017; Press, Woodrow, Logan, & Mitchell, 2018). During the 1990s *Te Whāriki* created a point of solidarity in an unsympathetic and, at times, adverse political climate (see Te One & Dalli, 2010; Te One, 2013). Since then, the primacy of market-driven policies alongside a discourse of vulnerability has impacted negatively on the early childhood education sector (Smith, 2016), and as Smith observed, despite funding increases the sector is still in "catch-up" mode (A. Smith, personal communication, 2016). In 2019, the sector is awaiting the release of a new strategic plan—*He taonga te tamaiti. Every child a taonga*: *The strategic plan for early learning 2019–2029* (Ministry of Education, 2018) which, in its draft form, foregrounds the re-worded aspiration of *Te Whāriki*. To fully reify *Te Whāriki* requires multiple-level actions through integrated policy (regulations and funding), research, and ongoing education and qualifications. The systems challenge was a significant rationale for the refresh and remains so; updating a policy document will not, in and of itself, create the changes needed to ensure children can indeed reap the benefits of a fully realised and rich curriculum.

As a conceptual framework that interweaves educational theory, political standpoints, and a profound acknowledgement of the importance of culture, *Te Whāriki* remains on the educational map as an innovative model of curriculum. This claim remains unchallenged and unchanged. But other challenges remain. There are still some important questions to consider as the education landscape in Aotearoa New Zealand continues in a state of change. Given the increasingly busy and complex lives children and families lead, will the promise of *Te Whāriki* be realised? Will all children's rights to reach their potential be taken to heart by kaiako, managers, owners, and others responsible for all children's overall wellbeing, including their rights to their language, identity, and culture, alongside their rights to be recognised as capable, competent, and actively contributing to their worlds?

To date, the response from the sector has been cautiously positive. Much depends on the outcome of the Education Conversation (Ministry of Education, 2018), a consultative forum for developing strategic directions in education in Aotearoa New Zealand over the next decade, whether or not there is cross-party political accord acknowledging that all children have the right to an education that enables them to reach their potential and enjoy a good quality of life. Cooper and Tesar (2017) note that, at the very least, the refreshed *Te Whāriki* has reclaimed prominence with teachers in early childhood centres who are curious to explore its content. Whether this exploration will lead to the promise of *Te Whāriki* being realised, only time will tell.

References

Action for Children and Youth Aotearoa (2015). *United Nations Convention on the Rights of the Child. Alternative report by Action for Children and Youth Aotearoa*. Retrieved from http://www.acya.org.nz/uploads/2/9/4/8/29482613/uncroc_alternative_report_by_acya_2015_final.pdf

Action for Children and Youth Aotearoa (2016a). *"Walk for a bit in my shoes … it isn't actually that easy." Supplementary information for the UN Committee on the Rights of the Child*. Retrieved from http://www.acya.org.nz/uploads/2/9/4/8/29482613/uncroc_-_acya_supplementary_information_-_walk_for_a_bit_in_my_shoes_-_i....pdf

Action for Children and Youth Aotearoa (2016b). *Counting what matters: Valuing and making visible the lives of children with disabilities. Supplementary information for the UN Committee on the Rights of the Child*. Retrieved from http://www.acya.org.nz/uploads/2/9/4/8/29482613/uncroc_-_acya_alternative_report_-_supplementary_information_-_counting_....pdf

Alcock, S., & Haggerty, M. (2013). Recent policy developments and the "schoolification" of early childhood care and education in Aotearoa New Zealand. *Early Childhood Folio, 17*(2), 21–26.

Alvestad, M., Duncan, J., & Berge, A. (2009). New Zealand ECE teachers talk about *Te Whāriki*. *New Zealand Journal of Teachers' Work, 6*(1) 3–19.

Bolstad, R. & Gilbert, J. (2012). *Supporting future-oriented learning and teaching—A New Zealand perspective*. Wellington: Ministry of Education. Retrieved from https://www.educationcounts.govt.nz/__data/assets/pdf_file/0003/109317/994_Future-oriented-07062012.pdf

Boston., J. & Chapple, S. (2014). *Child poverty in New Zealand*. Wellington: Bridget Williams Books.

Boston, J. & Holland, M. (Eds.) (1987). *The Fourth Labour Government: Radical politics in New Zealand*. Auckland: Oxford University Press

Carr, M. (2001). *Assessment in early childhood settings. Learning Stories*. London, UK: Sage.

Carr, M., Mitchell, L., & Rameka, L. (2016). Some thoughts about the value of an OECD international framework for early childhood services in Aotearoa New Zealand. *Contemporary Issues in Early Childhood, 17*(4), 450–454.

Child Poverty Action Group. (2014). *Child Poverty Action Group Policy Paper Series Part Three: Compulsory schooling and child poverty. Our children, our choice.* Auckland: Author, New Zealand. Retrieved from https://www.cpag.org.nz/assets/Publications/140630%20Our%20 Children%20Our%20Choice%20Part%203%20Comp%20Ed.pdf

Chzhen, Y., Gromada, A., Gwyther, R., Cuesta, J., & Bruckauf, Z., (2018). *An unfair start: Inequality in children's education in rich countries.* Florence, Italy: UNICEF Office of Research—Innocenti. Retrieved from https://www.unicef-irc.org/publications/995-an-unfair-start-education-inequality-children.html

Cooper, M. & Tesar, M. (2017). Editorial: *Te Whāriki* on the top shelves of early childhood centres in Aotearoa New Zealand. *The First Years: Ngā Tau Tuatahi. New Zealand Journal of Infant and Toddler Education, 19*(2), pp. 3–4.

Cribb, J., Lane, R, Penny, H., van Delden, K., & Irwin, K. (2011). Pragmatism and caffeine: Lessons from cross-agency, cross-sector working. *Policy Quarterly, 7*(4), 50–54. Retrieved from https:// ojs.victoria.ac.nz/pq/article/view/4399. doi: https://doi.org/10.26686/pq.v7i4.4399.

Cullen, J. (1996). The challenge of *Te Whāriki* for future developments in early childhood education. *delta, 48*(1), 113–125.

Cullen, J. (2008, November). *Outcomes of Early Childhood Education: Do we know, can we tell, and does it matter?* Paper presented at the Jean Herbison Lecture, New Zealand Association for Research in Education Annual Conference, Palmerston North, New Zealand.

Dalli, C. (2011). A curriculum of open possibilities: A New Zealand kindergarten teacher's view of professional practice. *Early Years, 31*(3), 229–243. doi: 10.1080/09575146.2011.604841

Duhn, I. (2006). The making of global citizens: Traces of cosmopolitanism in the New Zealand early childhood curriculum, *Te Whāriki. Contemporary Issues in Early Childhood, 7*(3), 191–201.

Duncanson, M., Oben, G., Wicken, A., Morris S., McGee, M., & Simpson, J. (2017). *Child poverty monitor: Technical report.* Dunedin: New Zealand Child and Youth Epidemiology Service, University of Otago. Retrieved from http://www.nzchildren.co.nz/

Early Childhood Taskforce. (2011). *An agenda for amazing children: Final report of the ECE Taskforce.* Wellington: Ministry of Education.

Education Review Office. (2009). *Implementing self review in early childhood services.* Wellington: Author. Retrieved from http://www.ero.govt.nz/National-Reports/Implementing-Self-Review-in-Early-Childhood-Services-January-2009

Education Review Office. (2011). *Positive foundations for learning: Confident and competent children in early childhood services.* Wellington: Author. Retrieved from http://www.ero.govt.nz/ National-Reports/Positive-Foundations-for-Learning-Confident-and-Competent-Children-in-Early-Childhood-Services-October-2011

Education Review Office. (2012) *Partnerships with whānau* Māori *in early childhood services.* Wellington: Author. Retrieved from http://www.ero.govt.nz/publications/partnership-with-whanau-maori-in-early-childhood-services/

Education Review Office. (2013). *Working with Te Whāriki.* Wellington: Author. Retrieved from http://www.ero.govt.nz/publications/working-with-te-whariki/

Education Review Office. (2015). *Infants and toddlers: competent and confident communicators and explorers.* Wellington: Author. Retrieved from https://www.ero.govt.nz/assets/Uploads/ ERO-Infants-Toddlers-WEB.pdf

Education Review Office. (2016). *Early learning curriculum.* Wellington: Author. Retrieved from http://www.ero.govt.nz/publications/early-learning-curriculum/

Education Review Office. (2018). *Engaging with Te Whāriki 2017.* Wellington: Author. Retrieved from https://www.ero.govt.nz/publications/engaging-with-te-whariki-2017/

Farquhar, S. (2010). *Ricoeur, identity, and early childhood.* Lanham, MD: Rowman & Littlefield Publishers.

Gilbert, R. (2015). Leading in collaborative, complex education systems. In *Leadership for communities of learning: Five think pieces.* (pp. 6–14). Wellington: Education Council, New Zealand | Matatū Aotearoa. Retrieved from https://www.educationcouncil.org.nz/sites/default/files/Education%20Council%20Five%20Think%20Pieces%200612.pdf

Grimmond, D. (2011). *1000 days to get it right for every child: The effectiveness of public investment in New Zealand children. Every Child Counts Discussion Paper No. 2.* Wellington: Every Child Counts.

Gunn, A. C., & Gasson, N. R. (2016). The spectre of standards in Aotearoa New Zealand early education and care. In M. Li, J. Fox, & S. Grieshaber (Eds). *Contemporary issues and challenge in early childhood education in the Asia-Pacific region* (Vol.10, pp 165–179). Springer.

Hedges, H. (2017). Reflecting on our aspiration statement: Competent, confident, and capable infants and toddlers. *The First Years: Ngā Tau Tuatahi. New Zealand Journal of Infant and Toddler Education 19*(2). pp. 5–8.

Kelsey, J. (1997). *The New Zealand Experiment: A world model for structural adjustment?* Auckland: Auckland University Press and Bridget Williams Books.

May, H. (2009). *Politics in the playground. The world of early childhood in New Zealand.* Dunedin: Otago University Press.

May, H. (2017). Te Whāriki 2017 launch. *The Space 48.* pp. 4–7.

May, H. & Carr, M. (2016).*Te Whāriki*: A uniquely woven curriculum shaping policy, pedagogy and practice in Aotearoa New Zealand. In T. David, K. Gooch, & S. Powell (Eds.), *Handbook of philosophies and theories of early childhood education and care* (pp. 316–326). London, UK: Routledge.

McLachlan, C. (2018). *Te Whāriki* revisited: How approaches to assessment can make valued learning visible. *He Kupu, 5*(3), 45–56. Retrieved from https://www.hekupu.ac.nz/article/te-whariki-revisited-how-approaches-assessment-can-make-valued-learning-visible

Ministry of Education. (1996). *Te whāriki: He whāriki mātauranga mō ngā mokopuna o Aotearoa: Early childhood curriculum.* Wellington: Learning Media.

Ministry of Education. (2007). *The New Zealand curriculum.* Wellington: Learning Media. Retrieved from http://nzcurriculum.tki.org.nz/The-New-Zealand-Curriculum.

Ministry of Education (2008). *Te Marautanga O Aotearoa.* Wellington: Learning Media.

Ministry of Education. (2013). *Ka Hikitia: Accelerating success 2013–2017 — The Māori education strategy.* Wellington: Author. Retrieved from https://www.education.govt.nz/assets/Documents/Ministry/Strategies-and-policies/Ka-Hikitia/KaHikitiaAcceleratingSuccessEnglish.pdf

Ministry of Education. (2015). *Report of the Advisory Group on Early Learning.* Wellington: Author. Retrieved from https://www.education.govt.nz/assets/Documents/Ministry/consultations/Report-of-the-Advisory-Group-on-Early-Learning.pdf

Ministry of Education. (2016). *Contract for Services: Update of Te Whāriki.* Jane Ewens' Personal archive.

Ministry of Education. (2017a). *Update of Te Whāriki: Report on the engagement process.* Wellington: Author. Retrieved from https://tewhariki.tki.org.nz/assets/Uploads/files/ONLINE-Te-Whariki-Update-Long-v21B.pdf

Ministry of Education. (2017b). *Enrolments in ECE*. Retrieved from https://www.educationcounts.govt.nz/statistics/early-childhood-education/participation

Ministry of Education. (2017c). *The National Picture: What does the ECE census 2017 tell us about ECE services?* Retrieved from https://www.educationcounts.govt.nz/__data/assets/pdf_file/0004/184540/ECE-Summary-page-Services.pdf

Ministry of Education. (2018). *He taonga te tamaiti. Every child a taonga: Strategic plan for early learning 2019-29 — Draft for consultation.* Retrieved from https://conversation.education.govt.nz/assets/ELSP/Early-Learning-Strategic-10-Year-Plan.pdf

Ministry of Education & CORE Education. (2017). *Te Whāriki: Whakamohio Introduction to Curriculum.* Retrieved from https://tewhariki.tki.org.nz/en/professional-learning-and-development/professional-learning-and-development/

Mitchell, L. M., Meagher-Lundberg, P., Arndt, S., & Kara, H. (2016). *ECE Participation Programme evaluation. Stage 4.* Wellington, New Zealand: Ministry of Education.

Mitchell, L. (2017). Discourses of economic investment and child vulnerability in early childhood education. *Waikato Journal of Education, 22*(1), 25–35. Retrieved from https://researchcommons.waikato.ac.nz/bitstream/handle/10289/12066/Mitchell%2c%20L%20%282017%29.%20Discourses%20of%20economic%20investment%20and%20child%20vulnerability%20in%20ECE.pdf?sequence=2&isAllowed=y

Morton, S. M. B., Atatoa Carr, P. E., Grant, C. C., Berry, S. D., Mohal, J., Pillai, A. (2015). *Growing Up in New Zealand: A longitudinal study of New Zealand children and their families. Vulnerability Report 2: Transitions in exposure to vulnerability in the first 1000 days of life.* Auckland: Growing Up in New Zealand.

Morton, S.M.B, Grant, C.C., Berry, S.D., Walker, C.G., Corkin, M., Ly, K., de Castro, T.G., Atatoa Carr, P.E., Bandara, D.K., Mohal, J., Bird, A., Underwood, L., & Fa'alili-Fidow, J. (2017). *Growing Up in New Zealand: A longitudinal study of New Zealand children and their families. Now We Are Four: Describing the preschool years.* Auckland: Growing Up in New Zealand.

Moss, P., Dahlberg, G., Greishaber, S., Mantovani, S., May, H., Pence, A., Rayana, S., Swadener, B., & Vandenbroeck, M. (2016). The Organisation for Economic Co-operation and Development's international early learning study: Opening for debate and contestation. *Contemporary Issues in Early Childhood. 17*(3), 343–351.

Nairn, K., Higgins, J., & Sligo, J. (2012). *Children of Rogernomics. A neoliberal generation leaves school.* Dunedin: Otago University Press.

Nuttall, J. (Ed.) (2003). *Weaving te Whāriki: Aotearoa New Zealand's early childhood curriculum document in theory and practice.* Wellington: NZCER Press.

Nuttall, J. (Ed.) (2013). *Weaving te Whāriki: Aotearoa New Zealand's early childhood curriculum document in theory and practice* (2nd ed.). Wellington: NZCER Press.

OECD (2004) *Starting strong: Curricula and pedagogies in Early Childhood Education and Care: Five curriculum outlines.* Paris, France: Author.

Office of the Children's Commissioner. (2018). *In-depth engagement with tamariki and rangatahi. Māori Series of focus group and interview for rich stories as part of Tama-te Rā Ariki series of engagement.* Retrieved from http://www.occ.org.nz/assets/Uploads/2018-June-Indepth-Maori-TTRA-case-study2.pdf

Office of the Children's Commissioner & Oranga Tamariki (2019). *What makes a good life? Children's and young people's views on wellbeing.* Retrieved from https://www.occ.org.nz/assets/Uploads/What-makes-a-good-life-report-OCC-OT-2019-WEB2.pdf

Press, F., Woodrow, C., Logan, H., & Mitchell, L. (2018). Can we belong in a neo-liberal world? Neo-liberalism in early childhood education and care policy in Australia and New Zealand. *Contemporary Issues in Early Childhood, 19* (4), 328–339.

Poulton, R. (2012). The early childhood education (ECE) sector in New Zealand: Opportunities galore? In S. Te One (Ed.). *Who gets to play?: Promoting participation in ECE for all children: Children 81* (pp. 37–39). Wellington: Office of the Children's Commissioner.

Rashbrooke, M. (Ed). (2013*). Inequality. A New Zealand crisis*. Wellington: Bridget Williams Books.

Ritchie, J. (2018). A fantastical journey. Reimagining *Te Whāriki. Early Childhood Folio*. 22(1) 9–14.

Royal Society of New Zealand. (2013). *Languages in Aotearoa New Zealand*. Retrieved from https://royalsociety.org.nz/what-we-do/our-expert-advice/all-expert-advice-papers/languages-in-aotearoa-new-zealand

Skerrett, M. (2018). Pedagogical intentions: Enacting a "refreshed" bicultural curriculum positioned at the crossroads of colonial relations, biocultural education, and critical literacy. *Early Childhood Folio* 22(1), 3–8.

Smith, A. (2013). *Does Te Whāriki need evidence to show that it is effective? A discussion paper*. Sarah Te One, Personal archive.

Smith, A. (2016). *Children's rights: Towards social justice*. New York: Momentum Press.

Taguma, M., Litjens, I., & Makowiecki, K. (2012). *Quality matters in early childhood education and care: New Zealand*. Paris, France: OECD. Retrieved from http://www.oecd.org/edu/preschoolandschool/NEW%20ZEALAND%20policy%20profile%20-%20published%203-8-2012.pdf

Te One, S. (2009). *Perceptions of children's rights in early childhood*. Unpublished doctoral thesis, Victoria University of Wellington.

Te One, S. (2013). *Te Whāriki: Historical accounts and contemporary influences 1990–2012*. In J. Nuttall (Ed.), *Weaving Te Whāriki. Aotearoa New Zealand's early childhood curriculum document in theory and practice*. (2nd ed., pp. 7–34). Wellington: NZCER Press.

Te One, S., & Dalli, C. (2010). The status of children's rights in early childhood education policy 2009. *New Zealand Annual Review of Education, 19*, 52–77.

UN Committee on the Rights of the Child (2016). *Concluding observations: New Zealand*. Retrieved from http://www.acya.org.nz/uploads/2/9/4/8/29482613/2016_un_committee_oncluding_observations.pdf

Wenmoth, D. (2015) Networked leadership. In *Leadership for communities of learning: Five think pieces*. (pp. 22–28). Wellington: Education Council New Zealand | Matatū Aotearoa. Retrieved from https://www.educationcouncil.org.nz/sites/default/files/Education%20Council%20Five%20Think%20Pieces%200612.pdf-

CHAPTER 2

Tōku Rangatiratanga nā te Mana Mātauranga: "Knowledge and Power Set Me Free…"

Tilly Te Koingo, Lady Reedy

ABSTRACT

This chapter, originally delivered as a keynote presentation to the 1995 Early Childhood Convention in Auckland, reflects on the sources of the Māori concepts that underpin *Te Whāriki*, both from the perspective of the author's own life and from her deep understanding of the Māori world view. The author expands on the meanings of these key concepts, sharing them with non-Māori readers whilst emphasising that they remain deeply and uniquely Māori. The chapter concludes with a reminder of the challenges that face Aotearoa New Zealand to develop and implement curricula that enhance the lives of all children.

Tilly Reedy's chapter is based on her keynote presentation to the 1995 Early Childhood Convention. We are grateful to Mrs Reedy and to the Te Kōhanga Reo National Trust for permission to reprint this material.

Tēnā rā koutou ngā kanohi ora ō ngā mātua-tīpuna kua ngaro atu ki te pō e …
Tēnā koutou, tēnā ra koutou katoa …

I believe in a freedom of the mind and spirit that is fearless yet controlled:
… a freedom that dreams dreams and seeks answers on distant horizons;
… a freedom that takes responsibility for the footprints left behind;
… a freedom that recognises the beauty of individuality;
… a freedom that weaves nations together for tomorrow's unity.

I believe in a freedom of the mind and of the spirit. That is my horizon—the heritage left to me by my ancestors who walked the ancient paths. Their horizon is my heritage.

They left me many treasures. They left me a heritage to set me free.

Ko Hikurangi te maunga	Hikurangi is my mountain
Ko Waiapu te awa	Waiapu is my river
Ko Ngāti Porou te iwi	Ngāti Porou is my people
Ko au e tū atu nei—	And I stand here before you—
He uri nā Porourangi …	A descendant of Porourangi …

They left me my whakapapa, my genealogical links: to Māui, the demigod of Māori mythology; to Paikea, the god who arrived in New Zealand on the back of a whale about 750 years ago; to our waka, *Horouta, Takitimu, Nukutere, Nukutaimemeha, Tereanini*, their leaders and their crews; to our larger-than-life ancestors, Toi, Rauru, Irakaiputahi, Kupe; to our eponymous ancestor Porourangi and his vibrant descendants, Materoa, Hinekehu, Te Rangitawaea, Pakanui, Te Aowera, Kapohanga …

I can trace my ancestry back to Māui, who "fished" this land up out of the sea. His canoe rests in petrified form on top of our famous mountain Hikurangi, the first place in the world to see the sun; Hikurangi, of special spiritual significance to us of Ngāti Porou. The magnificent birds of Ruakapanga, Tiungarangi, and Horongarangi rest there also. My 5-year-old granddaughter knows them well, and meets them often in creative, imaginative stories. She is also conversant with our famous ancestor Paikea and his whale. The whale is now an island at Whangara on the East Coast. They also left me their traditions and histories—about our waka *Horouta*, with its precious cargo of women and kūmara, and the very tapu *Takitimu*. They identified Porourangi as our eponymous ancestor, the culmination of our traditions, and the beginning of our "modern" histories.

Their horizon, my heritage

I grew up in a Māori-speaking community and Māori is my first language. It was the language of our home, the songs that were sung, the stories that were told. It was (and still is) the language of our marae, Hiruharama, and our meeting house, Kapohanga, the spiritual and emotional sanctuary of many. Kapohanga and the memories … of a young girl surrounded by powerful women who managed the marae and the community while their men were at war in Europe. I thought "women-in-charge" was the norm! My daughters think so too. I wonder where they got that crazy idea from. Last year, my daughter Riripeti wrote this poem for my birthday:

Poem To My Mother
He wahine toa!

Ngāti Porou woman
that sees to the future
with children,
mokopuna,
and mokopuna more

Shaped from behind
Jagged hills that drop to sea
Roll on inwards
to a "promised land"

Where embers glow
and a fire is poked
For warmth
welcome,
food,
and stories

to fill the imagined
the fantasy
the free
MINDS

of children,
mokopuna,
and mokopuna more

It was here also that I learnt about the power of place, tūrangawaewae, and of knowing I belonged. To know is to be empowered. To be empowered is to be free. It all seemed so simple then. Nothing was impossible. I think it was the sharing, the caring, the collective living and learning. But as with all things, there was a flip-side—and for me, learning to accommodate the idiosyncrasies of aunts, elders and those "big kids" was tough! I resented being "seen and not heard", and developed this belief that people least able to help themselves needed me to fly their flags. The arrogance of it! I was forever challenging my elders, my aunts and my uncles, and questioning decisions they made that smacked of injustice and unfairness. I was a constant embarrassment to my family, especially my mother. Today I still carry that legacy of non-acceptance of injustice, as I see it. I hope that age has mellowed the tone and the arrogance, but not the commitment to a fair and just society that recognises the beauty in differences as much as the comfort in similarities.

A tangata whenua perspective of early learning
The Māori child

> E tipu e rea mo nga ra o tou ao ...
> Grow up oh tender shoot and fulfil the needs of your generation ...
>   (Sir Āpirana Ngata, 1949)[1]

Māori tradition identified the Māori child as a valued member of the Māori world—before conception, before birth, before time. The child was the personification of the worlds of yesterday:

> He purapura i ruia mai i Rangiātea
> E kore e ngaro.

> Precious seeds dispersed from Rangiātea [the famed homeland of the Māori gods]
> Will never be lost.

As with all precious seeds, the child was nurtured for survival and inculcated with an understanding of their own importance, through the reciting of genealogies and stories of folk heroes. The indoctrination of their undisputed rights to their place in their time and age was also part of their teaching. They were left in no doubt that someone cared for them physically, mentally, spiritually.

Much of this indoctrination—of mana and pride, of knowledge of their aristocratic lineage, of histories, of descriptions of chiefly ornaments and cloaks—took place through the many lullabies that were composed on the birth of the child and sung to the child constantly. The following is the first verse of a very long, very well-known oriori which I learnt as a child. It is our tribal version of how the kūmara was brought to New Zealand, and makes many references to our Pacific ancestors and their stories. It identifies our genealogical ties to ancient times, and our historical knowledge base.

Po! Po!
E tangi ana Tama ki te kai mana
Waiho me tiki atu ki te Pou-a-hao-kai
Hei a mai te pakake ki uta ra
He waiu mo Tama
Kia homai e to tipuna e Uenuku
Whakarongo. Ko te kumara ko Parinui-te-Ra
Ka hikimata te tapuae o Tangaroa
Ka whaimata te tapuae o Tangaroa
Tangaroa! Ka haruru!
   (Ngata & Jones (eds), 1974, pp. 152–161)

My son, Tama, is crying for food!
Wait until it is fetched from the Pillars-of-netted food.
And the whale is driven ashore,
To give milk for you, my son.
Verily, your ancestor Uenuku will give freely.
Now listen! The kumara is from the Beetling-Cliff-of-the-Sun
Beyond the eager bounding strides of Tangaroa, God of the Sea;
Lo, striding to and fro is Tangaroa,
Tangaroa! Listen to his resounding roar!
   (Translation by P. Te Hurunui)

For some, indoctrination took place before they were born ...

"E takatakahi koe i roto ia a au he tāne, māu e ngaki te mate ō tō tipuna o Poroumata." Thus spoke Te Atakura to the unborn Tuwhakairiora as she set the path for his leadership role in a world of honour and revenge. He eventually avenged her father's death, and his prowess as a warrior and as a man is recited and recalled in Ngāti Porou today. A very powerful subtribe bears his name, and one of our most beautiful carved meeting houses is named for him as well.

The child was, and still is, "te uri a Papatūānuku", the child of Papatūānuku, the Earth Mother. When a child is born the placenta, whenua, is returned to the earth, also whenua. The umbilical cord is put in the special place selected long before by the child's ancestors, marking that child irrevocably for that tribe. The child is claimed. The child claims! Their tūrangawaewae, their right to a "standing place", is undisputed. They belong. But there are obligations also.

Take the word "aroha", for example. As I wrote in *He Matapuna*:

> Aroha is an overworked and misunderstood concept ... Misuse of this word is a result of our lack of responsibility to teach the rule of reciprocity on which aroha flourishes.

Aroha is not something anyone can command from others because they imagine it's their right. To accept and enjoy the loving, the sharing, the caring of aroha means you give back a little more than you received. This keeps the networks alive and functioning. The acceptance of aroha in any shape or form places one unequivocally under obligation to that person, that family, that group. Perhaps it is not too late for us to spell out the meaning of aroha, more especially the obligation and responsibility that go with it. (Reedy, 1979, p. 42)

The child was, and still is, the incarnation of the ancestors: te kanohi ora, "the living face". The child was, and still is, the living link with yesterday and the bridge to tomorrow: te taura here tangata, "the binding rope that ties people together over time". The child is the kāwai tangata, the "genealogical link" that strengthens whanaungatanga, "family relationships", of that time and place. The child is also te ūkaipō, "the favoured, the special". The child is also the repository of the teachings of yesterday, the enhancement of the dreams of today, and the embodiment of the aspirations for tomorrow—the hope for the survival of the family.

The following translation of a song by a modern songwriter encapsulates these ideas:[2]

Whiringa Wairua

Many Te Kōhanga Reo whānau have flourished
Enabling this sacred vine
To weave us to those departed
This woven fibre is the spirituality of man
Since time began
The fibre comes in many colours
Red, brown, purple, ochre
Weaving the spiritual link
To our ancestors departed
This woven fibre is the spirituality of man
Since time began
The path is crystal clear
For all Te Kōhanga Reo whānau
It is our genealogical links with our gods
Our relationships with each other
And to those departed
This woven fibre is the spirituality of man
Since time began
This is the call of Te Kōhanga Reo
This is the call of Aotearoa
Let us all weave together into the spiritual realm.
   (M. Reedy, 1990)

A further waiata expresses the aspirations for the high-born child Tutere Moana, and the absolute belief of his people that all things are achieved by the power of the mind. The disciplined power of the mind was a highly accomplished skill practised by the Māori for both good and not-so-good reasons. The translation of three lines of this very long lullaby is as follows:

Listen O son; there was only one determination

That transported Tāne to the uppermost heavens

And that was the determination of the mind …

In the same song, Tutere is encouraged to take hold of the three baskets of knowledge—te kete tūāuri, te kete tūātea, te kete aronui—procured by Tāne from the twelfth heaven.

The training that was promised was rigorous and precise. Mistakes meant death, so only the best survived. The training extended to all facets of life, with specialist teachers working with selected youth. It covered both the esoteric and the exoteric: from black magic to memorising traditions and genealogies; from carving, weaving and food-gathering to warfare. Every child was a valued member of the community. Every community was valued by the child.

The following is another well-known poem which explains the importance of the child in the Māori world. It likens the child to the central shoots of the flax plant, which are protected by the outer leaves to ensure its survival. If the shoots are removed, the plant will die. The Māori drew fibre from the flax plant to weave their mats, their clothing and their baskets, and from its roots they made medicine. The flax plant was vital to the survival of the Māori, as was the child—as is the child. As the leaves protected the central shoots, so did the family protect the child. This protection, along with the nurturing, the teaching and the training, was the responsibility of the whole family, not just the parents.

Unuhia te rito ō te harakeke

Kei hea te kōmako e kō?

Kī mai ki a au

He aha te mea nui ō te ao nei?

Māku e kī atu

He tangata, he tangata, he tangata.

Strip away the central shoots from the flax plant

Where will the bellbird sing?

Tell me

What is the most valued thing in this world?

I will say

Man, man, man.

For our ancestors, one could replace the last line with the words "He tamaiti, he tamaiti, he tamaiti"—"A child, a child, a child". The child was indeed a valued member of the Māori world of yesterday.

But what about today?

Today we witness the parlous state of the Māori child in a world without the "outer leaves" of the family. No protection. No sustenance. No nurturing. What has brought them to this state?

Dr Tamati Reedy, a former Secretary for Māori Affairs, in his submission to the Royal Commission on Social Policy in 1987, identified "the historical experience of the Māori people since the signing of the Treaty of Waitangi" as one possible reason. He saw the period 1840–90 as "the era of demoralisation", in which the aim of the colonial government was to amalgamate Māori and settlers as quickly as possible. Despite the skills of the Māori and their adaptation to the agricultural, animal husbandry, trading, and marketing worlds opened up by the Pākehā, the Māori by the 1890s were overwhelmed by the process of colonisation. The sheer extent and intensity of demographic and economic change hit them hard. The Māori ceased to command the process of change.

The period 1890–1940 was viewed by Reedy as "the era of social reconstruction", in which British-educated Māori began to appear, and to present and defend Māori interests in Pākehā institutions. Land development schemes, health and house-building programmes were implemented; tribal trust boards, the Māori Arts and Crafts Board, and the Māori Purposes Fund Board were set up to help the Māori economically, socially, and culturally.

Reedy identified the period from the 1940s to the 1980s as "the era of dislocation". As he saw it, the big problem for the Māori people was the loss of their lands by confiscation or sale. With the rising Māori population, there were not the opportunities for employment in the shrinking rural economy, so Māori moved into the cities. By the late 1950s, it was a government policy to encourage this trend. Māori institutions, including the transmission of language and cultural skills, were disrupted.

It is acknowledged that the government took responsibility for developing Māori land assets in the late 1920s, but no real effort has gone into developing the human resource of the Māori people. Educational under-achievement, coupled with a lack of resources, means that Māori are largely confined to unskilled and semi-skilled wage work. Access to professional careers and participation in new commercial opportunities are strictly limited. The Māori people bear a disproportionate share of the consequences of the depressed labour market of the 1980s, and face the grim prospect of permanent unemployment. They are severely disadvantaged.

This disadvantage is shown in research carried out by the New Zealand Planning Council (1989, 1990a, 1990b), and the effect on our target group. Census figures (1986) show that Māori children still live in extended family households, but that 43 percent of those aged 1–4 years and 50 percent of those aged 5–9 years live in families with two parents. Nearly 30 percent of all Māori children live with single adults. Māori families have shown the greatest increase in one-parent families, from 19 percent in 1976 to nearly 30 percent in 1986. In 1986 women made up 84 percent of all sole parents. So women are taking on the full responsibility for rearing the children in their early years. No extended family. No male role models.

This social disadvantage is exacerbated by economic disadvantage, with 70–80 percent of Māori children aged 1–9 years coming from families in the two lowest income quintiles. One-parent families are significantly worse off than their two-parent counterparts; in 1986 they had average incomes of less than $15,000 before tax. The relationship between social and economic disadvantage and family stress and instability is well researched. A poor start in life does not augur well for any child.

The economic disadvantage experienced by Māori children extends to the type of housing available to them. Māori children are more likely to be living in flats, units, and rental accommodation. Their health is adversely affected, and Māori infants are more likely to die in their first year of life. Those who survive are likely to require more hospital treatment for illnesses associated with poverty.

Economically, socially, and culturally, Māori children and their Māori world are disadvantaged. In the following poem, Rawiri Paratene captures the Māori situation graphically:

A Tribute to the Living Māori Race

The Pākehā
with his "steal" blades
has tried to gut us.
He almost succeeded.
A lot of blood has been lost
and our dangling hearts
are tied with flax
to our knees.
We are busy now
gathering severed limbs
transplanting vital organs
regenerating rich brown skin
re-embowelling disembowelled
bowels

And soon we'll be together
and we will stand as one
No longer hollow-stomached
For we are not extinct
Nor are we endangered!

The Pākehā
with his "beehive" matches
has tried to burn
our parents' tongues
He wants to slice ours out
with his brand new
rust resistant, ever efficient
disposable, bic-thinking
all new, all purpose, all empowering
all-uminium blades.

We are busy now
gathering scattered pieces
of the riddle of our language
Yes
all those pidgin-remnants
of an acrobatic tongue
that once was fluent as a river
And soon we'll be together
and we will speak as one
No longer tongue-tied
For we are not mutes
Nor are we illiterate!

The Pākehā
with his barter (and his bullets)
has tried to banish us.
And not content with that
he came armed with Holy Bible
to take possession of our souls.
We are busy now
gathering our people
reviving and recruiting
reclaiming what is ours

2: Tōku Rangatiratanga nā te Mana Mātauranga: "Knowledge and Power Set Me Free ..."

And soon we'll be together
and we will RISE as one
No longer razzle-dazzled
For we are not homeless
Nor are we lacking spirit!
Nor are we lacking spirit ...

The Māori people have, in the last decade, decided to take hold of their own destiny, despite the almost insurmountable hurdles placed before them. They have decided to return to their cultural roots for solutions to the issues they face. To return to their language, their culture, their values, and their practices for their identity—to return to their tribal roots to strengthen their minds and spirits. This return is the only hope for the survival of our young, the Māori child.

We have almost come full circle, and it has taken some of us 150 years to wake up to the fact that "the answer lies within us" (the catch-phrase of the World Indigenous Peoples Conference in 1990).

This challenge for the survival of the young Māori child, with an assured place in the twenty-first century, created the most vigorous and innovative educational movement in this country (dare one suggest, in the world): Te Kōhanga Reo, the Māori language nests. The movement is unique, imaginative. It has succeeded where nothing else has succeeded to unite us as a Māori people, working towards a common goal, and to motivate us to do something for ourselves. The language is us and it is ours. We are in control. Yet the language nests have done more than arrest the demise of a language—they have focused attention on the need to revitalise a generally dissipating culture and the marae, the last bastion of that culture. The marae is the cultural setting for the growing child.

Te Kōhanga Reo has brought together the child and a wide range of caregivers and teachers, and provided management and administration skills which have opened up exciting possibilities for the child's family.

The challenge has been carried into the primary schools of New Zealand—in immersion classes and Kura Kaupapa Māori. The latter continue the philosophy of Te Kōhanga Reo, with teachings only in Māori, and in an entirely Māori-speaking environment. Māori universities are being discussed, and one is operating with Ngāti Raukawa ki te Tonga. We have come full circle.

Yet all these achievements have had their difficulties. Hostility to the revival of Māori language and culture remains. Obstacles to the rebuilding and reinforcement of the Māori child's identity continue. Overt and covert racism persists.

Our Māori ancestors, in one of their many proverbs, provide an answer:

Whaia te iti kahurangi
Ki te tuohu koe, me he maunga teitei.

Seek ye the treasures of your heart
If you bow your head, let it be to a lofty mountain.

In other words, nothing worthwhile ever comes easy. The survival of the Māori in New Zealand is imperative for the survival of the Māori child. We must fight for that right as tangata whenua of New Zealand, as the first peoples of Aotearoa.

Nor are we lacking spirit . . .

Dimensions of the learner

Te Whāriki projects four dimensions for the holistic development of the child at all times—the physical (tinana), the mental (hinengaro), the spiritual (wairua), and the emotional (whatumanawa) (see Table 2.1).

Tinana

This dimension deals with the physical power and health of the body. The child learns that play, sport, and enjoyment are fundamental to good health; that knowledge of the biological functions and processes of the body is necessary; that the daily maintenance of the body, using old and new learnings, is important.

Hinengaro

This dimension deals with the power of the mind. The child learns about thoughts; about controlling their inner and external worlds, which builds this power of the mind; about "belief systems" that empower the mind; about explanations of the universe, from ancient Māori philosophies of te pō and te kore, to modern explanations of black holes and future/past time zones; about understanding themselves and their purpose in life.

To meet these needs, the Māori developed the very useful tool of karakia/incantation and affirmation. The karakia imprints within the mind the ability to focus on the purpose at hand, which may be to seek help for oneself or for someone else; to find a job; or to achieve some goal. This imprinting is similar to the rituals performed in the cultivation of the kūmara. It is no different from prayers calling on some divine agent, such as Jesus Christ, God or Allah, for guidance.

Wairua

This dimension deals with spiritual power and the sense of oneness with the universe. The child learns that all things are part of the universe; that all matter is made up of the same energy forces. They learn that past, present, and future are sources of trust, confidence, and self-esteem; that eternal questions about atua/gods and their place in the universe are challenges for the mind to explore; that tradition, religious beliefs, philosophy and modern science are not necessarily incompatible.

Whatumanawa

This dimension deals with the power of the emotions. The child, through knowledge and experience, builds an understanding of the range of human emotions—from love and happiness to hate and sorrow. These emotions manifest our inner world. If the child's experiences are positive and happy, the emotional responses will produce a child who is positive and happy, who is confident and has a positive self-image.

Ngā Taumata Whakahirahira

The following achievement aims will ensure that the learner is empowered in every possible way. The main achievement occurs in the development of the child's mana. The child is nurtured in the knowledge that they are loved and respected; that their physical, mental, spiritual, and emotional strength will build mana, influence, and control; that having mana is the enabling and empowering tool to controlling their own destiny.

Mana Atua

This is the development of personal wellbeing in the child, through an understanding of their own uniqueness and divine "specialness".

According to Māori there is a divine spirit, a spark of godliness, in each child born into this world. This belief is rooted in the teachings of old. When Tāne fashioned the human form from Papatūānuku, he breathed godliness into mankind. From that time to this, the teachings and understanding are that the essence of God is transmitted to each child born into this world. The Māori mind also determined that all things, both animate and inanimate, have their own mauri, their own spark of godliness. John Kehoe, in his book *Mind Power* (1991), reflects that "even a rock is a dance of energy".

It is therefore imperative that the teacher constantly celebrates and praises the learner. Whenever the child feels respected and accepted, their mauri thrives. When anything is correct, no matter how small, we must applaud and praise it! Only the child knows and feels the intensity and importance of this celebration.

We must also instil within the child the belief that they too can celebrate themselves. They need to be encouraged, each day and at all times, to use their own space to contemplate and ponder their own needs and successes.

Mana Tangata

This is the development of self-esteem through the individual's confidence to contribute to life. It encompasses the spirit of generosity and reciprocity; of caring for others and creating enduring personal relationships; of developing beliefs about prosperity that bring about the learning of skills for success and achievement; of developing physical powers through a strong and healthy body; of developing emotional maturity and awareness; of learning to deal with fears and inhibitions, which leads to joy and happiness. Children must learn early that life is a once-only experience. It is not a practice run.

Mana Reo

This is the development of communication, which enhances personal mana and wellbeing. The aim here is to empower the child in their ability to speak and to elucidate their learnings, knowledge, and abstract thoughts in te reo Māori. It is in the fluency of their delivery that their mana is enhanced.

Language is the window to a culture, and transmits the values and beliefs of its people. The many languages in this world have their own sounds and their own structures, yet they have but one purpose—to convey messages between the speaker and the listener.

Mana Whenua

This is the development of a sense of sovereignty, of identity, and of belonging. According to Māori, when a child is born their umbilical cord is cut and buried along with the placenta in their own land. In te reo Māori, the land and the placenta are both "whenua". Because of these traditions, the child has a spiritual unity with the land, with its people, and with the universe at large. A sense of identity with the land of their birth is inculcated in the child; love and respect for the land and its environment, and the geographic features of home, are learnt and imprinted in the child's mind. The spirit of the land lives in the child; their physical and emotional identification with the land is strengthened through myths, song, dance, and karakia. Confidence and self-esteem are the outcomes.

Mana Aotūroa

This is the development of a desire to explore and understand all aspects of this world and the universe; the development of curiosity, and of seeking answers.

The child learns and understands their uniqueness and their similarity with the rest of the universe. They learn that conquering the unknown through the power of the mind is possible; that understanding the physical world is exciting and challenging; that developing and practising the universal ideals of peace, compassion and harmony are a responsibility for us all.

Conclusion

Te Whāriki, the curriculum for early childhood education, is such a challenge for all of us. Our rights are recognised, and so are the rights of everyone else. For me, *Te Whāriki* encapsulates my horizon and the dreams I have for my mokopuna's heritage. It can be your horizon as well, and the heritage you leave behind, because *Te Whāriki* recognises my right to choose, and your right to choose. It encourages the transmission of my cultural values, my language and tikanga, and your cultural values, your language and customs. It validates my belief systems and your belief systems. It is also "home-grown".

Te Whāriki has a theoretical framework that is appropriate for all; common yet individual; for everyone, yet only for one; a whāriki woven by loving hands that can cross cultures with respect, that can weave people and nations together. *Te Whāriki* teaches us to respect ourselves and ultimately to respect others. It aims to ensure that children are empowered in every way possible, particularly in the development of their mana. They are nurtured in the knowledge that they are loved and respected; that their physical, mental, spiritual, and emotional strength will build mana, influence, and control; that having mana is the enabling and empowering tool to controlling their own destiny.

Te Whāriki encompasses the child in their uniqueness, as well as their being part of a whole. It reflects the child's holistic development, and the effect of the total environment on that development. In all of this, *Te Whāriki* also recognises the child as the living link to the past, the embodiment of the present, and the hope for the future. *Te Whāriki* perpetuates the cultural belief held by many Māori that the mokopuna is special.

Table 2.1

Te Whāriki: The Explanations

NGĀ TAUMATA WHAKAHIRAHIRA

Mana Atua
- The spiritual and sacred
- The unique and divine sense
- Developing a sense of wellbeing

Mana Tangata
- One's contribution to people, places, and things
- Developing self-esteem
- Developing ability to control

Mana Reo
- Speaking the language
- Communication
- Knowing the sacredness of the language

Mana Whenua
- Identity and belonging
- Rootedness
- Developing a sense of sovereignty with land

Mana Aotūroa
- Exploration
- Curiosity and adventure
- Developing understandings of self and the universe

TINANA

Power of the Body
- The body manifests its own atua/god
- The body projects its own powers

Physical Powers
Exercise and good nutrition build:
- A healthy body
- A strong body
- A fit body.

Body of Communication
- Language and its many forms—voice, sign, mind (telepathy)
- Language and its physical structures
- Expresses culture and people's mana

Physical Identity
- Cultural symbolism—houses, food, music
- Researching health of land and people
- Identifying with land of one's birth/ancestry

The Physical Universe
- Exploration of self, mankind, earth, and the universe
- Knowledge of the old and new
- Exploration of "large" and "small"

HINENGARO

Power of the Mind
- Training the mind to inquire, understand, and progress one's destiny through life
- Belief in "self"

Intellectual Powers
- Imprint belief systems
- Develop skills and knowledge for success
- Belief that opportunities abound in life
- No trials—this is life!

Power of Language
- Medium organised by the mind for communication
- Use of language skills enhances mana of the medium and person

Intellectual Identity
- Recognition and imprinting of home and place—land, rivers, mountains, people
- Self-esteem and love of "home"

Time and Space Orientation
- Conquering the unknown—internal or external
- Exploring and understanding one's uniqueness and similarity with the rest of the universe

WAIRUA

Power of the Spirit
- The spark of godliness in each human being
- Each is unique
- Mauri is in all things—animate and inanimate

Spiritual Powers
- Spirit of giving
- Caring for others
- Creating firm relationships

Spiritual Communications
- Every language carries its own spirit
- Every language is precious
- Language must be spoken to survive

Spiritual Identity
- Land, people, and universe are one
- Spirit of the land is in the person

Spiritual Universe
- The source of all energy in the universe is one
- Exploring and discovering is a spiritual experience

> **WHATUMANAWA**
>
> **Power of Emotions**
> - Emotions express our inner and outer worlds
> - Positive thoughts fuel happiness, success
> - Negative thoughts fuel negative outcomes
>
> **Emotional Powers**
> - Encouraging joy and happiness
> - Removing fears and inhibitions
> - Supporting fairness and justice
>
> **Emotional Communication**
> - Conveying emotions powerfully—love, happiness, sorrow, fear, hate
> - Language and a strong identity develop a healthy, confident person
>
> **Emotional Identity**
> - Identity with the land is developed through art, music, language, poetry, drama, and history
> - Understanding wars over land
>
> **Exploring the Emotional Universe**
> - Recognising universal "laws" of the emotions – love, greed ...
> - Developing those that bring peace, harmony, balance

References

Government Review Team (1988). *Government review of Te Kohanga Reo. Ripoata o te whakamatau o nga mahi a Te Kohanga Reo*. Wellington: Author.

Kehoe, J. (1991). *Mind power*. Toronto: Zoetic.

New Zealand Planning Council (1989). *From birth to death II*. Wellington: Author.

New Zealand Planning Council (1990a). *Māori information booklets 1, 2, 3, 4*. Wellington: Author.

New Zealand Planning Council (1990b). *Who gets what?* Wellington: Author.

New Zealand Planning Council (1990c). *Puna wairere*. Wellington: Author.

Ngata, A. T., & Jones, P. T. H. (Eds.). (1974). *Ngā mō teatea: He maramara rere nō ngā waka maha*. Part II. Auckland: Polynesian Society.

Reedy, M. (1990). 'Whiringa Wairua'. In Te Kohanga Reo booklet for World Indigenous Peoples Conference. Hamilton, New Zealand: The Conference.

Reedy, T. (1979). *He matapuna*. Wellington: New Zealand Planning Council.

2: Tōku Rangatiratanga nā te Mana Mātauranga: "Knowledge and Power Set Me Free ..."

Endnotes

1   The full text of Sir Āpirana Ngata's poroporoaki is as follows:

   E tipu e rea mo nga ra o tou ao
   Ko to ringa ki nga rakau a te Pākehā
   Hei ara mo to tinana
   Ko to ngakau ki nga taonga
   A o tipuna Māori
   Hei tikitiki mo to mahuna
   A ko to wairua ki te Atua
   Nana nei nga mea katoa.

   Grow up oh tender shoot and fulfil the needs of your generation
   Your hand mastering the skills of the Pākehā
   For your material well-being
   Your affections centred on the treasures
   Of your Māori ancestors
   As a plume upon your head
   Your soul given to God
   Creator of all things.

2   The original text of *Whiringa Wairua*, by Moehau Reedy, is as follows:

   Kua pua nga tini mano kawai
   O nga Kohanga Reo
   He whiriwhiri ano ki te putahi-tanga
   O rehua

   Whiringa wairua
   He muka tangata
   Whiria mai tawhiti nui i pamaomao
   He muka whero he parauri
   He muka papura kokowai
   Hei whiriwhiri ano ki te putahi-tanga
   O rehua

   Marakerake te huarahi
   Mo nga Kohanga Reo
   Ko te wairua ki te atua
   Ki te putahi-tanga
   O rehua

   Whiringa wairua, he muka tangata
   Whiria mai tawhiti nui i pamaomao
   Whiringa wairua he muka tangata
   Kohanga Reo karanga ra whiria mai
   Hei whakahoki ano ki te whiria mai
   Hei whakahoki ano ki te putahi-tanga
   O rehua

   Ki te putahi-tanga o rehua
   O rehua.

CHAPTER 3

Te hōhonutanga o *Te Whāriki*: Developing a deeper understanding of *Te Whāriki*

Lesley Rameka and Brenda Soutar

Introduction

Te Whāriki, the early childhood curriculum document, was published in 1996 and has shaped early childhood education practice in Aotearoa New Zealand for over 20 years. From the outset, the writers of *Te Whāriki*, Dr Helen May, Dr Margaret Carr, Dr Tamati Reedy, and Tilly Reedy, were committed to producing a document that honoured Aotearoa New Zealand's founding document, Te Tiriti o Waitangi.

In 2017 *Te Whāriki* was updated to reflect the changes to context, theory, and practice that had occurred over the years. The updated *Te Whāriki: He Whāriki Mātauranga mō ngā Mokopuna o Aotearoa: Early Childhood Curriculum* (Ministry of Education, 2017) includes a stronger focus on bicultural practices and greater stress on the importance of language, culture, and identity to the learning of mokopuna (children). Māori values and beliefs have been further embedded within *Te Whāriki* through the strengthened integration of te reo Māori; tikanga Māori; and Māori concepts, pedagogies, and practices.

This chapter explores the changes to *Te Whāriki* and discusses how Māori values and beliefs can support kaiako (teachers) to develop deeper understandings of Māori mokopuna and Māori culture, and ways of seeing and knowing the world from a Māori perspective. We firstly discuss the concept of 'te whāriki", including the importance of whakapapa (genealogy), kaitiakitanga (custodianship or stewardship), and spiritual elements such as tapu (sacredness) and mana (power). Next, we identify and explain some of the changes in *Te Whāriki*. We end with challenges to the implementation of *Te Whāriki* and potential ways forward for early childhood education.

Background

Titiro whakamuri kia anga whakamua
Look to the past in order to move forward

"Te whāriki" is a conceptual framework drawn from te ao Māori, the origin of which lies back beyond 1996 and 1993, when the draft was published , beyond even the introduction of the Gregorian calendar to Aotearoa New Zealand. Situated in another realm that spans aeons of time all the way back to the creation of the Māori world, the origin of te whāriki can be found where the whakapapa (genealogy) of harakeke[1] begins.

Barlow (1991) explains that everything has a whakapapa, including animals, trees, rocks, soil and mountains. Whakapapa links people to the environment and is closely associated with Māori notions of kaitiakitanga (custodianship or stewardship). One is obligated to interact in specific ways that are respectful, ways that maintain the tapu (sacredness) and mana (power) of people and the environment. There must always be reciprocity because relationships between people, places, things, and events involve interdependency. Harakeke, as a senior sibling to humankind, carries the same whakapapa that connects Māori to the original essence. This relationship is what guides the tikanga relating to planting, cultivation, and use of harakeke. Karakia recited during planting, cultivation, harvesting, and preparation, and those recited at the outset of a weaving project, are part of the narrative imbued in the weaving. Collectively these aspects are the mauri or life essence of any weaving, including whāriki or mats.

When a whāriki is woven, there is a tapu element because the tīpuna (ancestors) are present in spirit. Also present is the original essence, an energy often referred to as potential. The presence of tīpuna and the original essence is acknowledged through karakia (prayer) and ritual. "Animate and inanimate objects can also have *mana* as they also derive from the *atua* (gods) and because of their own association with people imbued with *mana* or because they are used in significant events" (Māori Dictionary, 2019).

A whāriki, like all woven artefacts, has mana from the original source. The mana and tapu of the whāriki will increase over time through use and through relationships with people, places, things, and events imbued with their own mana. It is the whāriki that communicates across the past, present, and future and holds the connection to the ancestors that allows mauri to flourish. When narratives regarding the whāriki cease to be told and rituals are not carried out, the ability of the whāriki to communicate is compromised, the mauri languishes, and the whāriki is considered no longer warm.

The weaver is considered to have inherited creative talent or pūmanawa directly from the original essence through the gods and ancestors. The weaver, therefore, is

---

[1] Phormium tenax; an evergreen perennial flax native to New Zealand.

a channel by which the spiritual realm expresses creativity. Reedy and Reedy (2013, p. 1) state:

> Its unique qualities stretch back to infinity, to ancient times, to ancestors and their deeds. *Te Whāriki* is built on a foundation of Māori values and belief systems, like mana, having authority, prestige, power; ihi, having rank and essential inner force; wehi, being awe-inspiring; manaaki, showing respect; and aroha, having love and compassion. It is also about whakapapa, genealogy; tūrangawaewae, identity; te reo, language; and tikanga, etiquette and behaviour.

Embedding a Māori worldview through the weaving of conceptual ideas described in *Te Whāriki* authenticates the document. Mana, for example, is not just a word sitting in isolation to describe an aspect of the child. The very concept is one of connectedness to people, place, things, events, and realms—past and present, physical and spiritual. It is impossible to have mana without relationships.

> The main achievement occurs in the development of the child's mana. The child is nurtured in the knowledge that they are loved and respected; that their physical, mental, spiritual and emotional strength will build mana, influence, and control; that having mana is the enabling and empowering tool to controlling their own destiny. (Reedy, 2013, p. 47)

Te Tiriti o Waitangi

Te Tiriti o Waitangi in the context of *Te Whāriki* is about the relationship between Māori and the Crown, which includes Pākehā (New Zealanders of European descent) and everyone who has come to join Māori on these islands. It relates to our shared obligations and our shared aspirations for today and tomorrow. The layout of the *Te Whāriki* as one framework and two pathways moves us closer to achieving this through an indigenous pathway, *Te Whāriki a te Kōhanga Reo*, and a Treaty-based pathway. The updated version of *Te Whāriki*, *He Whāriki Mātaurangae mō Ngā Mokopuna o Aotearoa Early Childhood Curriculum*, explains that the document was "developed using a partnership approach as envisaged by Te Tiriti o Waitangi … Each principle and strand was given dual Māori and English names which were not however synonyms as they had their origins in different world views" (Ministry of Education, 2017, p. 69).

The Māori worldview, which underpins *Te Whāriki*, positions it as authentic, as belonging here in Aotearoa New Zealand, and as an example of our Tiriti-based approach to learning. This was the attempt from the outset. Although not a perfectly balanced relationship, it would be fair to say early childhood and Kōhanga Reo, through *Te Whāriki*, have pioneered a pathway towards better Treaty relationships. The update brings more clarity to the notion of "one-framework-two-paths", where each worldview is perceived as having equal mana. "Each strand has dual English and Māori names; while closely related, different cultural connotations mean the two are not equivalents" (Ministry of Education, 2017, p. 22).

The original writing team of *Te Whāriki* consisted of Dr Helen May, Dr Margaret Carr, Dr Tamati Muturangi Reedy, and Tilly Te Koingo Reedy (on behalf of Te Kōhanga Reo National Trust). They attempted to take a Treaty-based approach to their work together, one that would affirm different worldviews. As a result, the Māori and English terms for the principles and strands were connected but neither was a translation of the other. The update of *Te Whāriki* (Ministry of Education, 2017) builds on this approach with additional text and definitions. It provides a strengthened platform for implementing Treaty-based practice and using it effectively. Reflective kaiako can consider how they might honour Te Tiriti o Waitangi through *Te Whāriki*.

Kaupapa Māori theory

An important change in the refreshed version is the recognition, affirmation, and validation of kaupapa Māori and kaupapa Māori theory in early childhood education. Kaupapa Māori theory is derived from Māori ways of knowing and being. The retention of the Māori language and culture is embedded in kaupapa Māori theory. Kaupapa Māori theory constitutes a distinctive, contextualised theoretical framework driven by whānau (extended family), hapū (subtribe), and iwi (tribe) understandings. Kaupapa Māori relates not only to Māori philosophies but also to actions and practices derived from such philosophies (Penehira, Cram, & Pipi, 2003; Pihama, Smith, Taki, & Lee, 2004; Smith, 2003). According to Smith (1997) it is both theory and transformative praxis. It has evolved from Māori communities and has succeeded in supporting fundamental structural changes in educational interventions. Kaupapa Māori theory has become an important and coherent philosophy and practice for raising Māori consciousness, supporting resistance, and encouraging transformative action and reflection (praxis) in order to progress Māori cultural capital and learning outcomes within education (Eketone, 2008).

Kaupapa Māori is able to express Māori aspirations and concepts that can, in turn, provide a guide for teaching and learning practices. Kaupapa Māori theory supports positive transformations and educational, social, and economic advancement through practices that empower Māori to achieve educational success as Māori. *Te Whāriki* (Ministry of Education, 2017, p. 61), reiterates the importance of kaupapa Māori theory in implementing educational practices that support mokopuna to succeed, stating, "The implementation of kaupapa Māori theory emphasises practices that enable Māori to achieve educational success as Māori". *Te Whāriki* emphasises that kaupapa Māori not only gives voice to Māori aspirations but also "expresses the ways in which Māori aspirations, ideas and learning practices can be framed and organised". Furthermore, it acknowledges the contextual nature of learning and development, and highlights the importance of a localised curriculum. It is stated that "Kaupapa Māori theory is situated within the land, culture, history and people of Aotearoa New Zealand, constituting a distinctive, contextualised theoretical framework driven by whānau, hapū and iwi understandings".

Te Whāriki also acknowledges the importance of a kaupapa Māori approach to assessment, in that it perceives the mokopuna as situated in Māori ways of knowing and being, and stresses the aspirations of families (whānau) for mokopuna learning and development. Kaiako must therefore develop an understanding of Māori ways of knowing and being, and be able to implement assessment practices that reflect a kaupapa Māori perspective of mokopuna. *Te Whāriki* states:

> Kaupapa Māori assessment is concerned with enhancing the mana of the child and their whānau. This means placing Māori constructs of the child and their whānau in the centre of the frame, ensuring that assessment captures the strengths, abilities and competencies of the mokopuna and their whānau. (Ministry of Education, p. 64)

Whakataukī

An addition to the updated *Te Whāriki* is the inclusion of whakataukī. Whakataukī are able to provide ideas, concepts, and values in concise and often poetic ways that resonate with the heart. They also often provide a focus for deeper consideration and critical discussions. Whakataukī can be viewed as sayings, proverbs, prophecies, witticisms, or mottos. They were traditionally used to establish, reinforce, and transmit beliefs and values (Karetu, 1992; Patterson, 1992). Traditional Māori society was founded on belief systems, principles, ideals, and values defined and handed down by ancestors, rather than on a set of laws as is more common in Western societies. This is highlighted in the whakataukī: "Kia heke iho rā i ngā tūpuna, kātahi ka tika. *If handed down by the ancestors, it would be correct*" (Ministry of Education, 2017, p. 60). Mead and Grove (2003) make the point that whakataukī are more than just historical relics; rather, they are a communication with tīpuna (ancestors). Through whakataukī one is able to gain insights into what tīpuna valued and thought about life. They provide clear messages for future generations, as illustrated by the following whakataukī: "Tū mai e moko. Te whakaata o ō mātua. Te moko o ō tīpuna. *Stand strong, o moko. The reflection of your parents. The blueprint of your ancestors*" (Mead & Grove, p. 17).

The whakataukī "He purapura i ruia mai i Rangiātea e kore e ngaro, *A seed sown in Rangiātea will never be lost*" (p. 6) emphasises that the speaker knows his or her whakapapa (genealogical links) to Rangiātea (the Māori spiritual homeland) so is confident and secure, with a positive future. Not only does the whakataukī stress the importance of a secure Māori identity to the wellbeing of the individual, but it also highlights an interpretive system that frames Māori worldviews and ideas of identity. Reedy (2003, p. 55) relates the whakataukī to the importance of the young child in Māori society, stating:

> Māori tradition identified the Māori child as a valued member of the Māori world—before conception, before birth, before time. The child was the personification of the worlds of yesterday:
>
> > He purapura i ruia mai i Rangiātea
> >
> > E kore e ngaro.
> >
> > Precious seeds dispersed from Rangiātea [the famed homeland of the Māori gods] will never be lost.
>
> As with all precious seeds, the child was nurtured for survival and inculcated with an understanding of their own importance [...]

Whakataukī are often able to transcend cultural bounds and present concepts that are applicable across cultures and communities, for example "Te manu i kai i te miro, nōna te ngahere; te manu i kai i te mātauranga nōna te ao. *The bird who partakes of the miro berry owns the forest; the bird who partakes of education owns the world*" (Ministry of Education, 2017, p. 51). This whakataukī exemplifies the value placed on education and learning. Acquiring appropriate skills, knowledge, and attitudes is critical for future generations. Another whakataukī underscores the importance of mokopuna in the Māori world. Young mokopuna were regarded as a tribe's greatest resource, as shown in the following whakataukī: "He taonga te mokopuna, kia whāngaia, kia tipu, kia rea. *A child is a treasure, to be nurtured, to grow, to flourish*" (Ministry of Education, 2017, p. 2). Another stresses the importance of ensuring the uniqueness of the child supports teaching and learning: "Mā te ahurei o te tamaiti e ārahi i ā tātou mahi. *Let the uniqueness of the child guide our work*" (p. 63). Both of these whakataukī have relevance for all early childhood services as does another well-known whakataukī: "Ehara taku toa i te toa takitahi engari he toa takitini, *I come not with my own strengths but bring with me the gifts, talents and strengths of my family, tribe and ancestors*" (p. 12). This whakataukī stresses a view of the child as inherently competent and capable, no matter what their age or ability.

Te reo Māori

A stronger emphasis on the promotion of te reo Māori (Māori language) is an important feature of the updated *Te Whāriki*. Reedy (2003, p. 48) states that "Language is the window to a culture, and transmits the values and beliefs of its people." It is both a communication tool and a transmitter of values and beliefs. It reflects the cultural environment and ways of viewing the world from one person to the next, and from one generation to the next. It is also an important factor in retaining connections to land and culture: "Toi te kupu, toi te mana, toi te whenua—*Hold on to the word, the mana, the land*" (Hemara, 2000, p. 79); "Ko te reo te mauri o te mana Māori—*The permanence of the language maintains the authority and land ownership*" (Early Childhood Development, 1999, p. 23). These whakataukī emphasise the critical importance of language in retaining mana, land, and culture. Language is a source of power and a vehicle for expressing identity; without language one loses power and a unique identity (Barlow, 1991).

The integration of te reo Māori throughout the updated *Te Whāriki* recognises the shared obligation to protect Māori language in early childhood. The use of Māori terms, such as *kaiako* to represent everyone involved in teaching young children and *mokopuna* for children, reflects this commitment to te reo Māori. Furthermore, these terms widen perspectives of kaiako and mokopuna and are inclusive of all. *Ako* can be translated as "to teach or learn" and *kai* expresses the person doing the action. Although it is typically used to refer to a teacher, the term kaiako also relates to being a learner. *Moko* is a term for tattoo and *puna* are springs. Mokopuna have been described as the "temporal signs or manifestations of the tupuna" (ancestors) (Love, 2004, p. 50).

Not only is te reo Māori used throughout the revised *Te Whāriki*, there are also a number of statements that stress the importance of kaiako valuing, learning, and including te reo Māori in the programme.

- "All children should be able to access te reo Māori in their ECE setting, as kaiako weave te reo Māori and tikanga Māori into the everyday curriculum." (Ministry of Education, 2017, p. 12)
- "Kaiako develop their own knowledge of te reo Māori, tikanga Māori and Māori worldviews so that they are better able to support children to understand their own mana atuatanga." (p. 28)
- "It is important that te reo Māori is valued and used in all ECE settings. This may involve, for example, using correct pronunciation, retelling stories, and using Māori symbols, arts and crafts." (p. 41)
- "Through te reo Māori children's identity, belonging and wellbeing are enhanced." (p. 41)
- Children demonstrate "An appreciation of te reo Māori as a living and relevant language." (p. 42)
- "Language and culture are inseparable. Kaiako enhance the sense of identity, belonging and wellbeing of mokopuna by actively promoting te reo and tikanga Māori." (p. 43)

- "Kaiako pronounce Māori words correctly and promote te reo Māori using a range of strategies based on relevant language learning theories." (p. 43)
- "Te reo Māori is included as a natural part of the programme." (p. 44)
- "The use of te reo Māori in the programme is encouraged. Kaiako are supported to learn te reo Māori and to understand what it means for a child to be growing up bilingual." (p. 45)

The *Te Whāriki* strand *Mana reo—Communication* also strongly promotes the use of te reo Māori in early childhood. *Mana reo* refers to the development and power of language and communication (Barlow, 1991). *Mana reo* supports mokopuna wellbeing through empowering them to communicate their thoughts, knowledge, and learnings, and so enhances their mana (Reedy, 2003). It emphasises mokopuna abilities to express themselves, verbally and non-verbally, in English and in Māori.

Tikanga Māori

According to Patterson (1992), the word *tikanga* comes from the word "tika" and means the nature or function of a thing. Tikanga relates to things such as actions, habits, appearance and customs, including how and why people behave in certain ways. Mead (2003) describes *tikanga* as a rule, method, habit or "the Māori way" or in accordance with Māori customs (p. 11). Patterson (1992, p. 103) states that:

> The all-important quality here is that of being in accord with human nature, or rather, being in accord with tribal nature, being "natural" and hence being reasonable and correct. To a Māori this means being in accord with custom and common practice. By following the customs and practices laid down by tribal ancestors, you can be a full human being.

Te Whāriki (Ministry of Education, 2017) makes a number of statements that provide tikanga expectations and guide practice in relation to particular cultural customs.
- "... kaiako need understanding of a world view that emphasises the child's whakapapa connection to Māori creation, across te kore, te pō, te ao mārama, atua Māori and tīpuna" [the nothingness, the night, the world of light, Maori gods, and ancestors]. (p. 12)
- "Viewed from a Māori perspective, all children are born with mana inherited from their tīpuna. Mana is the power of being and must be upheld and enhanced." (p. 18)
- "For Māori the spiritual dimension is fundamental to holistic development because it connects the other dimensions across time and space." (p. 19)
- "It is important that kaiako develop meaningful relationships with whānau and that they respect their aspirations for their children, along with those of hapū, iwi and the wider community." (p. 20)

- "Connections to past, present and future are integral to a Māori perspective of relationships. This includes relationships to tīpuna who have passed on and connections through whakapapa to, for example, maunga, awa, moana, whenua and marae" [mountains, rivers, seas, land and ancestral houses]. (p. 21)
- "Cultural beliefs influence which learning dispositions are valued and how. *Te Whatu Pōkeka* highlights rangatiratanga [leadership], whakatoi [cheekiness], manaakitanga [caring] and aroha [loving] as learning dispositions that are valued in te ao Māori. Others include hūmārie [humility] and whakahī [pride]." (p. 23)
- "Kaiako should have an understanding, of Māori approaches to health and wellbeing and how these are applied in practice." (p. 26)

Challenges and potential

Despite the promise the updated *Te Whāriki* offers, a scan of recent Education Review Office (ERO) reports highlights that the early childhood sector has much to work on in order to actualise the promise. A 2012 ERO report, *Partnership with Whānau Māori in Early Childhood Services* (Education Review Office, 2012), found that only 10% of early childhood services developed a high level of partnership with whānau Māori. While most services expressed a desire to support Māori mokopuna and whanau, they lacked the required knowledge and skills to move beyond being welcoming, and expected Māori mokopuna and their whānau to fit in to the service's culture. This expectation was derived from a belief shared across most early childhood services that all mokopuna and whānau should be treated the same which was often based on the assumption that Māori mokopuna and whānau did not need to be treated differently to the normal (Pākehā) perspectives of knowing and being. Some made deficit assumptions as to why Māori were not involved in the service, including the claim that Māori did not value education. Others expressed the view that whānau were incapable of helping with learning, which revealed their lack of understanding of whānau skills, knowledge, and expertise.

Another ERO report, *Working with Te Whāriki* (Education Review Office, 2013), identified that many services made reference to New Zealand's dual cultural heritage, Te Tiriti o Waitangi, and bicultural practice in their philosophies. However, most did not fully realise the intent of te Tiriti o Waitangi in practice by offering a programme that was responsive to the language, culture, and identity of Māori mokopuna. It also highlighted that there were misunderstandings about the difference between providing a bicultural curriculum for all children and implementing a curriculum that supports Māori mokopuna to experience success as Māori.

A more recent ERO report *Awareness and Confidence to Work with Te Whāriki* (Education Review Office, 2017) also made reference to kaiako understandings of the differences between promoting educational success for Māori children and implementing a bicultural curriculum, stating that it was not well understood in many services. A lack of support to develop pedagogical knowledge was a key issue for services where kaiako were not confident to work with *Te Whāriki* to support Māori mokopuna.

Te Whāriki: He Whāriki Mātauranga mō ngā Mokopuna o Aotearoa: Early Childhood Curriculum establishes the curriculum to be used in early childhood education services across Aotearoa New Zealand. It also provides guidance for kaiako on its implementation. However, what is clear from these ERO reports is that there is much work to be done and that *Te Whāriki* alone cannot make the required changes. *Te Whāriki* can be a lever to agitate for change if it is supported through structural and professional initiatives.

An important point to make is that implementing *Te Whāriki* requires that all members of early childhood teams take individual and collective responsibility for ensuring Māori worldviews, cultural knowledge, and language are embedded within early childhood practice. With such commitment, mokopuna can enjoy and achieve educational success as Māori, within an environment that reflects the dual heritage of Aotearoa New Zealand. Furthermore, to effect authentic and sustainable change, this team effort requires ongoing growth in knowledge and understandings of Māori worldviews, values, and language, and of ways to model these insights in practice.

Achieving such change involves the teaching teams firstly exploring their own cultures, worldviews, values, and pedagogical frames, thereby opening themselves up to not only other ways of seeing the world, but also to practices associated with those worldviews. Kaiako will then be able to develop authentic understandings of Aotearoa New Zealand's dual cultural heritage and histories, Māori cultural ways of knowing and being, and associated practices. Appropriate professional learning and development is critical to the deepening of kaiako understandings of how to respectfully implement practices that value Māori ways of knowing, being, and doing in their services. We know from the ERO reports discussed previously that goodwill by individuals can only go so far. A cohesive programme of professional learning and development that focuses on all areas of Māori culture, language, and identity is required. An arguably more important platform, which can sustain change over time, is Initial Teacher Education (ITE) programmes. We must ask whether ITE programmes are able to provide the required support to equip kaiako with the knowledge, skills, and attitudes required to implement *Te Whāriki* in a culturally authentic and respectful way.

Finally, kaiako must recognise the knowledge and expertise within whānau and community. They must collaborate with whānau and community to weave together the principles and strands to create a localised curriculum for their service that is reflective of their context. This localised curriculum is situated within Aotearoa New Zealand and is underpinned by the Treaty of Waitangi. It requires acknowledgement of Māori and tangata whenua, and the shared responsibility to protect te reo and tikanga Māori. Early childhood education has a critical role in providing mokopuna with culturally located environments that recognise the right of all mokopuna to be exposed to, and learn, te reo and tikanga Māori.

If our goal is to actualise *Te Whāriki*, there must be a concerted effort not only across the early childhood sector but also across and within government agencies and institutions. It will require that all those associated with early childhood education—kaiako working with mokopuna, service leaders, professional learning and development providers, Initial Teacher Education providers, and the Ministry of Education—to commit to and take individual and collective responsibility for supporting the implementation of the bicultural intent of *Te Whāriki*.

References

Barlow, C. (1991). *Tikanga whakaaro: Key concepts in Māori culture*. Auckland: Oxford University Press.

Early Childhood Development. (1999). *Ahuru moowai—Parents as first teachers*. Wellington: Early Childhood Development.

Education Review Office. (2012). *Partnership with whānau: Māori in early childhood services*. Wellington: Author.

Education Review Office. (2013). *Working with Te Whāriki*. Wellington: Author.

Education Review Office. (2017). *Awareness and confidence to work with Te Whāriki*. Wellington: Author.

Eketone, A. (2008). Theoretical underpinnings of Kaupapa Māori directed practice. *MAI Review, 1*, 1–11.

Hemara, W. (2000). *Māori pedagogies: A view from the literature*. Wellington: New Zealand Council for Educational Research.

Karetu, T. (1992). Language and protocol of the marae. In M. King (Ed.), *Te ao hurihuri: Aspects of Māoritanga* (pp. 29–42). Auckland: Reed Books.

Love, C. (2004). *Extensions on Te Wheke*. Wellington: Open Polytechnic of New Zealand.

Māori Dictionary. (2009). Retrieved from https://maoridictionary.co.nz.

Mead, H. (2003). *Tikanga Māori: Living by Māori values*. Wellington: Huia Press.

Mead, H., & Grove, G. (2003). *Ngā pēpeha a ngā tīpuna*. Wellington: Victoria University Press.

Ministry of Education. (2017). *Te whāriki: He whāriki mātauranga mō ngā mokopuna o Aotearoa: Early childhood curriculum*. Wellington: Author. Retrieved from https://education.govt.nz/assets/Documents/Early-Childhood/ELS-Te-Whariki-Early-Childhood-Curriculum-ENG-Web.pdf

Patterson, J. (1992). *Exploring Māori values*. Palmerston North: Dunmore Press.

Penehira, M., Cram, F., & Pipi, K. (2003). *Kaupapa Māori governance: Literature review & key informant interviews*. Wellington: Katoa. Retrieved from www.tpt.org.nz/downloads/Kaupapa%20Māori%20Governance%20-%20Literature%20Review%20-%20Final%20report.pdf

Pihama, L., Smith, K., Taki, M., & Lee, J. (2004). *A literature review on kaupapa Māori and Māori education pedagogy.* Auckland: International Research Institute for Māori and Indigenous Education (IRI). Retrieved from https://www.academia.edu/7909873/a_literature_review_on_kaupapa_maori_and_maori_education_pedagogy

Reedy, T. (2013). Toku rangitiratanga na te mana-mātauranga: "Knowledge and power set me free ...". In J. Nuttall (Ed.), *Weaving Te Whāriki* (pp. 35–53). Wellington: New Zealand Council for Educational Research.

Reedy, T., & Reedy, T. (2013, December). *Te Whāriki:* A tapestry of life. Keynote address presented to the New Zealand conference on ECEC in cooperation with the OECD ECEC Network, *Curriculum implementation in ECEC:* Te Whāriki *in international perspective*, Wellington.

Smith, G. (1997). *The development of kaupapa Māori: Theory and praxis.* Unpublished doctoral thesis, The University of Auckland, New Zealand.

Smith, G. (2003, December). *Kaupapa Māori theory: Theorizing indigenous transformation of education & schooling.* Paper presented at 'Kaupapa Māori Symposium' NZARE/AARE Joint Conference, Auckland, New Zealand.

CHAPTER 4

Reconceptualising professional learning as knotworking: Actualising the transformative potential of *Te Whāriki*

Maria Cooper, Helen Hedges, and Joanna Williamson

> He rangi tā matawhāiti, he rangi tā matawhānui.
> *A person with restricted vision has a restricted horizon; a person with wide vision has plentiful opportunities.*

Introduction

Actualising the potential of *Te Whāriki* relies on kaiako/teachers having a broad range of professional knowledge and capabilities to draw on when interpreting the document and creating curriculum in specific communities. It also depends on kaiako/teachers being well supported to continue to grow their understandings. In Aotearoa New Zealand, policy makers have identified the implementation of *Te Whāriki* as a variable and complex issue to be explored in situ: inquiry-based and localised research is validated and encouraged (Education Review Office, 2017b; Ministry of Education, 2015). Our chapter draws attention to implementation in relation to professional knowledge, policies, and practices to support ongoing professional learning support. We argue that for kaiako/teachers to enact the refreshed *Te Whāriki*, professional learning and development (PLD) needs to be reconceptualised. Those involved in rethinking PLD have thus far advocated for a shift from simplistic information-sharing and short-term workshop provision to professional learning embedded in learning communities that value critical debate and dialogue (Thornton & Cherrington, 2018). We propose the idea of a culture of "knotworking" (Engeström, 2008) to extend current PLD provision in more fluid and flexible ways. This "knotworking" approach is responsive to research on effective teacher professional learning (Mitchell & Cubey, 2003) and to the capabilities required of kaiako/teachers outlined in *Te Whāriki*.

The transformative potential of *Te Whāriki*

The original early childhood curriculum document *Te Whāriki* (Ministry of Education, 1996) is internationally acclaimed due to its bicultural focus, non-prescriptive and play-based nature, inclusion of children from birth, and emphasis on holistic learning outcomes. The curriculum document was viewed as a way to unify a diverse sector around shared beliefs, goals, and practices that played out in ways specific to local communities. It was designed so that each setting could weave a locally responsive curriculum aligned with the principles, strands, goals, and outcomes described in *Te Whāriki*. These features have been retained and, arguably, strengthened in the revised document (Ministry of Education, 2017).

Te Whāriki was designed to be a catalyst for change in early childhood education (ECE) understandings and practices (Cullen, 2003). ECE researcher Cullen identified early on that attention needed to be paid to beliefs and theories that had historically dominated teacher thinking and practice. Cullen drew attention to the concepts of holism and diversity central to *Te Whāriki*. She argued that the professional knowledge of kaiako/teachers needed to grow in order to interpret and enact the framework in relation to curriculum content and outcomes. Attention to professional knowledge would reduce surface understandings of the document being considered sufficient, or existing practices being reinterpreted using new terminology.

Ten years later, researcher Hedges (2013) noted that the fluctuating policies the ECE sector had experienced meant that the promise of *Te Whāriki* had yet to be realised. Given that kaiako/teachers are the key decision makers about what children experience in ECE settings, Hedges raised concerns about the levels of professional knowledge throughout the sector, including in teacher education and among professional learning providers. She noted this as a constraint to building a systematic research and practice base in ECE for the benefit of children. Our chapter echoes Cullen's and Hedges' concerns and focuses specifically on support for professional learning. Where are we several years later? What has changed? What still remains a challenge? What are the new challenges? What is it that the revised *Te Whāriki* draws attention to? How can *Te Whāriki* help those in the ECE sector navigate international discourses and encourage the continuation of children's care and education in keeping with the aspiration statement of "confident and competent learners" (Ministry of Education, 2017, p.12)? What kinds of PLD might assist such capability development? What kind of policy support is needed to champion the creation of a new model for knowledge growth? Our chapter addresses these questions. It raises concerns about the level of support the sector has received for professional learning and offers guidance on how knowledge might be extended and grown within services.

Implementing *Te Whāriki*: A complex issue

Since the advent of *Te Whāriki*, policy makers have raised concerns about the quality of professional knowledge amongst kaiako/teachers to support its implementation. For example, following an Early Childhood Education Taskforce report suggesting that the implementation of *Te Whāriki* "be reviewed in order for strengths and weaknesses to be identified and learned from" (Early Childhood Education Taskforce, 2011, p. 112), the Education Review Office (ERO) explored ways services were working with the curriculum framework to ensure success for every learner (Education Review Office, 2013). Based on information gathered from their reviews of 627 early childhood services in 2012, ERO reported that although most services were using *Te Whāriki* as a guide for curriculum, only 10% of services were working in depth with theory in relation to the document. ERO (2013) highlighted that the problem was not *Te Whāriki* itself, but rather insufficient in-depth professional knowledge to implement a non-prescriptive curriculum. They urged the Ministry of Education to provide the sector with additional guidance and support to work with the intent of *Te Whāriki* in local curriculum design and implementation.

Similarly, the report of the Advisory Group on Early Learning (AGEL) (Ministry of Education, 2015) included a recommendation to improve the implementation of *Te Whāriki*. The differing values and purposes of *Te Whāriki* for kaiako/teachers and policy makers were apparent in the AGEL report's description of *Te Whāriki* as a "curriculum policy document owned and mandated by the New Zealand government" (p. 9) and also as a "potentially powerful tool for mediating teacher and teaching-team decision-making" (p. 10). The report's recommendations included an update of the curriculum document then undertaken in 2016 and 2017.

Both reports (Education Review Office, 2013; Ministry of Education, 2015) acknowledged the complexities of implementing *Te Whāriki* and the need for professional knowledge and appropriate guidance and support. The findings and recommendations of these reports are even more critical now, given that the refreshed *Te Whāriki* explicitly identifies, on p. 59, some of the professional knowledge kaiako/teachers require.

ERO's evaluation of kaiako/teacher implementation of the revised *Te Whāriki* has led, thus far, to the publication of two reports. The first report (Education Review Office, 2017a) focused on awareness and confidence to work with *Te Whāriki*. Based on data from 290 services, leaders and kaiako/teachers were found to have a high degree of awareness of, and growing confidence to begin to work with, the refreshed curriculum. However, barriers to implementation were noted. The key barriers were time and leader/kaiako knowledge and understanding of *Te Whāriki*.

The second report, focused on engaging with the 2017 version of *Te Whāriki*, was based on data from 167 services and six governing organisations (Education Review Office, 2017b). It raised similar concerns and was more explicit about issues related to access to and engagement in PLD. ERO (2017b) reported that while many individual services had engaged in PLD related to the revised *Te Whāriki*, including workshops, webinars, and online support—and, in a few cases, utilising participants' knowledge and expertise, support from organisations (umbrella organisations such as kindergarten associations) and/or external PLD providers—this engagement had been highly variable. In some cases, PLD was not reaching all those within services, compromising the ability for all teams to develop shared understandings and practices. There was also variability in the ways early childhood organisations were supporting their services, with only one organisation reported as actively working with an external PLD provider to support kaiako/teachers with implementation. Similar to the previous report, barriers to implementing *Te Whāriki* were identified as kaiako/teachers having limited time to engage with both *Te Whāriki* and PLD, varying levels of understanding about the curriculum, different levels of enthusiasm and commitment to ongoing learning, and inconsistent access to PLD. ERO acknowledged that PLD and effective leadership were both needed to improve understandings and practice in relation to *Te Whāriki*, and that either one on its own was insufficient for effective curriculum implementation. To these matters we add that policy and funding to grow professional knowledge through an effective model of practice-focused professional learning are also required.

Such findings are troubling, as they sit against a backdrop of explicit expectations from significant policy makers and advisors—the Ministry of Education, ERO, and the Teaching Council of Aotearoa New Zealand—for kaiako/teachers and leaders to engage in high-level PLD. For example, ERO (2017b) expect that individual services and organisations will engage more deeply with *Te Whāriki* while determining next steps and priorities for PLD. In the recent standards for the teaching profession published by the Teaching Council, teachers are expected to be able to "use inquiry, collaborative problem-solving and professional learning to improve professional capability to impact on the learning and achievement of all learners" (Teaching Council of Aotearoa New Zealand, 2017, p. 18). The ability to meet these expectations is impacted by issues of inequitable access to high-quality PLD, varying levels of support for kaiako/teachers and leaders to identify their PLD needs, and access to participants' expertise and support from external PLD providers/researchers (Cherrington, 2017). Such issues affect how kaiako/teachers and leaders across the sector might grow and deepen their professional knowledge for effective implementation. In short, policy makers are finding fault with curriculum implementation but are yet to advocate for or fund models of PLD that would improve the situation. One-off workshops and short digests of information have long been found inadequate to support professional knowledge-building; they are "episodic and piecemeal … doom[ing] any attempts to sustain intellectual community" (Grossman, Wineburg, & Woolworth, 2001, p. 948). Yet current Ministry of Education investment means these continue to be the primary modes of PLD provision, albeit now via technology that has afforded useful websites with information, resources, and webinars. As we discuss shortly, technology might improve access and reach, but it does not guarantee engagement with the content in sufficient depth to address the issues outlined. There remains a need to offer PLD over a sustained period, and for that PLD to be responsive to research on effective PLD. This will create opportunities for the potential of *Te Whāriki* as a catalyst for changed knowledge and practices to be realised. We provide an overview of that research shortly. Before doing so, we offer an illustrative example of why in-depth knowledge and engagement are needed.

Theory and pedagogy

The refreshed *Te Whāriki* invites engagement with developmental, sociocultural, bioecological, kaupapa Māori, neuroscience, and critical theories. The intention is to increase the richness of the weaving of theories underpinning pedagogy. However, there is a risk that some theoretical ideas might be narrowly interpreted unless there is time to engage with recent research, time to reflect, and opportunities to dialogue with others. We exemplify our concern in relation to infant and toddler pedagogy.

Current popular approaches to infant and toddler pedagogy appear to draw quite narrowly, and at times uncritically, on emphases related to Western developmental theory, neuroscience, and/or a focus on the individual child (Education Review Office, 2013; Nutbrown & Page, 2008). These approaches also appear to respond to studies promoting an inwards focus on the self (e.g., self-concept, self-esteem, self-confidence, self-regulation) as a key factor in life-course outcomes. Yet these emphases and ideas are just one part of a much broader range of theoretical knowledge that is available to inform pedagogical decisions about what matters in weaving local whāriki for all infants and toddlers. A diverse range of theory is endorsed in *Te Whāriki*, policy reports (e.g., Education Review Office, 2013), an extensive literature review on quality pedagogy for children under two (Dalli et al., 2011), and on the Te Kete Ipurangi website (Ministry of Education, 2019).

Significantly, some of the Western infant and toddler pedagogies underplay the social and broader relational worlds, lives, and identities of children and families, and the interdependent values and dispositions honoured in bioecological, sociocultural, and kaupapa Māori theories. Māori ECE researchers Rameka et al. (2017) critiqued Western ideas about infant and toddler pedagogy. Through a series of purposeful local inquiries, they reclaimed and repurposed some culturally located practices and pedagogies in their project with kaiako/teachers of infants and toddlers. Our example later in this chapter of extending professional learning communities with knotworking features illustrates that theoretical interweaving relies on kaiako/teachers having relevant professional knowledge and opportunities to critically discuss and debate the range of contemporary concepts, theories, and perspectives most relevant and appropriate for their community whāriki. To do this, kaiako/teachers need flexible and collective opportunities to interrogate practices, negotiate, and add in-depth knowledge in collaboration with colleagues and internal and external experts, including high-quality PLD providers. Without this, kaiako/teachers can understandably fall back on early under-examined interpretations of theories and practices.

Professional learning and development: History and research findings

Having made a case for the knowledge, time, and expertise required by kaiako/teachers if they are to engage with the refreshed curriculum more fully, we now overview PLD provision and research on what constitutes effective PLD. However, as a significant constraint, we note that Aotearoa New Zealand, like many countries, currently maintains policy where a range of staff with no qualification educate children alongside qualified kaiako/teachers. This makes PLD provision complex, as it is attempting to cater for an almost impossibly wide range of needs. As Ball (2013) noted, "Policies [on PLD] are enacted in material conditions, with varying resources, in relation to particular 'problems' that are constructed nationally and locally. They are also set against existing commitments, values and forms of experience" (p. 11). Locally, these constraints were noted by Meade et al. (2012) in their collective case studies of early childhood centres. These case studies compared practices in centres operating in the funding band where 50–79% of staff are qualified against centres operating in the funding band where 100% of staff are qualified. The settings with fewer qualified teachers "displayed less 'know-how' and 'know-why'", and while they spoke of teams being made up of equals, "the data suggested that 'equal' was at the level of the 'lowest common denominator'" (p. 105), especially in relation to pedagogy that is most effective in promoting positive outcomes for children. In addition, logistics regarding the work responsibilities of qualified teachers—who were required to guide unqualified staff and student teachers in their work—had consequences for children. These consequences included qualified teachers spending less time with children due to spending more time supporting unqualified adults with "on-job professional education" (p. 107).

As a main funder of PLD provision in Aotearoa New Zealand, the Ministry of Education has historically allocated funding based on their chosen priority areas

4: Reconceptualising professional learning as knotworking:
Actualising the transformative potential of *Te Whāriki*

(Cherrington, 2017). ECE researcher Cherrington noted that from 1997 to 2010, funding was allocated to services committed to PLD programmes that addressed priority areas at that time, such as understanding and implementing the original version of *Te Whāriki* (Ministry of Education, 1996), assessment, and self-review. However, this situation changed when targeted contestable funding was introduced in 2010 and the PLD funding was halved. A smaller range of services were able to access funding for PLD, on a narrower range of topics (Cherrington, 2017). Moreover, the funding was limited to those services needing to improve the rates of children's participation in ECE and/or needing to improve the quality of their service, with less emphasis on the high-quality reflection and inquiry PLD we are arguing for. While inquiry-based self-review and internal evaluation continue to be prioritised at policy level (see Education Review Office, 2009), since 2010 such priorities are reflected in rhetoric and external evaluation, not in the funding of provision for professional learning opportunities so that settings can engage collectively in knowledge-building.

In short, at the time that policy organisations were critiquing the implementation of *Te Whāriki*, there appear to have been few well-designed, systematic, and sustained programmes of PLD in Aotearoa New Zealand to build capability and capacity in kaiako/teachers. This situation is not proposed to change judging by the vague reference to PLD in the current draft strategic plan for early learning 2019–29 (Ministry of Education, 2018). However, the use of technology has been identified as a way to share resources and build community (Cherrington & Thornton, 2013). For example, following the release of the refreshed curriculum document, CORE Education was contracted by the Ministry of Education in 2017 to 2018 to support teacher/kaiako implementation of *Te Whāriki*. CORE Education introduced curriculum champions to support pedagogical leaders with curriculum implementation in their services, and promoted the use of online resources and webinar recordings to stimulate teacher/kaiako and leader discussions (CORE Education, 2019). Another recent Ministry of Education response to the PLD need has been to initiate the development of the Te Kete Ipurangi (TKI) *Te Whāriki* website. This open-access site includes a wide range of presentations, podcasts, key resources, and short guides to support the content of *Te Whāriki*. The site is continually updated with new materials as they are commissioned. Similarly, The Education Hub, described as a "one stop shop" of "up-to-date, usable research" (Education Hub, 2019), disseminates brief digests aimed at kaiako/teachers in the profession. In a digital age, these resource banks of information reflect a positive step towards actioning the recommendations of policy makers.

Nevertheless, we propose there is risk of superficial engagement with condensed ideas and materials unless kaiako/teachers are provided with structural support for critical debate and dialogue grounded in evidence of their own practices alongside research and theory. Kaiako/teachers also need external provocation to challenge, reframe, and collectively update their professional knowledge in ways that go beyond their setting and are responsive to literature on effective PLD.

There is a plethora of literature about effective PLD in school settings but only one systematic review of such literature in ECE. ECE researchers Mitchell and Cubey (2003) identified eight principles of effective PLD:

1. incorporating participants' own knowledge and understandings
2. providing theory and research knowledge
3. investigating pedagogy in participants' own settings
4. analysing teaching and learning data generated in own settings
5. promoting critical reflection to challenge assumptions and extend thinking
6. supporting diverse educational practices
7. changing practice, beliefs, understandings and attitudes
8. raising awareness of own beliefs.

These principles could be applied to PLD that offers systemic and systematic support in local contexts, such as through professional learning communities (PLCs) (Thornton & Cherrington, 2018), in order to get to grips with the revised document.

Cherrington and Thornton have been advocates for the use of PLCs in Aotearoa New Zealand (Cherrington & Thornton, 2013; Thornton & Cherrington, 2018). PLCs are collectives of teachers who are supported by policy and leadership to inquire into and reflect on their practices together. PLCs rely on the idea that teachers will take control of their own learning and commit to a culture that prioritises debate, critical reflection, multiple perspectives, and children (Cherrington, 2017).

Certain features of PLCs generate opportunities for successful outcomes and improved teaching and learning: an emphasis on professional learning, supportive leadership, a shared focus, commitments to reading research, deprivatising (sharing openly) and discussing teaching practices, and plenty of opportunities for dialogue (Cherrington & Thornton, 2013; Thornton & Cherrington, 2018). Such communities may not need to be geographically co-located and may be virtual given the technologies available now (Cherrington & Thornton, 2013). It is critical that expert external facilitation is involved to ensure that robust debate and dialogue occur to move past an illusion of collaboration (Orland-Barak & Tillema, 2006). Such external expertise could be involved at different points and reflect research knowledge and capability, knowledge of the national and local context, and high levels of facilitation and communication skills. This expertise is reflected in the questions we propose shortly that could be part of an ongoing, high-functioning, and critically reflective professional learning culture.

Examples of funded PLC-type activities that promote research and professional dialogue in Aotearoa New Zealand include Centres of Innovation, the Teaching and

Learning Research Initiatives (TLRIs), and the more recent Teacher-Led Innovation Funded projects (TLIFs). These funded studies, along with postgraduate studies, have the potential to provide in-depth understandings to guide shifts in professional knowledge, pedagogy, and related practices connected to *Te Whāriki*. These studies and practice examples foreground the importance of research and PLD that offers examples of contextually relevant implementation of *Te Whāriki* consistent with policy makers' expectations.

To summarise so far, addressing professional knowledge for the implementation of *Te Whāriki* is a complex challenge that continues to trouble the sector. We argue that funding for more effective forms of collaboration between early childhood kaiako/ teachers, services, researchers, and PLD providers is needed. Such investment will assist the sector in working towards addressing the expectations of the Education Review Office and the Teaching Council of Aotearoa New Zealand. It will also support ECE researchers and kaiako/teachers to improve outcomes for children and families. We now draw upon cultural–historical activity theory to understand how teaching teams, PLD providers, and other experts might connect and collaborate around the professional knowledge needed to implement *Te Whāriki* in ways that extend the idea of a PLC. We propose "negotiated knotworking" (Engeström, 2008, p. 19) as central to a culture that can support professionals, both internal and external to a specific early childhood service, to come together in dynamic ways to expand collective learning with the aim of implementing *Te Whāriki* in depth.

A CHAT reconceptualisation of PLD: Negotiated knotworking

Cultural–historical activity theory (CHAT) offers a broad theoretical lens with which to understand how ECE communities might actualise the transformative potential of *Te Whāriki*. Extending the cultural–historical work of Vygotsky (1978) and Leont'v (1978), Engeström's (2000, 2008) third generation activity theory focuses on understanding object-oriented systems that are collective in nature. "Object" in this sense refers to the focus or motive that individuals are oriented towards, which gives rise to the collective activity. In our case, an early childhood service reflects an activity system focused primarily on the object of implementing the renewed *Te Whāriki*. This object is what subjects, or kaiako/teachers in the service, talk about, focus on, and carry out actions in relation to. In this way, the object provides direction and meaning for their collective activity (Engeström, 2008).

A CHAT concept of value is "knotworking" (Engeström, 2008; Engeström, Engeström, & Vähäaho, 1999). Knotworking describes the fluid, organic, and distributed patterns of collaboration between participants who come together from across boundaries, such as kaiako/teachers, external PLD providers, and others offering relevant expertise. Their purpose of connecting and collaborating in this manner is to negotiate meaning, which in this case is about implementing *Te Whāriki* effectively. Collaboration across boundaries is dynamic, assumed to be long-term rather than simple and short-term, and facilitated by negotiated knotworking (Engeström, 2008). This means that services, PLD providers, and other experts would see their connection as developing over time, rather than for the short-term only.

Negotiated knotworking is defined as "rapidly pulsating, distributed, and partially improvised orchestration of collaborative performance between otherwise loosely connected actors and activity systems" (Engeström, 2000, p. 972). To illustrate, as an early childhood service and PLD provider/external expert work on their common object, they would each generate separate threads of activity that need to be tied, untied, or re-tied. They would do this by coming together to form temporary "knots", a metaphor for the coming together of different professionals for the purpose of transforming understandings and practices, leading to new knowledge (Engeström, 2008). Kaiako/teachers may bring to these knots their current challenges, internal inquiry foci, and practice-based evidence. The provider/external expert might offer external insights and critique of practices, and respond with suggestions, readings, and online resources. The kaiako/teachers and leaders would try out ideas and then come back together to engage in critical debate and dialogue about possible ways forward. Hence, negotiated knotworking is an intentional process characterised by complexity and uncertainty (Engeström, 2008) and, in this case, driven by the object of implementing *Te Whāriki*. The fluidity of such a process suggests that respect for differing expertise, rather than central authority, would be valued. This means that while professional leaders might be involved, they would not necessarily lead the collaboration at all times. Consequently, the overall group would generate new collective knowledge and new levels of activity. Given the learning potential and mutual benefits of negotiated knotworking, we propose that PLD provision embeds information and resource-sharing and short-term workshops *within* the purposeful and sustained activity of knotworking cultures.

Creating a knotworking culture

One of the most significant challenges for actualising the transformative potential of *Te Whāriki* lies in creating opportunities for kaiako/teachers to grow their professional knowledge through dynamic, long-term connection and collaboration with other groups and individuals. Next, we proffer reflective questions and provocations to assist groups in establishing a knotworking culture focused on professional knowledge for implementing *Te Whāriki*, with the outcome of understanding and fostering children's learning. These questions are guided by Engeström's (2008)

4: Reconceptualising professional learning as knotworking: Actualising the transformative potential of *Te Whāriki*

CHAT principles and the concept of negotiated knotworking and prompted by our analysis of the findings of Cherrington and Thornton (2013), Thornton and Cherrington (2018), and Mitchell and Cubey (2003).

- *Mediating tools and signs*—each group needs clarity about the mediating tools of their activity. What resources, technologies, materials, and other tools can we use in our collective work? Do we need to introduce new tools to mediate new understandings and practices? What potential tensions might arise when introducing new tools to our activity? The relational tools of robust dialogue and debate can centre on research-based readings and practice experiences.
- *Mutual constitution of actions and activity*—each group needs to understand the relationships between their individual actions, collective activity, and improving the implementation of *Te Whāriki*. What changes do we need to make to foster alignment between our practices and desired outcomes? What time will we give to addressing these changes and who else might be involved? These actions and activities would be supported by effective professional leadership and opportunities for dialogue on purposes and directions.
- *Contradictions and deviations as sources of change*—through the knotworking, tensions may arise that provide additional opportunities for professional learning. Viewing tensions in this way moves beyond the illusion of collaboration, as knotworking involves professionals with different expertise coming together as knots for high levels of collaboration, collective critical inquiry, debate, and decision-making regarding professional knowledge to implement *Te Whāriki*.
- *Historicity*—groups can gain a fuller appreciation of their shared focus by understanding the historical landscape of their activity: What changes over time have occurred? What new practices and processes are we proposing and how are these responsive to contemporary understandings?

Creating a knotworking culture within PLCs to underpin PLD facilitation is consistent with realising the strength of the weaving metaphor inherent in *Te Whāriki*. If *Te Whāriki* is to be a catalyst for change (Cullen, 2003) and have transformative potential (Hedges, 2013), we argue that kaiako/teachers need to develop collective capacity and grow their professional knowledge through sufficient, dynamic opportunities to think critically and engage in debate and dialogue with others, including those with external expertise, who are also deeply invested in ECE. Such an open-ended and flexible learning culture fosters robust mutual engagement with beliefs, practices, research, theory, and literature, and welcomes rich dialogue, an openness to provocation, new learning, and trusting relationships.

Conclusion

Te Whāriki is recognised internationally as a rich and progressive document, but the effectiveness of its localised implementation in Aotearoa New Zealand has raised concerns. We suggest that lack of attention to the ongoing provision of high-quality PLD decreases the potential for kaiako/teachers to grow professional knowledge and realise Te Whāriki's potential, with consequences for understanding and fostering children's learning. Taking a CHAT lens in this chapter has helped us to suggest ways that PLD might be reconceptualised to support a culture of knotworking in PLCs that reflect the principles of quality PLD. In such a culture, opportunities for high levels of collaboration, collective critical inquiry, debate, and decision-making across boundaries are needed to actualise the potential of Te Whāriki as a catalyst for change with transformative potential. It also means positioning the ever-evolving object of implementing Te Whāriki as involving a rich interweaving of knowledge, pedagogy, and practices.

> Ehara taku toa i te toa takitahi, he toa takitini.
> *My strength is not as an individual, but as a collective.*

References

Ball, S. (2013). *The education debate* (2nd ed.). Bristol, UK: The Policy Press.

Cherrington, S. (2017). Professional learning and development in early childhood education: A shifting landscape of policies and practice. *New Zealand Annual Review of Education, 22*, 53–65. doi:https://doi.org/10.26686/nzaroe.v22i0.4148

Cherrington, S., & Thornton, K. (2013). Continuing professional development in early childhood education in New Zealand. *Early Years: An International Research Journal, 33*(2), 119–132.

CORE Education (2019). *Te Whāriki 2017*. Retrieved from http://core-ed.org/about-core/our-projects/te-whariki-online/

Cullen, J. (2003). The challenge of *Te Whāriki*: Catalyst for change? In J. Nuttall (Ed.), *Weaving Te Whāriki: Aotearoa New Zealand's early childhood curriculum document in theory and practice* (pp. 269–296). Wellington: New Zealand Council for Educational Research.

Dalli, C., White, E. J., Rockel, J., Duhn, I., Buchanan, E., Davidson, S., ... Wang, B. (2011). *Quality early childhood education for under-two year-olds: What should it look like? A literature review*. Retrieved from https://www.educationcounts.govt.nz/publications/ECE/Quality_ECE_for_under-two-year-olds/executive-summary

Early Childhood Education Taskforce. (2011). *An agenda for amazing children: Final report of the ECE Taskforce*. Wellington: Author.

Education Council of Aotearoa New Zealand. (n.d). *Our code, our standards. Code of professional responsibility and standards for the teaching profession*. Retrieved from https://teachingcouncil.nz/content/our-code-our-standards

Education Review Office. (2009). *Implementing self review in early childhood services*. Retrieved from https://www.ero.govt.nz/assets/Uploads/imp-selfreview-ece-jan09.pdf

Education Review Office. (2013). *Working with Te Whāriki*. Wellington: Author.

Education Review Office. (2017a). *Awareness and confidence to work with Te Whāriki*. Retrieved from https://www.ero.govt.nz/assets/Uploads/Awareness-and-confidence-to-work-with-Te-Whariki.pdf

Education Review Office. (2017b). *Engagement with Te Whāriki (2017)*. Retrieved from https://www.ero.govt.nz/assets/Uploads/Engaging-with-Te-Whariki.pdf

Engeström, Y. (2000). Activity theory as a framework for analyzing and redesigning work. *Ergonomics, 43*, 960–974.

Engeström, Y. (2008). *From teams to knots: Activity-theoretical studies of collaboration and learning at work*. New York, NY: Cambridge University Press.

Engeström, Y., Engeström, R., & Vähäaho, T. (1999). When the center does not hold: The importance of knotworking. In S. Chaiklin, M. Hedegaard, & U. J. Jensen (Eds.), *Activity theory and social practice* (pp. 345–374). Aarhus, Denmark: Aarhus University Press.

Grossman, P., Wineburg, S., & Woolworth, S. (2001). Toward a theory of teacher community. *Teachers College Record, 103*(6), 942–1012.

Hedges, H. (2013). The future of *Te Whāriki*: Political, pedagogical and professional concerns. In J. Nuttall (Ed.), *Weaving Te Whāriki: Aotearoa New Zealand's early childhood curriculum document in theory and practice* (2nd ed., pp. 277–298). Wellington: NZCER Press.

Meade, A., Robinson, L., Smorti, S., Stuart, M., Williamson, J., with Carroll-Lind, J., … Te Whau, S. (2012). *Early childhood teachers' work in education and care centres: Profiles, patterns and purposes*. Wellington: Te Tari Puna Ora o Aotearoa / New Zealand Childcare Association.

Ministry of Education. (1996). *Te whāriki. He whāriki mātauranga mō ngā mokopuna o Aotearoa: Early childhood curriculum*. Wellington: Learning Media.

Ministry of Education. (2015). *Report of the advisory group on early learning*. Wellington: Author.

Ministry of Education. (2017). *Te whāriki. He whāriki mātauranga mō ngā mokopuna o Aotearoa: Early childhood curriculum*. Wellington: Author.

Ministry of Education. (2018). *Early learning 10 year strategic plan*. Retrieved from https://www.education.govt.nz/our-work/information-releases/information-releases-from-2018/early-learning-10-year-strategic-plan/

Ministry of Education (2019). *Te Whāriki online*. Retrieved from https://tewhariki.tki.org.nz/

Mitchell, L., & Cubey, P. (2003). *Characteristics of professional development linked to enhanced pedagogy and children's learning in early childhood settings: Best evidence synthesis*. Wellington: Ministry of Education. Retrieved from http://www.educationcounts.govt.nz/publications/series/2515/5955

Nutbrown, C., & Page, J. (2008). *Working with babies and children: From birth to three*. London, UK: SAGE.

Orland-Barak, L., & Tillema, H. (2006). The 'dark side of the moon': A critical look at teacher knowledge construction in collaborative settings. *Teachers and Teaching: Theory and Practice, 12*(1), 1–12.

Rameka, L., Glasgow, A., Howarth, P., Rikihana, T., Wills, C., Mansell, T., Burgess, F., … Iosefo, R. (2017). *Te whātu kete mātauranga: Weaving Māori and Pasifika infant and toddler theory and practice in early childhood education*. Wellington: TLRI. Retrieved from http://www.tlri.org.nz/tlri-research/research-completed/ece-sector/te-whatu-kete-matauranga-weaving-m%C4%81ori-and-pasifika

The Education Hub (2019). *Research guides*. Retrieved from https://theeducationhub.org.nz/research/

Thornton, K., & Cherrington, S. (2018). Professional learning communities in early childhood education: A vehicle for professional growth. *Professional Development in Education.* 45:3, 41–432. https://doi.org/10.1080/19415257.2018.1529609

PART 2

Te Whāriki in practice

CHAPTER 5

Frayed and fragmented: *Te Whāriki* unwoven

Jenny Ritchie and Mere Skerrett

Introduction

Te Whāriki: He Whāriki Mātauranga mō ngā Mokopuna o Aotearoa: Early Childhood Curriculum (Ministry of Education, 1996) developed via a long process of careful, collective, and wide consultation during the first half of the 1990s, and was published in its final form in 1996. It was subsequently updated in 2017. In this chapter we consider how, and to what extent, the 'refreshed' *Te Whāriki 2017* upholds Tiriti-based commitments. These include Māori self-determination over their lands, resources, and everything else that they valued, including the sustenance of te reo Māori (the Māori language) me ngā tikanga Māori (Māori values and aspirations) as essential to our diverse bioculture that is Aotearoa. In the two decades between the two versions of *Te Whāriki*, global consciousness has turned to the impacts of global warming and climate change, which, along with other human impacts on the biosphere, have resulted in an alarming crisis for the world's biocultural diversity, and in fact to the wellbeing of all life on Earth (Costello et al., 2009; World Wildlife Fund, Grooten, & Almond, 2018).

We therefore explore barriers that remain—both discursive and political—to a heightened focus on biocultural diversity, sustaining te reo Māori as the repository of ancestral wisdom and biocultural identity for the islands of Aotearoa New Zealand. The term 'biocultural diversity' considers linguistic, cultural, and biological diversities representing life on our planet (Skutnabb-Kangas, Maffi, & Harmon, 2003). Indigenous languages index Indigenous cultures in relationship with their environs. Indigenous languages and cultures recognise the interdependence of all living organisms, plants, animals, bacteria, and humans living and flourishing together in networks of complex and delicate relationships alongside all things inanimate.

Further, Indigenous worldviews recognise that damage to any part of these delicate relationships or networks (with or among humans and/or the ecosystem) will result in unforeseen, perhaps unintended, and likely harmful consequences for the whole biocultural system. Human environmental adaptation has been remarkable in its reach (Flannery, 2010; Wilson, 2012).

Languages, too, diversify and adapt as they connect to new lands and ecosystems. Human (biological) diversity and linguistic diversity are intimately and intricately related. Therefore, as Skutnabb-Kangas et al. (2003) assert, the diversity of life goes beyond respecting biodiversity to include cultural and linguistic diversity, which is what is meant by the term 'biocultural diversity'. Unfortunately, as humankind advances in both technology and territory, scant regard has been paid to the impacts on either Indigenous peoples or the biodiversity that they protect (Gorenflo, Romaine, Mittermeier, & Walker-Painemilla, 2012; Raygorodetsky, 2018).

After exploring these issues in more detail, in the final section of this paper we examine the implications for early childhood education (ECE) in response to demographic changes and to the anthropocentric crisis of climate change through the lens of the international commitment to the United Nations' Sustainable Development Goals which include a strong focus on responding to climate change, and protecting life on land and in the sea (United Nations General Assembly, 2015).

Te Whāriki and Te Tiriti o Waitangi: Two versions, differing outcomes

In this first section we introduce key constructs from Te Tiriti o Waitangi, and then critique how *Te Whāriki 2017* has shifted the discourse in relation to upholding these commitments away from the 1996 recognition of Te Tiriti. We argue that the dual recognition of both versions of Te Tiriti/the Treaty is an ambiguous positioning that detracts from recognition of tino rangatiratanga and defies international obligations to uphold Indigenous treaty versions. We further consider the tensions generated by binarisation of the new 'flipped' format of *Te Whāriki 2017*, which has shifted Part B of the 1996 document, the Māori text, now calling it *Te Whāriki a te Kōhanga Reo*, at the behest of the National Te Kōhanga Reo Trust (Bell, personal communication, 12 June, 2017)[1], and positioned it upside down and underneath in relation to *Te Whāriki: He Whāriki Mātauranga mō ngā Mokopuna o Aotearoa*.

In the preamble of Te Tiriti o Waitangi, Queen Victoria acknowledges the rangatiratanga of the chiefs over their lands and assures them that she has sent the governor to ensure that no harm will come to Māori or to Pākehā (Network Waitangi Otautahi, 2018). In Article I, *governance* (kawanatanga) over the lands is entrusted to the Queen. In Article II, Māori retain their tino rangatiratanga, their absolute sovereign authority over their lands, villages, and everything that they value (taonga

---
1 Ministry of Education briefing on *Te Whāriki 2017*.

katoa). Article III states that the Queen will care for all Māori of New Zealand and ensure that Māori have the same rights (ngā tikanga katoa rite tahi) as the people of England. In the fourth Tiriti protocol, verbally agreed at the Waitangi signing, the governor undertook to ensure that Māori beliefs would be cared for equally alongside those of the other religions present (Network Waitangi Otautahi, 2018).

The 1996 version of *Te Whāriki* referenced Te Tiriti o Waitangi, the Māori language text of the 1840 treaty, stating in its introduction that: "In early childhood settings, all children should be given the opportunity to develop knowledge and an understanding of the cultural heritages of both partners to Te Tiriti o Waitangi" (Ministry of Education, 1996, p. 9). It included the expectation that: "The curriculum should include Māori people, places, and artefacts and opportunities to learn and use the Māori language through social interaction" (p. 43). It furthermore emphasised the Article II Tiriti obligation to uphold Māori tino rangatiratanga, stating that "Decisions about the ways in which bicultural goals and practices are developed within each early childhood education setting should be made in consultation with the appropriate tangata whenua" (p. 11).

In contrast, *Te Whāriki 2017* recognises both Te Tiriti o Waitangi and the Treaty of Waitangi, opening its explanation of the document as follows:

> Te Tiriti o Waitangi | the Treaty of Waitangi is New Zealand's founding document. Signed in 1840 by representatives of Māori and the Crown, this agreement provided the foundation upon which Māori and Pākehā would build their relationship as citizens of Aotearoa New Zealand. Central to this relationship was a commitment to live together in a spirit of partnership and the acceptance of obligations for participation and protection. Te Tiriti | the Treaty has implications for our education system, particularly in terms of achieving equitable outcomes for Māori and ensuring that te reo Māori not only survives but thrives. Early childhood education has a crucial role to play here, by providing mokopuna with culturally responsive environments that support their learning and by ensuring that they are provided with equitable opportunities to learn. (Ministry of Education, 2017a, p. 3)

The statement positions the two versions of the treaty as having equal standing, ignoring the historical record that around 540 Māori chiefs signed the version in the Māori language, and only 39 signed a version in the English language. The British naval captain William Hobson had been appointed as consul to the independent state of New Zealand which had been confirmed by the promulgation of the 1835 document *He Whakaputanga o te Rangatiratanga o Nu Tireni—Declaration of Independence* (New Zealand History, n.d.). When, in 1840, Hobson sent copies of the treaty texts to the British Secretary of State, "the Māori text was entitled 'Treaty' and the English text was provided as the 'Translation'" (Suter, 2014, p. 11). The final section in the quote from *Te Whāriki 2017* above reflects a reliance on what are commonly referred to as the "three 'p's" of the treaty: partnership, participation, and protection, and their implications for Māori language education and teacher responsibilities.

In *Te Whāriki 2017* the two treaty versions are positioned as if they are synonymous, yet the English translation has been used to justify the colonialist assumption of sovereignty which led to the settler imposition of rafts of legislation and policies that discriminated against Māori, including within education. It has long been established that the different language versions are not interchangeable nor are they direct translations (Mutu, 2010; Walker, 2004). Māori have consistently rejected the British assumption of sovereignty in Waitangi Tribunal claims (Mutu, 2018), since Te Tiriti confirmed Māori self-determination and allowed for British *governance* (kawanatanga) rather than sovereignty. Further, the international legal convention of contra proferentem stipulates that it is the Indigenous language version that must prevail when there are issues surrounding the English translation, and this was affirmed by the Waitangi Tribunal in 1983 (Suter, 2014).

Whilst it could be said that the intent of referencing both Te Tiriti and the Treaty in *Te Whāriki 2017* reflects a sentiment of commitment one to the other or in a "spirit of partnership" as it were between Māori and Pākehā, the embedded colonial structures of English language dominance (and Pākehā power) and Māori language subordination still dominate curriculum in New Zealand. These 'partnership' relationships, it is argued here, are merely a fabrication; simultaneously concealing and revealing in what has been described as a 'flipped' document. The *Te Whāriki 2017* document separates the now two curricula with a graphic of a whāriki (woven mat). The Māori language side is allegedly only for Kōhanga Reo, which currently serve only 17% of Māori children (Ministry of Education, 2017b), and is not the official curriculum for Māori immersion settings other than Kōhanga Reo. The bulkier curriculum is written in English, incorporating te reo constructs, for an unspecified demographic but presumably for every other child in the country not in Kōhanga Reo, and is discoursed as the 'bicultural' side of the pathway. Two distinct curriculum pathways are defined as:

> … one bicultural, derived from a synthesis of traditional Māori thinking and sociocultural theorising and one indigenous, each with its own pedagogy. The Ministry of Education chose the flipbook format to showcase this unique bicultural, one-framework-two-paths curriculum and to make it clear that both pathways are of equal status and have mana in their own right … Neither part of the combined document is a translation of the other. (Ministry of Education, 2017a, p. 69)

Even though at the outset of the document it states "It emphasises our bicultural foundation, our multicultural present and the shared future we are creating" (p. 2), the languages divide can be seen as problematic. The relationship between languages and cultures has well been established as integral to each other. Language encapsulates and reflects its culture, as it indeed shapes it. It is impossible to have deep insights into a culture without knowing its language. Additionally, one cannot be bicultural if one is a monolingual. Too much focus on being bicultural has resulted in pedagogies of distraction in terms of the value, the place, and importance of te reo Māori in the curriculum. The Māori-medium pathway has additive learning outcomes of Māori/English bilingualism. However, the history of languages learning in New Zealand has been via a subtractive monolingual English-medium pathway. It is an irony that this essentially monolingual pathway is referenced in ECE as the 'bicultural' and perhaps even the 'bilingual' pathway when the result is the opposite. It is duplicitous to convey the idea that having a dual (but separate) Māori/English language binary in a curriculum document will solve the monolingual assimilatory aims of English-medium education. Paradoxically, the bilingual/bicultural pathway of Māori immersion education is positioned as 'monolingual' Māori, when it is from this pathway that the very eloquent Māori/English bilinguals are graduating.

To summarise the notion of differing texts, differing pathways, differing outcomes in a colonising context, the notion of a "one-framework-two-paths curriculum" document that claims, "all children grow up in New Zealand as competent and confident learners, strong in their identity, language and culture" (Ministry of Education, 2017a, p. 2) without sufficient ideological clarification, research, and policy development is problematic. Further, in terms of Treaty claims, it is argued here that the signed Māori version of Te Tiriti o Waitangi conveys far more nuanced and important meanings than the banal generalities of the "three 'p's", a trope which has served as a convenient mechanism that not only over-simplifies the important commitments made to Māori, but which allows the Crown to be diverted from enactment of Tiriti obligations. It is that diversion that is being signalled above. The wording explaining treaty expectations in *Te Whāriki 2017* does not reflect the strong sentiment of the actual commitment to Te Tiriti o Waitangi that was signed up to by the Chiefs in 1840 and 1841, and to which the early childhood care and education sector has demonstrated its commitment.

Changing contexts of curriculum development

A great deal has changed in the intervening years since the early 1990s when *Te Whāriki 1996* had been created via a 5-year-long, deeply consultative and inclusive process. The world has experienced increasingly intensifying human-generated impacts of climate change and pollution, along with economic policies that have heightened disparities between rich and poor within and between countries, and exploited our Earth's resources to the point that our planet's biodiversity is seriously under threat through loss and despoliation of wild habitats. This scenario in fact threatens our very survival, since "without a dramatic move beyond 'business as usual' the current severe decline of the natural systems that support modern societies will continue" (Grooten & Almond, 2018, p. 8). Meanwhile, Aotearoa New Zealand has in the past two decades changed demographically to now be officially classed as 'superdiverse' (Royal Society of New Zealand, 2013). In 2006, the Deaf community of Aotearoa had their languages (both Māori and English Sign) recognised officially. Yet, our first language, te reo Māori, remains endangered, with 11% of Māori people at the 2013 census reporting they spoke te reo well, and only 3.44% of non-Māori able to speak te reo (Statistics New Zealand, 2013). A recent study found that:

> Providing educational opportunities that support adults and tamariki to attain high proficiency in te reo Māori is key to increasing the use of te reo Māori on a wide and significant scale. Tamariki play a pivotal role in language revitalisation. (Hutchings et al., 2017, p. xviii)

In the final year of the 2008–17 National led Government, the then Minister of Education, Hekia Parata, pushed through what may have been intended to be a legacy project, the 'refreshing' of *Te Whāriki*. This was a very rushed process which lacked a preliminary consultation with the wider early childhood care and education sector as to what was valued about the existing curriculum or what changes the sector might have considered to be necessary or useful. After a short period of writing by a Ministry-appointed team, a draft was released on 4 November 2016. The Ministry allowed only a very brief 6-week consultation period, which coincided with the always rushed and extremely busy end-of-year period, until 16 December, 2016. Following the receipt of 774 submissions (Ministry of Education, 2017b) amendments resulted in the final 'refreshed' document, launched in April, 2017. The Ministry acknowledged that concerns raised in submissions on the draft document included the sense that:

> the bicultural essence of the original curriculum had been lost and needed to be reinstated. More emphasis on tikanga and kaupapa was needed to get the balance right. More specific feedback included the need to reference more [Māori] socio-cultural theory, support bilingual practices, emphasise whānau involvement, and carefully use language that placed equal value on both cultures. (Ministry of Education, 2017b, p. 9) [Note: [Māori] appears bracketed in original, somewhat conflating the two concepts.]

In the final 2017 version, the number of learning outcomes was reduced from 118 to 20. Despite criticism it retained a very brief section on theoretical perspectives, a page on 'Responsibilities of Kaiako', and three pages on assessment. Fortunately, in response to submissions, the questions for reflection component, which had been missing in the draft, was reinstated, and the embarrassingly inadequate list of references removed. In the next section, we discuss implications of *Te Whāriki 2017* with regard to the sustenance of te reo Māori, a taonga that is protected under Te Tiriti (Waitangi Tribunal, 1986).

(Mis)understandings of Te Tiriti o Waitangi

In the intervening two decades between *Te Whāriki* versions, the use of te reo across our nation remains fragile, Tiriti obligations notwithstanding. *Tau Mai te Reo*, the Ministry of Education's Māori language strategy, stresses that "The Ministry of Education and education sector agencies play a critical role in supporting Māori language acquisition and revitalisation" (Ministry of Education, 2013, p. 4).

Theories of 'replacement' of Indigenous knowledges, perhaps under the guise of valuing and respecting those knowledges, are ultimately theories of eradicating those knowledges (Tuck & Gaztambide-Fernández, 2013). That is the irony. In policy documents, what can often look like the valuing of Indigenous knowledge is really about co-option and control. According to Tuck and Gaztambide-Fernández (2013), replacement is a process that masks the 'ensurance' of settler futurity. This section focuses on the processes of 'displacement' and 'replacement' which started to happen soon after signing the nation's founding document, Te Tiriti o Waitangi, in 1840. Just how white-settler futurity is achieved through the curricular co-option of Indigenous knowledges is described next. Co-option of curricula assists with displacement and replacement theory. Here, the term 'linguafaction' is introduced to theorise this displacement. That is the legacy and ever-consuming future of colonisation in Aotearoa.

Encounter history

As previously mentioned, Article III of Te Tiriti o Waitangi guaranteed certain rights to Māori, the same rights as British citizens. As British citizens have a right to their British English language, so too then do Māori have a right to our Māori language. However, that is not the way it has panned out in our colony, structurally. Colonisation is a structural process, not a one-off event. It doesn't happen overnight or at the signing of a treaty, but as part of an ongoing structural system that continually reinvents itself to entrench itself, and, simultaneously, conceal itself. It is this notion of concealment that Tuck and Gaztambide-Fernández (2013) refer to as a process that masks the 'ensurance' of white-settler futurity. That is, it sets up a system of privilege (the descendants of the settlers) and oppression (of the original Indigenous inhabitants of the land). British settler colonisation is a particular type of colonisation. It has nothing to do with 'civilisation' (one of its fake narratives), but all to do with access to land or territory. Aotearoa is Māori land, but much of it has been alienated through the processes of colonisation, threatening the lives of its Indigenous inhabitants and the languages they speak, referred to here as linguafaction. Indigenous language/s undergo shift (from languages of the land to foreign colonial languages) in direct ratio to the rate of shift of land from Indigenous utilisation to that of the coloniser. There is a power-cum-racist element to linguafaction—the power of a dominant hegemonic structure to create unequal hierarchies based on the languages one speaks and the cultures those languages represent. One language dominates and exploits for political and economic power, while the other (colonised) languages are quagmired, or, in the case where children have stopped acquiring them as native languages, become moribund (Miyaoka, 2001). In a colony, the result is a forced language shift away from the now minoritised Indigenous language to the dominant (colonising) language. In this way, Māori were forced into a deficit position which has played out in the New Zealand education system ever since it was instituted. Fanon (1970) puts it this way: that knowledge of the colonial language is precisely what inserts 'black' subjectivity into a racist social order and to speak it is to take on that world, that culture, that social order. To interpolate, this then highlights the importance of mandating te reo Māori in the curriculum if Māori are to live as Māori in accordance with the Māori Education Framework (Durie, 2001).

Returning then to Te Tiriti o Waitangi of 1840: it guaranteed rights. Articles II, III, and IV are germane to the premise that Te Tiriti is fundamental to education in Aotearoa New Zealand in 2019. Article II guaranteed 'taonga' rights (Māori language being one of those taonga). Article III guaranteed citizenship rights (in the same manner of rights that British citizens had to the English language, Māori citizens have to the Māori language). Article IV guaranteed Māori religious rights and freedoms. In what ways is the curriculum reflective of these rights? They may be seen as, albeit obscurely, reflected in the 2017 update of *Te Whāriki* as evidenced in the following statement:

> Te Tiriti | the Treaty has implications for our education system, particularly in terms of achieving equitable outcomes for Māori and ensuring that te reo Māori not only survives but thrives. Early childhood education has a crucial role to play here, by providing mokopuna with culturally responsive environments that support their learning and by ensuring that they are provided with equitable opportunities to learn. The importance of such provision is underscored throughout *Te Whāriki: He whāriki mātauranga mō ngā mokopuna o Aotearoa Early childhood curriculum.* (Ministry of Education, 2017a, p. 3)

However, the juxtaposition of 'Tiriti o Waitangi | Treaty of Waitangi' in *Te Whāriki 2017* is no guarantee of equitable outcomes for Māori or an assurance that te reo Māori will survive and thrive. More needs to be done, especially around initial teacher education, which we touch on later in this chapter.

Demographic challenges

One of the most dramatic changes in Aotearoa New Zealand in recent decades has been in the area of immigration policies. We are now classed as culturally and linguistically 'superdiverse', which indicates a level of cultural complexity surpassing anything previously experienced. New Zealand is now home to 160 languages, with multi-ethnic depth forecasted to deepen even further (Royal Society of New Zealand, 2013, p. 1).

One aspect of 'refreshment' that was clearly needed was a response to these changed demographics. Fundamental to welcoming others to our shores, is to do so from a stance that acknowledges the tangata whenua status of Māori. This statement in *Te Whāriki 2017* does not make this positioning explicit:

> New Zealand is increasingly multicultural. Te Tiriti | the Treaty is seen to be inclusive of all immigrants to New Zealand, whose welcome comes in the context of this partnership. Those working in early childhood education respond to the changing demographic landscape by valuing and supporting the different cultures represented in their settings. (Ministry of Education, 2017a, p. 3)

This bland statement of 'multiculturalism' presents a danger of Māori being relegated to being 'just another minority' in the country in which they are the original peoples. Later in the document we read that:

> Increasingly, children are likely to be learning in and through more than one language. Besides English, te reo Māori and New Zealand Sign Language (NZSL), some 200 different languages are in use in New Zealand, with Samoan, Hindi, Northern Chinese, French and Yue (Cantonese) being the most common. Children more readily become bi- or multilingual and bi- or multiliterate when language learning in the education setting builds on their home languages. (Ministry of Education, 2017a, p. 12)

Whilst this brief recognition of multilingualism is undoubtedly important, what is missing again here is acknowledgment of the Tangata Whenua/Tangata Tiriti dynamic, which includes all immigrants within 'Tangata Tiriti' as previously highlighted by Sir Edward Taihakurei Durie KNZM (as cited in King, 2003) and which ensures ongoing recognition of the status of Māori as tangata whenua. This is increasingly important lest te ao Māori and te reo Māori be submerged in the deluge of diversity.

Closely related to Tangata Whenua are Tagata Pasifika. Specific articulation in *Te Whāriki 2017* of the challenges of the complexities and specificities of Tagata Pasifika conceptualisations should have more strongly identified the implications for teachers that "an evolving Pasifika child with multiple identities and, in some cases, multiple linguistics, [is] a reality in our current ECE social and political landscape" (Leaupepe, Matapo, & Ravlich, 2017, p. 36).

New Zealand Sign Language (NZSL) became our third official language in 2006, with the passing of the New Zealand Sign Language Act 2006. The Act recognises "the distinct linguistic and cultural group of people who are deaf and who use New Zealand Sign Language as their first or preferred language" (section 4). It also affirms the status of signed te reo Māori which is not acknowledged in *Te Whāriki 2017*. The Act further advises that "the Deaf community should be consulted on matters relating to NZSL" (section 9). It is important to acknowledge that, as with any language, NZSL gives expression to the culture from which it has emanated, as Whaea Rangimārie Rose Pere so evocatively pointed out:

> Language is the life line and sustenance of a culture. It provides the tentacles that can enable a child to link up with everything in his or her world. It is one of the most important forms of empowerment that a child can have. Language is not only a form of communication but it helps transmit the values and beliefs of a people. (Pere, 1991, p. 9)

This is equally true for Deaf children and the Deaf community:

> New Zealand Sign Language (NZSL) is crucial to many deaf people's ability to learn, communicate and participate in society. The language is vital to the expression of deaf culture and identify. Deaf culture is well documented and includes shared values, norms, behaviours, history, humour, art, stories, poetry and traditions of deaf people. Deaf culture is passed on from generation to generation through NZSL. (New Zealand Sign Language Board, 2018)

It is useful that *Te Whāriki 2017* acknowledges the important consideration of both Deaf languages *and* culture:

> It is desirable that children in ECE settings should also have the opportunity to learn NZSL, an official language of New Zealand, and to learn about Deaf culture. For some children, NZSL is their first language, and services have a responsibility to support its use and development. (Ministry of Education, 2017a, p. 12)

This commitment means that all teachers in early childhood settings in Aotearoa New Zealand now need to consider their capacity to be authentic models of both official languages: te reo Māori *and* New Zealand Sign Language in English and Māori. Yet even though te reo Māori was finally recognised as an official language over 30 years ago (Maori Language Act 1987), our education system continues to struggle to give full expression to te reo and te ao Māori.

Responding to the crisis of the Anthropocene and the challenge of meeting the SDGs

As identified earlier in this chapter, a key shift in awareness since 1996 is in response to our increasingly exponentially damaged Earth and her biocultures. This damage is the direct result of industrialised agriculture and industry, and of economic and values systems that allow such plunder of the Earth, her lands, forests, rivers, and seas, our biosphere, without penalty. Our allegedly 'democratic' Western systems of government are being bypassed by the hyper-capitalist corporate entities that operate beyond the restraints of national boundaries and regulatory systems, enriching a very few at the expense of the many and the wellbeing of our planet. As we experience the increasing frequency and severity of impacts of climate change such as cyclones in the South Pacific, hurricanes and fires in the US, droughts in many African countries, sea-level rise inundating Pacific Islands nations, and fires, flooding, and drought in both Australia and Aotearoa New Zealand, the poorest and most vulnerable people, including children, are the worst affected everywhere (Lawler, 2011).

There are complex interactions within the Earth's systems that we know very little about, and the increasing disparities between rich and poor between and within countries is compounding our biospheric crisis: "inequality is not just a socioeconomic issue that divides communities and nations; it is also a significant driving force behind social-ecological dynamics and feedbacks within the biosphere" (Hamann et al., 2018, p. 74). It is admittedly very difficult to comprehend the enormity of our situation, the implications of the Anthropocene, our current epoch, described by Rosi Braidotti as "a multi-layered posthuman predicament that includes the environmental, socio-economic, and affective and psychic dimensions of our ecologies of belonging" (2018, p. 2). It is nonetheless indelibly marked by the imprint of human-generated impacts on the planet and biosphere, whereby the technosphere is parasitically overtaking the biosphere (Zalasiewicz et al., 2016). Such is this impact, that in future years the scarring and despoiling of the Earth will be marked as a distinct epoch, one that is Anthropogenic, or of human origin. One of the saddest impacts is the huge loss of biodiversity which continues unchecked (Mace et al., 2018). Of our 168 native bird species, just 20% are in good health, whilst 48% are in some trouble, and 32% are in serious trouble (Parliamentary Commissioner for the Environment, 2017, p. 28).

River scientist Dr Mike Joy has documented impacts such as the decimation of biodiversity due to loss of habitats through the obliteration of wetlands and the toxification of waterways due to intensification of dairying. New Zealand now has "the invidious statistic of the highest global per-capita frequency of the zoonoses coliform enteritis, campylobacteriosis, cryptosporidiosis and salmonellosis" (Joy, 2015, p. 19). In attributing the unfortunate impacts that his work reveals, Joy implicates "the negative impacts of neo-liberalisation on New Zealand both socially and economically [and] environmentally, the same movement of resources from all to a select few—private gain through public loss" (Joy, 2015, p. 5). Another very sad statistic demonstrative of holistic malaise is that, in Aotearoa New Zealand, we have the highest youth suicide rate in the 'developed' world (OECD, 2017). From a te ao Māori perspective, human wellbeing is deeply interwoven with the wellbeing of our environment, we are all inter-related and inter-connected, and we have a responsibility as kaitiaki to uphold ethics of care and of guardianship (Henare, 2001).

In September 2015, our Government, along with 192 other nations, signed up to the United Nations' Sustainable Development Goals (SDGs) which stipulate targets that all countries should meet by 2030. Goal 4.7 requires educators to ensure that:

> all learners acquire knowledge and skills needed to promote sustainable development, including, among others, through education for sustainable development and sustainable lifestyles, human rights, gender equality, promotion of a culture of peace and nonviolence, global citizenship and appreciation of cultural diversity and of culture's contribution to sustainable development. (UNESCO, 2017, p. 8)

Te Whāriki 2017 makes no mention of the SDGs, and no reference to the important educational implications in Goal 4.7 above.

This chapter has signalled the issue of the denial of rights of Māori enshrined in Te Tiriti, yet racism remains an ongoing breach of human rights experienced by Māori (and others) on a daily basis. We are concerned that *Te Whāriki 2017* resonates with a political 'blanding' regarding serious issues related to the ongoing legacy of colonisation and our responsibility as educators to intervene in the perpetuation of racist injustices. For example, the curriculum no longer contains the reflective question: 'In what ways do the environment and programme reflect the values embodied in Te Tiriti o Waitangi, and what impact does this have on adults and children?' (Ministry of Education, 1996, p. 56). Nor has it retained the expectation that: "The early childhood curriculum actively contributes towards countering racism and other forms of prejudice" (p. 18). In fact, *Te Whāriki 2017* doesn't mention racism at all and mentions challenging prejudice just once. We believe that it is a core responsibility (response-ability) of all education/educators to challenge the ongoing prevalence of racism (even if it somehow makes it easier to do so by naming it as 'unconscious bias' to be less threatening and/or more palatable). Miles Ferris, the president of Māori school principals' association Te Akatea, has recently pointed out that "There's a high level of racial bias, discrimination throughout our system that's not often talked about. And it's not till we address those issues that I think we're going to see long-term and effective change" (Radio New Zealand News, 2 May, 2018).

Te Whāriki 2017 briefly mentions the notion of global citizenship as follows (and once more in the *Belonging—Mana whenua* strand):

> A curriculum must speak to our past, present and future. As global citizens in a rapidly changing and increasingly connected world, children need to be adaptive, creative and resilient. They need to 'learn how to learn' so that they can engage with new contexts, opportunities and challenges with optimism and resourcefulness. For these reasons, *Te Whāriki* emphasises the development of knowledge, skills, attitudes and dispositions that support lifelong learning. (Ministry of Education, 2017a, p. 7)

Sustainability is mentioned only once in *Te Whāriki 2017*, merely acknowledging its presence in the New Zealand school curriculum. However, *Te Whāriki 2017* does bring to the fore the notion of kaitiakitanga, our responsibility as carers for and guardians of the environment. In introducing the strand of *Exploration—Mana aotūroa*, *Te Whāriki 2017* acknowledges that:

> Diverse ways of being and knowing frame the way respect for the environment is demonstrated. Kaiako develop understandings of how children and their whānau make sense of the world and respect and appreciate the natural environment. Children may express their respect for the natural world in terms of respect for Papatūānuku, Ranginui and atua Māori. Kaitiakitanga is integral to this. (Ministry of Education, 2017a, p. 46)

Implications for teacher education and the Ministry of Education

The recent Education (now Teaching) Council's *Code of Professional Responsibility and Standards for the Teaching Profession* (Education Council, n.d.) contains clearly stated commitments to Te Tiriti o Waitangi, te reo, social justice, and sustainability. In this instance, it seems that our profession has taken the lead where the Ministry of Education, under previous National Government oversight, had abdicated its responsibilities. We recommend that the Teaching Council require all teacher education qualifications to have an entry requirement for te reo, since it is very difficult within the limited space available in a 3-year degree, and nearly impossible in a 1-year qualification, to develop sufficient fluency. An entry level te reo requirement would provide a strong platform for building on teacher candidates' reo during the duration of their qualification programme. Next, we need to ensure that all teachers in teacher-led early childhood settings are degree-level qualified. It is very difficult to uphold a shared team commitment when some of the team (currently up to 50%) are unqualified (Westerbeke, 2016). Developing a sophisticated level of fluency in te reo takes years, so we therefore recommend that the Ministry fund all teachers to participate in ongoing reo courses. We also recommend that the entire education sector, led by our Ministry of Education, take note of and respond to the expectations contained within the SDGs, in particular with regard to the education competencies espoused by UNESCO (2017) which aim to equip our future generations to meet the global challenges that are crucial for the survival of humanity, of our fellow planetary co-habitants, and for the wellbeing of the planet itself.

Conclusion

Whilst *Te Whāriki 2017* acknowledges our changing demographics and seeks to be inclusive of superdiversity, this inclusion must build on a platform affirming that all who have come to live in this land must recognise and honour the foundational commitments made to Māori in Te Tiriti o Waitangi. It has been argued here that the over-simplification of Te Tiriti in the "three p's" (partnership, participation, and protection) reflected in *Te Whāriki 2017* (but not reflected in the actual wording nor the intent of Te Tiriti o Waitangi) have become a short-cut enabling people to avoid directly engaging with the clearly stated meanings, obligations, and implications of Te Tiriti. In addition to our obligations under Te Tiriti o Waitangi, and the SDGs, the United Nations Declaration on the Rights of Indigenous Peoples (United Nations, 2007) also requires nations to prioritise Indigenous knowledges as sources of wisdom and of specific place-based knowledges unique to their contexts, and that provide time-tested sustainable ways of living in those places.

Without expressly acknowledging the requirement for educators to challenge racism, *Te Whāriki 2017* is in danger of being an instrument that perpetuates racism. Without our curriculum naming racism as the source of great historical and contemporary injustice in our country, teachers, children, and families can remain oblivious to our racist history and its ongoing perpetuation. It is well overdue that our education sector be woken into consciousness about this. Fortunately, the 2017 Teaching Council Code of Professional Responsibility and Standards for the Teaching Profession, *Our Code, Our Standards*, requires all teachers to respect their "trusted role in society and the influence [we] have in shaping futures by promoting and protecting the principles of human rights, sustainability and social justice [and] demonstrating a commitment to a Tiriti o Waitangi based Aotearoa New Zealand" (Education Council, n.d., p. 12). This must be at the heart of our work as teachers in Aotearoa New Zealand.

References

Braidotti, R. (2018). A theoretical framework for the critical posthumanities. *Theory, Culture & Society*, doi:10.1177/0263276418771486

Costello, A., Abbas, M., Allen, A., Ball, S., Bell, S., Bellamy, R., ... Patterson, C. (2009). Managing the health effects of climate change. *The Lancet, 373*(9676), 1693–1733.

Durie, M. (2001). *A framework for considering Māori educational advancement*. Opening address. Hui taumata mātauranga, Taupō, New Zealand.

Education Council of Aotearoa New Zealand. (n.d). *Our code, our standards. Code of professional responsibility and standards for the teaching profession.* Retrieved from https://teachingcouncil.nz/content/our-code-our-standards

Fanon, F. (1970). *Black skin, white masks.* London, UK: Paladin.

Flannery, T. (2010). *Here on Earth. A natural history of the planet.* Toronto, Canada: HarperCollins.

Gorenflo, L. J., Romaine, S., Mittermeier, R., A., & Walker-Painemilla, K. (2012). Co-occurrence of linguistic and biological diversity in biodiversity hotspots and high biodiversity wilderness areas. *Proceedings of the National Academy of Sciences of the United States of America, 109*(21), 8032-8037. Retrieved from https://doi.org/10.1073/pnas.1117511109

Grooten, M., & Almond, R. E. A. (Eds.). (2018). *Living planet report—2018: Aiming higher.* Gland, Switzerland: World Wildlife Fund, Institute of Zoology (Zoological Society of London). Retrieved from: https://wwf.panda.org/knowledge_hub/all_publications/living_planet_report_2018/

Hamann, M., Berry, K., Chaigneau, T., Curry, T., Heilmayr, R., Henriksson, P. J. G., . . . Wu, T. (2018). Inequality and the biosphere. *Annual Review of Environment and Resources, 43,* 61–83. doi:10.1146/annurev-environ-102017-025949

Henare, M. (2001). Tapu, mana, mauri, hau, wairua: A Māori philosophy of vitalism and cosmos. In J. A. Grim (Ed.), *Indigenous traditions and ecology. The interbeing of cosmology and community* (pp. 197–221). Cambridge, MA: Harvard University Press.

Hutchings, J., Higgins, R., Bright, N., Keane, B., Olsen-Reeder, V., & Hunia, M. (2017). *Te Ahu o te Reo. Te reo Māori in homes and communities. Overview Report. He Tirohanga Whānui.* Wellington: Te Taura Whiri i te Reo Māori/New Zealand Council for Educational Research. Retrieved from https://www.nzcer.org.nz/system/files/Te%20Ahu%20o%20te%20Reo%20Overview%20Report%20_0.pdf#page=1&zoom=auto,-108,842.

Joy, M. (2015). *Squandered—the degration of New Zealand's freshwaters.* Retrieved from: https://freshwaternz.files.wordpress.com/2015/05/squandered.pdf

King, M. (2003). *The Penguin history of New Zealand.* Auckland: Penguin.

Lawler, J. (2011). *Children and climate change. Children's vulnerability to climate change and disaster impacts in East Asia and the Pacific.* Bangkok, Thailand: UNICEF East Asia and Pacific Regional Office. Retrieved from: http://www.unicef.org/malaysia/children_and_climate_change.pdf

Leaupepe, M., Matapo, J., & Ravlich, E. P. (2017). *Te Whāriki* a mat for "all" to stand: The weaving of Pasifika voices. *Curriculum Matters, 13,* 21–41.

Mace, G. M., Barrett, M., Burgess, N. D., Cornell, S. E., Freeman, R., Grooten, M., & Purvis, A. (2018). Aiming higher to bend the curve of biodiversity loss. *Nature Sustainability, 1*(9), 448–451. doi:10.1038/s41893-018-0130-0

Ministry of Education. (1996). *Te whāriki. He whāriki mātauranga mō ngā mokopuna o Aotearoa: Early childhood curriculum.* Wellington: Learning Media. Retrieved from: https://education.govt.nz/assets/Documents/Early-Childhood/Te-Whariki-1996.pdf

Ministry of Education. (2013). *Tau mai te reo. The Māori language in education strategy 2013 – 2017.* Wellington: Ministry of Education. Retrieved from https://www.education.govt.nz/assets/Documents/Ministry/Strategies-and-policies/Ka-Hikitia/TauMaiTeReoFullStrategyEnglish.pdf

Ministry of Education. (2017a). *Te whāriki. He whāriki mātauranga mō ngā mokopuna o Aotearoa. Early childhood curriculum.* Wellington: Author. Retrieved from: https://www.education.govt.nz/early-childhood/teaching-and-learning/te-whariki/

Ministry of Education. (2017b). *Update of te whāriki. Report on the engagement process.* Wellington: Author. Retrieved from: https://tewhariki.tki.org.nz/en/te-whariki-foundations/the-story-of-te-whariki/

Miyaoka, O. (2001). *Endangered languages: the crumbling of the linguistic ecosystem.* Retrieved from http://www.accu.or.jp/appreb/09/pdf34-2/34-2P003-005.pdf.

Mutu, M. (2010). Constitutional intentions: The Treaty texts. In M. Mulholland & V. Tawhai (Eds.), *Weeping waters* (pp. 13–40). Wellington: Huia.

Mutu, M. (2018). Behind the smoke and mirrors of the Treaty of Waitangi claims settlement process in New Zealand: No prospect for justice and reconciliation for Māori without constitutional transformation. *Journal of Global Ethics, 14*(2), 208–221.

Network Waitangi Otautahi. (2018). *Te Tiriti o Waitangi* (poster). Retrieved from: https://trc.org.nz/content/te-tiriti-o-waitangithe-treaty-waitangi-translation-maori-text

New Zealand History. (n.d.). *He Whakaputanga—Declaration of Independence, 1835.* Retrieved from https://nzhistory.govt.nz/media/interactive/the-declaration-of-independence

New Zealand Sign Language Board. (2018). *About New Zealand Sign Language.* Retrieved from: http://www.odi.govt.nz/nzsl/about/

OECD. (2017). *CO4.4: Teenage suicides (15–19 years old).* Retrieved from: https://www.oecd.org/els/family/CO_4_4_Teenage-Suicide.pdf

Parliamentary Commissioner for the Environment. (2017). *Taonga of an island nation: Saving New Zealand's birds.* Wellington: Author. Retrieved from: http://www.pce.parliament.nz/publications/taonga-of-an-island-nation-saving-new-zealands-birds

Pere, R. R. (1991). *Te wheke.* Gisborne: Ao Ake.

Radio New Zealand News. (2018, 2 May). *Ministry urges 'bold step' for Māori education.* Retrieved from: https://www.radionz.co.nz/news/te-manu-korihi/356413/ministry-urges-bold-step-for-maori-education

Raygorodetsky, G. (2018). Indigenous peoples defend Earth's biodiversity—but they're in danger. from National Geographic website: https://www.nationalgeographic.com/environment/2018/11/can-indigenous-land-stewardship-protect-biodiversity-/

Royal Society of New Zealand. (2013). *Languages in Aotearoa New Zealand.* Retrieved from Royal Society of New Zealand website: https://royalsociety.org.nz/what-we-do/our-expert-advice/all-expert-advice-papers/languages-in-aotearoa-new-zealand/

Skutnabb-Kangas, T., Maffi, L., & Harmon, D. (2003). *Sharing a world of difference. The Earth's linguistic, cultural and biological diversity.* Paris, France: UNESCO. Retrieved from: http://unesdoc.unesco.org/images/0013/001323/132384e.pdf

Statistics New Zealand. (2013). *Te Kupenga 2013 (English).* Retrieved from: https://www.stats.govt.nz/information-releases/te-kupenga-2013-english

Suter, B. (2014). *The contra proferentem rule in the reports of the Waitangi Tribunal. LLM Research Paper. LAWS 547: The Waitangi Tribunal and New Zealand legal history.* Wellington: Victoria University of Wellington. Retrieved from https://core.ac.uk/download/pdf/41339669.pdf

Tuck, E., & Gaztambide-Fernández, R. A. (2013). Curriculum, replacement, and settler futurity. *Journal of Curriculum Theorizing, 29*(1).

UNESCO. (2017). *Education for sustainable development goals. Learning objectives.* Paris, France: UNESCO. Retrieved from: http://unesdoc.unesco.org/images/0024/002474/247444e.pdf

United Nations. (2007). *United Nations Declaration on the Rights of Indigenous Peoples. A/RES/61/295.* Retrieved from: https://www.un.org/development/desa/indigenouspeoples/declaration-on-the-rights-of-indigenous-peoples.html

United Nations General Assembly. (2015). *Transforming our world: The 2030 Agenda for sustainable development.* Retrieved from: http://www.un.org/ga/search/view_doc.asp?symbol=A/RES/70/1&Lang=E

Waitangi Tribunal. (1986). *Report of the Waitangi Tribunal on the Te Reo Maori Claim (WAI 11).* Wellington: GP Publications. Retrieved from: http://www.justice.govt.nz/tribunals/waitangi-tribunal

Walker, R. (2004). *Ka Whawhai Tonu Matou. Struggle without end* (revised ed.). Auckland: Penguin.

Westerbeke, L. (2016). *Understanding the construction of belonging in a for-profit ECE centre: An ethnographic study.* Unpublished doctoral thesis, University of Waikato, Hamilton.

Wilson, E. O. (2012). *The social conquest of Earth.* New York, NY & London, UK: Liveright.

World Wildlife Fund, Grooten, M., & Almond, R. E. A. (Eds.). (2018). *Living planet report—2018: Aiming higher.* Gland, Switzerland: World Wildlife Fund.

Zalasiewicz, J., Williams, M., Waters, C. N., Barnosky, A. D., Palmesino, J., Rönnskog, A.-S., . . . Wolfe, A. P. (2016). Scale and diversity of the physical technosphere: A geological perspective. *The Anthropocene Review,* 1–14. doi:10.1177/2053019616677743

CHAPTER 6

Towards an authentic implementation of Teu Le Va and Talanoa as Pacific cultural paradigms in early childhood education in Aotearoa New Zealand

Diane Mara

Introduction

This chapter seeks to demonstrate how policy frameworks, models, and metaphors have the potential to embed innovative and culturally responsive pedagogical knowledge that is characteristic of quality early childhood education (ECE) provision for Pacific children and their families. Through a small-scale study, it is demonstrated that kaiako can be encouraged to work within the Talanoa framework (Vaioleti, 2006) of professional discussion and decision making, whilst establishing the safe 'va' through implementing the concept of Teu Le Va (Mara, 2013) to responsively include and empower Pacific children and families within early childhood educational settings.

The history of the development of Pasifika ECE in Aotearoa New Zealand is well documented elsewhere (Mara, 2013, 2017). In my view, the policy context that prevailed when the cited articles were written has, to some extent, been altered through the latest iteration of *Te Whāriki*, the early childhood curriculum (Ministry of Education, 2017). It is suggested that in the latest ECE curriculum document, the priority of meeting the needs and interests of the Pacific child remains less valued and less professionally evident (Leaupepe, Matapo, & Ravlich, 2017). Together with the proposed confirmation of the *Pasifika Education Plan 2013–2017* and the recent release of *Tapasā: Cultural competencies for teachers of Pacific students* (Teaching Council of New Zealand, 2018), which details competencies required of student and registered teachers working with Pacific students, it can be argued that the ECE policy discourse has undergone some qualitative change.

The chapter begins with an analysis and critique of the development of the early childhood curriculum documents between 1993 and 2017 with respect to the ways in which the needs and interests of the Pacific child and their family have been and are currently articulated. To what extent can early childhood teachers confidently apply their knowledge and professional judgements as they implement the intent of curriculum documents into transformative practice? The main focus of this chapter is to provide a progress report on the planning, data collection, and data analysis within a small-scale study carried out by four kindergartens, all members of the Heretaunga Kindergarten Association. All stages of the study were carried out and interpreted through key Pasifika frameworks. The analysis of evidence was carried out using Pacific frameworks of analysis: Teu Le Va (Mara, 2013), Talanoa (Vaioleti, 2006), and a Pasifika topology of culturally responsive pedagogy in ECE (Mara & Kumar, 2013). The chapter concludes with reflections on the potential of achieving more equitable outcomes for Pacific children and their families by addressing some remaining barriers in the contemporary ECE sector.

Analysis of *Te Whāriki* and Pasifika ECE in Aotearoa New Zealand

Any curriculum document is a reflection of its historical context and articulated priorities, as expressed by its writers and the quality of contemporary evidence. Those researchers and teachers who have been part of the history of early childhood curriculum development processes in Aotearoa New Zealand have a role in informing new generations of kaiako regarding where the sector has come from, so that decisions about the future can include qualities of the past for contexts of the future. In my view, one aspect that must continue is to further social justice and equity for all tamariki in Aotearoa New Zealand.

This analysis considers the three major early childhood curriculum documents published in New Zealand between 1993 and 2017, and the ways in which the Pacific child and their needs and interests are visible. Wendt Samu (2006) provides a comprehensive and forward-thinking discussion on quality teaching and responsiveness to diversity as inseparable notions. She discusses the multiple uses and interpretations of what she refers to as the "Pasifika umbrella", which was a contemporary response to the Best Evidence Syntheses commissioned by the Ministry of Education to inform policy (Alton-Lee, 2005, cited in Wendt Samu, 2006), which remains relevant to curriculum and learning debates. Wendt Samu writes, in reference to the schooling sector:

> I am of the view that what can be developed for teachers of Pacific students in New Zealand classrooms is a framework of principles to guide their efforts to develop

specific and relevant teaching and learning environments for their specific Pacific students. (2006, p. 46)

The terms referring to Pacific children and their families have changed across the following three documents, and, to some extent, it is argued such iterations may not have been useful for kaiako in understanding Pacific paradigms and values.

From 1993 onwards

The first publication of *Te Whāriki: Draft Guidelines for Developmentally Appropriate Programmes in Early Childhood Services* (Ministry of Education, 1993) in its introduction makes the first reference to "Pacific Islands Language groups" (p. 12), acknowledging the engagement of Pacific communities in ECE provision and as a recognised part of the ECE sector. Indeed, consultation within Pacific communities was also evident in this document. Examples of references that are made to Tangata Pasifika programmes (beyond Pacific language groups) are on p. 31, *Principle: Holistic Development*, and again within this principle, on p. 37, referring to *Relationships*. On p. 101, under *Aim: Exploration* are specific examples for teachers under a section aimed at practice within Tagata Pasifika programmes. This document also contained examples of practice under Home-Based and Special Needs sections. In the final version of the 1996 *Te Whāriki* (Ministry of Education, 1996) all three sections were removed and guidelines for teachers for specific 'diversities' were no longer available.

From 1996 onwards

In the 1996 version of *Te Whāriki* there was a greater focus on the child at the centre of curriculum, with clearer articulation of the importance of sociocultural approaches to learning and teaching and the inclusion of Bronfenbrenner's ecological model (Ministry of Education, 1996, p. 19). On p. 12 there is a Foreword entitled *Tagata Pasefika: Pacific Islands early childhood centres*. Note the focus was still on programmes and centres, not on the Pacific child or the fact that the majority of Pacific children attending ECE attended services other than Pacific services. This paragraph, probably unwittingly, suggests, "Because of the diversity of Pacific Islands cultures there is no single Pacific Islands curriculum" (p. 12). In fact, *Te Whāriki* was and is the curriculum for Pacific children and their families and was always referred to as "the place to stand for all".

There are some mentions of Pacific/Tagata Pasefika in the 1996 version, but Pacific is often grouped with Māori; for example, on pp. 46 and 47 under the strand *Wellbeing* where there is a mention of the importance of spirituality in the sentence: "Adults should acknowledge spiritual dimensions ... are of prime importance to Māori and Tagata Pasefika families." On p. 64 under *Strand 3 Contribution* there is also a sentence ending "respect the process of working as āiga and showing respect for Tagata Pasefika elders". Not only was this a paragraph in which the first two sentences were describing Māori, but āiga is a Samoan word, not one that applies across all Pacific communities. On p. 73, under *Strand 4 Communication,* kaiako are appropriately encouraged to recognise the place of oral traditions, including stating that storytelling is important in Māori and Pacific Islands cultures.

It is true that the writers in 1993 and 1996 reflected contemporary views and perspectives about Pasefika ECE, because key Pacific leaders were involved in the development process and provided their input to both documents. However, potential alienation is exerted by repeated use of confused terminology and the influence of majority discourses in constructing knowledge and understandings. It was therefore hoped that the next version of *Te Whāriki* in 2017 would provide clearer and more informed frameworks for professional knowledge and practice of kaiako in relation to Pasefika/Tagata Pasefika/Pacific terminology. It was expected by Pacific authors and researchers in ECE that their work, including that of Pacific teacher educators between 1996 and 2016, would be cited to ensure Pasifika knowledges are more accessible to all early childhood teachers. However, a clarification of terms under the 'Pasifika umbrella' remained absent.

From 2017 onwards

The 2017 edition of *Te Whāriki* (Ministry of Education, 2017) clearly outlines "a curriculum for all children" (p. 12) and foregrounds concepts of identity, language, and culture, including mention of one Pacific language, Samoan, as one of the most widely spoken Pacific languages in Aotearoa New Zealand. Three paragraphs on p. 62 describe "Pasefika approaches" and helpfully lists four Pacific ethnic communities of the seven main communities that live within Aotearoa New Zealand. However, these paragraphs contain generalisations such as "Pasifika and non Pasifika world views" and the use of metaphors "to connect the familiar and the unfamiliar". Neither of these generalisations are usefully defined or contextualised to extend understanding. Within the strands of *Wellbeing* and *Belonging,* mention is made of Pasifika (pp. 26 and 31). Under *Wellbeing,* kaiako are encouraged to "be sensitive to the different ways of diverse families represented in their setting" (p. 26) but it does not mention that such sensitivity must be evidenced within the content and pedagogy of programmes. Under *Belonging,* the advice is for kaiako to strengthen wellbeing by "acknowledging the interconnectedness of people, place and time" (p. 31). In my view, such statements can be made of all peoples and, yet again, it is unclear how kaiako can usefully move beyond acknowledgement of an over-arching principle into professional culturally responsive practice where there already exists diversity across Pacific ethnic groups.

The advice to be responsive to the communities represented within any early childhood service is important, and the nature and authenticity of relationships with whānau is essential; in my view, this should have been emphasised to a greater extent in the curriculum document. However, the continued use of Pasifika, followed by mention of only one Pacific ethnic group—such as Samoan—as an example, needs to be closely examined. The term 'Pasifika' was coined by the Ministry of Education over a decade ago as a shorthand way of encompassing the diversity of the Pacific communities represented in New Zealand. Whilst the term can be used for programmes, policies, or frameworks, when mention is made of people, children, or families then different Pacific ethnic group names must be mentioned. This argument about consistency of usage of terms is advanced because, if we are truly relating to time, place, and things, as advised in *Te Whāriki* (Ministry of Education, 2017), there is no such place as Pasifika, and there are no Pacific peoples who trace their heritages back to Pasifika in geographic terms. Such cultural and historical facts should determine the ways in which ECE discourses mention Pacific peoples and should instead be framed by Pacific peoples themselves.

It is clear that, over time, the visibility of Pacific children and their families in the national curriculum documents has reduced, terminology has changed, and the diversity of Pacific origins, ethnicities, and languages still remains to be articulated clearly and unequivocally for kaiako. Whether other remaining policy documents can address such gaps in professional knowledge and advice remains to be seen. In the context of this partial acknowledgement of diverse Pacific peoples, the next section of this chapter turns to the potential of the *Tapasā* framework for supporting teachers to work effectively with Pacific families.

Tapasā: A framework for Pacific professional cultural competence

The significance of the *Tapasā* framework (Teaching Council of New Zealand, 2018) in the context of this volume is its timeliness in relation to the publication of *Te Whāriki* in 2017. *Tapasā* is a comprehensive guide, one that has been much needed and anticipated by the Pasifika ECE sector. It brings together the work of Pacific teachers and education researchers who, over time, have articulated their research and professional practice approaches. The bibliography of the framework, on pp. 28 to 32, is a valuable resource and very useful for ECE kaiako for referencing and underpinning their pedagogical decisions. However, one important criticism of this document is its development in the absence of consultation with Pacific families and communities, in contrast to that which occurred in the original development of *Te Whāriki*. Early childhood kaiako must work alongside and empower Pacific families and communities, but *Tapasā* has not incorporated the necessary diversity of Pacific communities' perspectives and cultural knowledge.

Tapasā includes clear links to *Our Code Our Standards* (Education Council Aotearoa New Zealand, 2017), the professional practice standards for New Zealand teachers. Indicators of competency range from student teacher level through to experienced teachers and pedagogical leaders. It is still early days to discern whether these levels are indeed useful in building innovative and responsive practice, and questions remain regarding the validity of these indicators as authentic assessment of teacher performance and accountability to Pacific learners and their families. What are the Pacific cultural competencies of the assessors? Can one assume that an experienced qualified teacher would automatically meet all the indicators under each category, including cultural competence?

Authentic assessment of cultural competencies is not just behavioural but must also take into account contextual factors. For example, in centres and services in which there is a small number of Pacific children, or where a range of Pacific heritages are represented, kaiako will inevitably be faced with professional and cultural dilemmas. How can they exercise their professional knowledge and pedagogical judgements in relation to being responsive to Pacific children and Pacific communities using a range of Pacific models and approaches? To address this question, kaiako must engage in authentic talanoa with colleagues, and with their Pacific parents and communities to inform their curriculum decision making.

The research models on p. 27 of *Tapasā* are clearly summarised and referenced for kaiako, although as an example, Tivaevae (included in the table on p. 27) could also usefully be included in the pedagogical models, particularly in early childhood contexts, because of its close relationship between elements of collaboration, respectful relationships, and co-construction of knowledge, and the collaboration that is required to produce a beautiful Cook Islands and Tahitian artefact. The pedagogical models and frameworks presented, whilst useful, could potentially be challenging to kaiako without informed and responsive collaborations. The models are presented in ethnically distinct groups, which must have some particular caveats placed on any formulaic or direct, uncritical application.

Further, *Tapasā* was written to serve as a resource across all sectors of education. Early childhood contexts are unique because services have *Te Whāriki* as a curriculum, and there is a diversity of Pacific communities that kaiako are required to empower consistent with *Principle 3 Family and Community* (Ministry of Education, 2017, p. 2). So, which Pacific pedagogical framework would be the best guide to follow when implementing *Tapasā*? There are always limitations to ethnic-specific categories, because ethnicity and identity are not synonymous, so how can teachers avoid making stereotypical assumptions or reinforce stereotypes when considering the use of any or all Pacific models? With intermarriage and migration, increasing numbers of Pacific learners can also claim multiple ethnic identities, hinted at in *Te Whāriki 2017*:

6: Towards an authentic implementation of Teu Le Va and Talanoa as Pacific cultural paradigms in early childhood education in Aotearoa New Zealand

The identities, languages and cultures of Pasifika children are strengthened by acknowledging the interconnectedness of people, place, time and things. (Ministry of Education, 2017, p. 31)

The implications of these realities for early childhood teachers are considerable. Not only do multiple identities include ethnicities, but identities are also socially constructed, taking into account gender, social class, sexuality, ability, and disability. Consequently, kaiako have to be prepared to negotiate and navigate the deeper nuances of Pacific knowledge paradigms (referred to in *Tapasā* as pedagogical models and frameworks). The term used in the footnote on p. 26 is "phenomenology" which is defined as kaiako understanding social and cultural realities *from the perspectives of those experiencing social interaction and perspectives*. This means that the insertion and incorporation of Pacific voices and funds of knowledge must be integral to all teaching and learning opportunities to authentically validate the strengths of Pacific children and Pacific parents. Unless kaiako gain an understanding of the diversity of Pacific worldviews, learnt through relationships, their dispositions and their attitudes to learning and knowledge-sharing of Pacific families, and their cultural competencies, will remain surface, stereotypical, or even worse, potentially tokenistic.

A small-scale study with early childhood kaiako: Culturally responsive pedagogy focused on Pasifika models and approaches

Early in 2018 I was approached by the Heretaunga Kindergarten Association in Hawke's Bay to assist in improving their responsiveness to Pacific children and families engaged in their services. This chapter records the planning and work in progress of action research projects within four kindergartens within the Heretaunga Kindergarten Association, and my contribution as facilitator and Pacific researcher working under the auspices of Te Rito Maioha Early Childhood New Zealand. This was an opportunity to employ culturally responsive Pacific research methodology through each stage of the inquiry, including the analysis of evidence collected by the kaiako during the period of the study.

Preparation and planning

Kaiako teams in each of the kindergartens developed their own inquiry questions aimed at increasing their responsiveness and professional practice in meeting the needs and interests of their Pacific children and strengthening relationships with Pacific families. One such question was: "In what ways can we recognise and respect the identities of our Pasifika tamariki in their profile books?". Another kindergarten posed the question: "How do we ensure Pasifika children experience an environment where (their) stories, languages, and symbols are acknowledged?". The process we described as a Talanoa process was employed to decide on the final topic and on the wording of the question that shaped each centre's 8-month review cycle. The inquiry process followed an action research methodology, which is defined and contextualised by Goodfellow and Hughes (2009) as practitioner inquiry. In essence, we followed a form of social inquiry that involves thoughtful practice and the creation of local knowledge. This approach is characterised by a clear process of planning, analysing, and acting. Alongside this approach, the Pasifika Education Research Guidelines (Auckland Uniservices, 2001), the concept of Teu Le Va (Mara, 2013), and Talanoa (Vaioleti, 2006) were shared with the kaiako. The aim was to provide an understanding of the cultural parameters of an inclusive methodological paradigm, in terms of Pacific values, beliefs, and perspectives.

A planning template was developed for the kindergartens that recorded the contexts for each of the four inquiries. Together with their agreed question, kaiako had to demonstrate how their inquiry made direct links to each of the following: *Te Whāriki* (Ministry of Education, 2017); the *Pasifika Education Plan 2013–2017, Early Learning Goals* (Ministry of Education, 2013); and the *Code of Professional Responsibility and Standards for the Teaching Profession* (Education Council Aotearoa New Zealand, 2017). In the latter stages of collecting evidence it was fortuitous that reference could be made even more appropriately to the relevant competencies contained in the just released *Tapasā* competency framework.

The reason kaiako were asked to link their question to each of these frameworks in their planning was to reinforce the principle that cultural responsiveness to Pacific children and their families and communities is *core* business and a professional responsibility of all reflective practitioners. The key Ministry of Education policy documents are now in place to implement responsive and inclusive pedagogy with a focus on Pacific needs and interests. However, the ongoing challenge is to contextualise the laudable aims and principles of the policy documents into respectful, responsive, and reciprocal relationships between Pacific families and kaiako, with the learning needs and interests of the Pacific child always placed at the centre.

Although the wording of the inquiry questions initially included the term 'Pacific' the focus in each kindergarten moved very quickly to the specific Pacific communities and ethnic identities represented there. Indeed, the teachers very quickly became motivated to be more knowledgeable and sensitive to all of the kindergarten tamariki they taught and the diversity of their backgrounds. There is an increasing number of Pacific-specific resources and information available on the internet that kaiako could draw from when planning their learning and teaching experiences. Although a selection of these sources was accessed by the kaiako during the study, it was encouraging that, in all cases, they also asked their respective Pacific families and communities to provide their final approval before these were included in the curriculum to assist in their children's learning.

The planning for the collection of evidence to answer the inquiry questions was relatively straightforward. Kindergarten teachers already employ professional practices of gathering evidence of learning and teaching, including learning stories, photographs, observations, conversations with parents, reflective discussions, notes from meetings, and other anecdotal and formative evidence. A point of difference in this study was that kaiako were advised to ensure their collections foregrounded the perspectives of the Pacific children and the Pacific families during this process.

Across the four kindergartens, there were similarities in the questions the teachers decided to focus on, but this was not an issue. It was crucial that the focus of their inquiry was already a priority in their own context, could be easily integrated into their own strategic planning, and could engage their Pacific communities within their programmes. In addition, the use of Talanoa was important (in other words, sustained and respectful dialogue and power sharing) so that all kaiako were committed to continuing with their aims even where staff changes occurred during the data collection stage of the study.

Gathering of evidence phase

At the time of preparing this chapter, all evidence has been collected and will be included in the final report by the kindergartens at a later date. Examples of the types of evidence gathered included learning stories, photographs, notes from staff meetings, narratives recording interactions with whānau, and incidental observations of children's engagement with new resources and adults. The study built upon the professional expertise and skills in pedagogy already evidenced by the kaiako, but the distinctive feature in this study was that kaiako were mentored to incorporate Pacific lenses and frameworks as further interpretations in their culturally responsiveness repertoire.

Analysing the evidence using Pacific frameworks

The kaiako were briefed on the Pacific frameworks that would be used for the analysis stage: Talanoa (Vaioleti, 2006); Teu Le Va (Mara, 2013); and culturally responsive pedagogy with a focus on Pasifika ECE (Mara & Kumar, 2013). The aim was to show how Pacific frameworks can be applied to provide evidence of culturally responsive teaching and learning, and how that evidence can be shared with families, external assessors, and other stakeholders. Once this step has been completed, the kindergartens will Talanoa once again about their next steps in the inquiry cycle. Each of these frameworks invites particular forms of evidence to support inquiry:

1. Talanoa framework of analysis

Evidence within this framework could include the ways in which kaiako have engaged with their families in a respectful and ongoing way. As a result of these encounters, the Pacific families' contributions would have been accepted and incorporated into planned and enacted changes in pedagogy and practice.

2. Teu Le Va framework of analysis

The concept of Teu Le Va is detailed in Mara (2013). Teachers were provided with this reading, drawing their particular attention to pp. 61 and 62, where the links between *Te Whariki* (1996) and Teu Le Va are clearly made. At the basis of the 'va' is the holistic context within which balance is worked for and achieved by all participants—materially, cognitively, emotionally, and spiritually. Evidence within this framework could include the changes in the environment (physical, social, emotional, linguistic, spiritual, and cultural) noted by the kaiako, or evidenced by responsiveness in how families and parents are welcomed into the kindergarten. Pacific families who feel increasingly comfortable and welcomed into the va show willingness to share their knowledge, seek advice, and to trust kaiako. The trust within the va of the centre must be built up over time. Equality and mutual respect in relationships are dominant features, whereby the wellbeing of everyone is enhanced. In other words, is this a place where Pacific children are flourishing in all aspects of the learning environment, and where Pacific languages and identities are enhanced?

3. Culturally responsive pedagogy with a focus on Pasifika ECE

This framework is an adaptation of the Hernandez-Sheets (2005) typology cited in *Tapasā* (Teaching Council of New Zealand, 2018, p. 26). Originally, this typology was adapted for Pacific students in a study in New Zealand secondary schools (Ferguson, Gorinski, Wendt Samu, & Mara, 2008). However, it is not clear whether this framework has ever been used to inform Pacific culturally inclusive pedagogy in secondary schools or taught in teacher education degree courses on cultural responsiveness.

Mara and Kumar (2013) sought to address the perceived chasm between the discourses of education policy frameworks in ECE and how these can be translated effectively and authentically to transform professional and pedagogical knowledge in the early childhood context. This framework has the wider aim of addressing many of the inequitable educational outcomes for Pacific children and students within existing educational structures and services. The importance of quality education and optimal holistic development in the first years is widely acknowledged, so the use of this typology at ECE level is important.

A drawback with teacher competency frameworks is that they sometimes focus on teacher behaviour and performance in isolation, without any contextual consideration or evidence of the quality and nature of the educational interactions between learners and teachers. The strength and utility of the original Hernandez-Sheets typology is that it provides contextual indicators, not only of teacher practice and attitudes, but, in its adapted form, details the expected cultural 'displays' of Pacific learners. The sociocultural approaches in ECE discourses in Aotearoa New Zealand, the focus on relationships, and the co-construction of knowledge match well with the more transactional approach and method of analysis of pedagogy detailed by Hernandez-Sheets (2005).

Mara and Kumar (2013) have followed the pedagogical dimensions of Hernandez-Sheets' typology but these have been adapted to assess culturally responsive Pacific ECE contexts in Aotearoa New Zealand, consistent with *Te Whāriki* and reframed under the headings below:

I Diversity and difference
II Identity and Pacific ethnic identity development
III Social interaction and interpersonal relationships
IV Culturally safe context and self-regulated learning
V Language and language learning
VI Culturally inclusive content and co-construction of knowledge
VII Pedagogy and cognitive and reasoning skills
VIII Assessment and Pacific child's voice

In this small-scale study, the evidence was collected for analysis under all the dimensions of the typology (Mara & Kumar, 2013). However, for reasons of brevity, just two examples from the typology follow: namely, Language and language learning and Assessment and Pacific child's voice.

V Language and language learning

The first group of indicators are teacher responsibilities, the second are expected child responses to the teacher's pedagogy and practice

- Understands language is a cultural tool to communicate thoughts, feelings, beliefs, ideas
- Accepts and embraces all language symbols and forms communicated by Pacific children
- Understands link between language and identity, and never judges what children cannot change
  - Growing in their language development in their Pacific language as well as English
  - Literacy skills and fluency growing in one or more language including their Pacific heritage language
  - Are able to easily switch between their languages and feel encouraged to do so.

VIII Assessment and Pacific child's voice

The first group of indicators are teacher responsibilities, the second are expected child responses to the teacher's pedagogy and practice
- Systematic observation, recording, and documentation of dispositions for learning
- Documentation for parents to be written in the appropriate Pacific language
- Regular invitation and involvement of Pacific parents and whānau in assessment processes and evidence
  - Pacific child's voice is evident at all stages of assessment documentation and interpretation
  - Articulating the child's own successes, problem solving, thinking, questioning
  - Plurilingual expressions of own learning, needs, interests, ideas, contributions.

For example, Pacific children participate in reflections about their learning and these are recorded; Pacific children are provided with time to think and problem solve in one or more language; and express themselves without self-consciousness in the language they feel most comfortable as they are learning.

The purpose of the typology is not for kaiako to treat Pacific children and families as 'other' but to reframe and use negotiated Pacific lenses so that their ways of being, doing, and thinking are understood and interpreted more accurately by kaiako. In so doing, kaiako are better positioned to innovate and be culturally accountable to all children within their early childhood service, including Pacific children and their families. This small-scale study provided opportunities for kaiako to work with Pacific paradigms and concepts. In doing so, they found growing confidence in working with Pacific children and families.

Conclusion

Concern about levels of achievement for some groups of students within the New Zealand education system, including Pacific students, remains a government focus. Early learning and development policies being implemented by the current Government to address child poverty and abuse, child health outcomes, and mental health mean that ECE will be expected to play its part in advancing equity and positive outcomes. Whilst there is reason for some optimism regarding the future of quality Pasifika ECE, barriers remain to its full realisation in the wider context of Pacific wellbeing.

The first barrier for Pacific children and their families receiving and being engaged in culturally responsive early childhood pedagogy is the fact that most Pacific children attend education and care centres where not all kaiako are qualified or registered teachers. Quality implementation of culturally responsive pedagogy (as expected and described within *Te Whāriki 2017*) relies upon expertise in reflection, communication, establishing and maintaining positive and professional relationships, keen observation, rigorous assessment and evaluation processes, and knowledgeable decision making in response to Pacific children's observed needs and interests. In my view, it is not sufficient to provide leadership in skills that reside in only one or two qualified kaiako amongst a team of unqualified and casual assistants within a service.

Another barrier is the lack of cultural and linguistic diversity within the teaching profession itself in Aotearoa New Zealand. Not only does the profession not reflect growing ethnic and linguistic diversities within the wider community, but neither are there sufficient numbers of linguistically and culturally skilled Pacific teachers qualifying to be professional leaders, mentors, or professional support staff. Nor are there enough Pacific professionals appointed to curriculum or management leadership positions within Pacific early childhood services or in other services accessed by Pacific children.

The third barrier to reaching innovative, culturally responsive practice is the need for quality professional development to support the implementation of Pasifika methods and approaches, as described in *Te Whāriki* (Ministry of Education, 2017), and the realisation of *Tapasā* (Teaching Council of New Zealand, 2018). It would seem a waste of time to develop the frameworks including Teu Le Va and Talanoa without access to appropriate resources and professional support that takes into account specific contexts and the composition of services' distinct communities.

Kaiako must be accountable, not only to the government policies and regulations, but also to Pacific children and their families. In addition, full implementation of culturally responsive pedagogy with a focus on Pacific children meets the Pacific child's right to access the richness and resilience of their Pacific culture, language, and identity in Aotearoa New Zealand. This study demonstrates that in ECE settings, when kaiako are appropriately supported to employ the Pacific paradigms of Teu Le Va and Talanoa, confidence in their Pacific cultural responsiveness can be enhanced. Most importantly, strengthened by accessible Pacific paradigms, kaiako can exercise their professional judgement within existing pedagogical frameworks and in their own unique settings to ensure the needs, interests, and priorities of Pacific children and their families are met.

Acknowledgements

The author acknowledges the kind support of the Heretaunga Kindergarten Association and the kaiako of the four kindergartens for their professionalism and commitment to the study described in this chapter.

References

Auckland Uniservices (2001). *Pasifika education research guidelines*. Wellington: Ministry of Education. Retrieved from https://www.educationcounts.govt.nz/publications/pasifika/5915

Education Council Aotearoa New Zealand. (2017). *Our code our standards: Code of professional responsibility and standards for the teaching profession*. Wellington: Author. Retrieved from: https://educationcouncil.org.nz/content/our-code-our-standards.

Ferguson, B., Gorinski, R., Wendt Samu, T., & Mara, D. (2008). *Literature review on the experiences of Pasifika learners in the classroom*. Wellington: New Zealand Council for Educational Research.

Goodfellow, J., & Hedges, H. (2007). Practitioner research. In L. Keesing-Styles and H. Hedges (Eds.), *Theorising early childhood education: Emerging dialogues* (pp. 187–210). Castle Hill, NSW: Pademelon Press.

Hernandez-Sheets, R. (2005). *Diversity pedagogy. Examining the role of culture in the teaching–learning process*. Boston, MA: Pearson Education.

Leaupepe, M., Matapo, J., & Ravlich, P. (2017). Te Whāriki a mat for "all" to stand: The weaving of Pasifika voices. *Curriculum Matters, 13*, 21–41. https://doi.org/10.18296/cm.0021

Mara, D. (2013). Teu Le Va: A cultural knowledge paradigm for Pasifika early childhood education in Aotearoa New Zealand. In J. Nuttall (Ed.), *Weaving te whāriki: Aotearoa New Zealand's early childhood curriculum document in theory and practice* (2nd ed., pp. 55–70). Wellington: NZCER Press.

Mara, D. (2017). Voyaging the oceanic terrains: Sustainability from within Pasifika early childhood education. *Waikato Journal of Education Te Hautaka Mātauranga o Waikato, 22*(1), 37–43.

Mara, D., & Kumar, A. (2013, July). *Culturally responsive pedagogy in Pasifika early childhood education*. Paper presented to the Annual Conference of Te Rito Maioha Early Childhood New Zealand, Hamilton, Aotearoa New Zealand.

Ministry of Education. (1993). *Te whāriki: Draft guidelines for developmentally appropriate programmes in early childhood services*. Wellington: Learning Media.

Ministry of Education. (1996). *Te whāriki. He whāriki mātauranga mō ngā mokopuna o Aotearoa: Early childhood curriculum*. Wellington: Learning Media.

Ministry of Education. (2013). *Pasifika education plan 2013–2017*. Wellington: Author.

Ministry of Education. (2017). *Te whāriki. He whāriki mātauranga mō ngā mokopuna o Aotearoa. Early childhood curriculum*. Wellington: Author.

Teaching Council of New Zealand. (2018). *Tapasā: Cultural competencies framework for teachers of Pacific learners*. https://teachingcouncil.nz/content/tapas%C4%81-cultural-competencies-framework-teachers-of-pacific-learners

Vaioleti, T. (2006). Talanoa research methodology: A developing position on Pacific research. *Waikato Journal of Education, 3*, 175–189.

Wendt Samu, T. (2006). The 'Pasifika Umbrella' and quality teaching: Understanding and responding to the diverse realities within. *Waikato Journal of Education, 12*, 35–49.

CHAPTER 7

The paradox of age for the infants and toddlers of *Te Whāriki*

E. Jayne White

Introduction

Te Whāriki (Ministry of Education, 1996) was the first early years curriculum in the world to grant status to the place of infants and toddlers, and it set a precedent for their legitimate and specialised inclusion in formal education (White & Mika, 2012). In the recently refreshed *Te Whāriki* (Ministry of Education, 2017), a similar positioning was immediately evident—in the English language version at least—that maintained its stance concerning overlapping categories and age groupings. These categories and groupings persistently and persuasively delineate between infants, toddlers, and young children in terms of "growing interests and capabilities" (p. 14) and in examples of practice that appear for each curriculum strand. A rationale for these distinctions is provided: "It can be useful to think of child development in terms of three broad, overlapping age ranges: infants (birth to 18 months), toddlers (one to three years) and young children (two and a half years to school entry)" (p. 13).

In a text that concurrently situates its locus in bioecological, sociocultural, kaupapa Māori, Pasifika, critical and "emerging" theories (Ministry of Education, 2017, pp. 60–62), the retention of a developmental stance seems, at first glance, somewhat paradoxical. Many of the ideas that underpin these theories reject universal categorisations of age in favour of sociocultural/socio-historical/ecological/metaphysical approaches to understanding childhood as a socially, morally, and/or culturally constructed event in time and place. Indeed, many scholars in early years research actively caution against an exclusive allegiance to "developmentally appropriate" practices and orientations as limiting, if not downright immoral, when used to categorise learners as competent or otherwise (Farquhar & White, 2016; Moss,

2006; Murris, 2016; Urban, 2018). Such thinking is also loosely asserted in the context of *Te Whāriki* in a sustained contemplation of the "competent and confident child" (Ministry of Education, 2017, p. 12) and enshrined in statements that persuasively assert the rights of all children to exercise agency, to participate actively in the world, to collaborate with others based on their cultural heritage—*irrespective of age*—and to be viewed as full of potential. As the curriculum states in and through its woven imagery: "The whāriki is unfinished, with loose strands still to be woven. This acknowledges the child's potential and their ongoing educational journey" (Ministry of Education, 2017, Cover note).

Sitting alongside this view, a developmental stance is retained in the document in orienting pedagogical practice. While Lee, Carr, Soutar, and Mitchell (2013, p. 21), in discussing the 1996 version of *Te Whāriki*, suggested that the curriculum outrightly rejected any "staged or levelled" developmental stance, age demarcations were categorically implicated through its pages. This is no less true for the 2017 "refresh" where the same (albeit overlapping) developmental distinctions are made between infant, toddler, and young child. Reasserting its careful framing around the idea that "fluctuations" will occur, the "refreshed" document continues to assert developmental differences in age-specific ranges that are characterised as sets of unique interests and capabilities based on a developmental continuum to learning mastery on entry to school. Such positioning is persistent in the curriculum over time—calling for reflections on pedagogy that take into account the specialised needs of infants as well as toddlers, which are different, albeit aligned, to those of young children as learners.

In this chapter I will argue that the simultaneous positioning of a persistent age-oriented approach alongside the tentative promotion of critical theories represents a necessary paradox of age in consideration of infants and toddlers in the Aotearoa New Zealand early childhood curriculum. A paradox, by definition, is based on the concurrent location of seemingly incommensurable propositions that cohabit a discourse. It may appear contradictory and will often be treated in a binary or polarising manner as a consequence. However, a paradox can also act as a mechanism for examining the underpinning assertions that orient its status. Seen in this light, both propositions concerning age may hold true—thus reconciling the location of infants and toddlers in curriculum when both are brought into alignment.

Neither a developmental stance nor its poststructural antithesis—which arises out of postmodern critique of all universal categorisations, including age—are necessarily new in scholarly contemplations of infants and toddlers (although certainly the former has held more historical sway in *Te Whāriki*). As Elkind explains:

> Whereas modern childhood was defined in terms of differences between age groups, postmodern childhood is identified with differences within age groups. This

metamorphism of our conception of childhood has radically transformed educational practice quite independently of any reform movement or agenda. (Elkind, 1998, p. 1)

However, I want to assert that it is the contemplation of both—articulated in bicultural approaches to learning—that holds the key to their necessary irreconcilable coexistence in New Zealand's early childhood curriculum. Contemplating the essential paradox that arises, the chapter concludes by suggesting that *a developmentally informed notion of being* is a necessary stance for the infants and toddlers of *Te Whāriki*, but only when it is accompanied by *socially just participation in "here and now" encounters of becoming* in the world. Such an alliance orients pedagogy towards the competent and confident "child-in-the-universe", while at the same time recognising the specialist issues concerning diversity, vulnerability, and *modus operandi* that come with consideration of age.

Contemplating the paradox of age

The two seemingly oppositional stances that underpin the paradox of age for the infants and toddlers of *Te Whāriki* have puzzled scientists and philosophers alike for centuries.[1] Both stances draw from origins of thought that are concerned with "being" and "becoming" in the world as a kind of status or movement (White & Mika, 2019). When being and becoming are viewed as a binary encounter, two very different views of learning arise.

1. Being: Where a set of known stages or states of "being" are prescribed, learning can be marked out as a series of developmental coordinates or progressions. If age-defined states of being are essential for learning, then so too is a curriculum that delineates pedagogy by age or stage.

2. Becoming: Where movement is oriented towards constant lifelong "becoming", established age delineations collapse and learning is less predictable or knowable. Where lifelong becoming is given weight, it follows that learning will be a much more fluid adventure that exceeds the parameters of age and perhaps even of culture.

Both viewpoints will be explored in the sections that follow, each lending weight to the irreconcilable status in *Te Whāriki* of the treatment of infants and toddlers.

---

1 It is beyond the scope of this chapter to explore this issue to its fullest extent—suffice to say that thinkers such as Aristotle and Darwin are key protagonists in these discussions.

1. Being: Developmental age-stage

Loosely conceptualised as nature vs. nurture, a developmental stance explains human life through biological processes of metamorphosis (sometimes known as ontogenesis). Its logic is founded on the idea that individuals develop in an orderly, universal fashion through the lifespan as they follow known sequences of development. New experiences may hasten or slow down their development, but the same processes take place for all human beings (Hawley, 2014). This idea took root in early childhood thought in the last century through the well-known work of biologist Jean Piaget (1926), who determined a series of incremental stages of development. Piaget famously marked out a special place for infants as a sensorimotor period, while simultaneously situating them in an "initial ego-centrism" (p. 281). While Piaget has not retained the theoretical stronghold seen in the 1996 edition of *Te Whāriki*, the 2017 version picks up on the related constructivist ideas of Margaret Donaldson and her colleagues (Donaldson, Grieve & Pratt, 1983). We can see this somewhat tempered developmental thinking in statements in *Te Whāriki* such as: "*Although learning and development generally follows a predictable sequence*, for some children progress in some areas may require further assessment, planning, intervention and support" (Ministry of Education, 2017, p. 13, emphasis added).

Over the years between 1996 and 2017, persistent attention has been given to this view, not least through the rise of neurological science. Neurological science has strongly and persuasively asserted the importance of the environment on the developing brain and its emphasis on critical periods for learning during infancy (Fox, Leavitt, & Nelson, 2010). Correspondingly, this knowledge is much more dominant in the 2017 version of *Te Whāriki*, evidenced in statements such as "Neural pathways are formed during this period which are the foundations for all future learning" (Ministry of Education, 2017, p. 13) and in a theoretical subsection that argues the special significance of early experience for optimum brain development:

> The major difference between the brain of a young child and that of an adult is that the child's brain is more impressionable. This difference, known as plasticity, has both a positive and a negative side ... the brain of a young child is more receptive to learning and to enriching influences, but it is also more vulnerable. (p. 62)

This turn towards infant vulnerability, in a document that simultaneously emphasises the competent child, brings the paradox of age into sharp relief. In 2013 Nuttall asserted the necessary absence of such terms within *Te Whāriki*, based on the argument that they present a deficit view of infants. Arguing instead for descriptions of infant learning in terms of "opportunity, respect and relationships" (p. 3), Nuttall (2013) posed a more positive stance in consideration of the "competent" learner. Yet in 2017 we see the introduction of "vulnerability" into the text based on the very same principles of respect, presumably now informed by neuroscientific research that highlights this critical period of development and opportunity. By drawing increased evidence-based attention to (and perhaps accountability for) the importance of nurturing experiences for infants in early childhood settings than had been promulgated in the earlier document, the 2017 version correspondingly and more vehemently calls for "specialised knowledge and practice" (Ministry of Education, 2017, p. 14) for this age group. This shift, in the wake of more powerful evidence (see, for example, Rayna & Laevers, 2011; Dalli & White, 2016), sets in motion an increased accountability for teachers to engage with infants and toddlers as developmental "beings" who have specific developmental needs, as well as interests and capabilities, that must be taken seriously.

A second, related, developmental stance orienting the status of infants and toddlers in curriculum refers to the evolutionary processes that frame human adaptation (sometimes called phylogenesis). This approach permits dynamic changes in development in accordance with the environment, while simultaneously retaining an emphasis on developmental pathways (Darwin 1877; Honneth & Joas, 1988). John Bowlby's well-known attachment theory (1969/1982) established a related orientation for infants to maintain close and secure adult attachments, with dire consequences cautioned for infant mental wellbeing in the absence of these attachments. More recently, however, such claims have been challenged in consideration of infants and toddlers in group care situations (White et al., 2018). As Trevarthen and Delafield-Butt (2017) point out, group caregiving arrangements present additionally nuanced complex social circumstances which "celebrate the child's agency and well-being made in intersubjective engagement with teachers and professional caregivers as a priority for practice" (p. 34), disrupting traditional notions of attachment theory that have dominated the field. In alignment with this view, *Te Whāriki* (Ministry of Education, 2017) pays special attention to the group learning environment, ascribing the "familiar adult that is nearby" (p. 14) as central to learning by paying attention to the child's developmental needs for consistency of care. The teacher (now re-visioned as "kaiako") is consequently called upon as a caregiver and relational partner with infants and as a mediator for toddlers. The teacher's work is first and foremost to support the learner "by participation in valued social and cultural activities" (p. 61) according to the child's fluctuating developmental needs as they encounter a widening circle of people, places, and things. *Te Whāriki* (Ministry of Education, 2017) takes a cautious view in this regard, advocating for a kaiako who "has primary responsibility for each infant"[2] (p. 33), while also recognising that toddlers need predictable, yet widening, relationships within the world as members of a peer group.

---

2 Interestingly, at the time of writing, New Zealand has not legislated for primary caregivers for infants, nor have they (yet) changed their minimum ratio from 1:5.

The underpinning premise of this positioning is that the individual will progress from primitive to more advanced states of being given the right conditions *within the constraints of age*. This view is further promulgated through the sociocultural theory that continues to hold sway in *Te Whāriki* (Ministry of Education, 2017).

The forefather of sociocultural theory—Lev Vygotsky—in his essay on "The Problem of Age" (1934), argued that the development of mental functioning only begins when the child is able to perceive. Since he also claimed that infants up until age 3 cannot perceive themselves separately to adults or use oral language (which he believed was essential to mental development), Vygotsky argued they do not possess mental functioning. Such a view, if unmoderated, potentially casts infants and toddlers as sensory novices who will eventually gain entry into society as learners through a developmental route that must be passed through, albeit at a different pace according to mediation by sociocultural contexts. This emphasis may partially explain why transition to school features strongly in the 2017 version of *Te Whāriki* (as opposed to earlier transitions, which are given only brief acknowledgement), and why emphasis is persistently given to mediated progression over time in asserting learning outcomes, for example repetition of the phrase: "*over time* and with guidance and encouragement children become increasingly capable ..." (Ministry of Education, 2017, pp. 52–56, emphasis added).

Such emphasis on developmental progression in the context of the mediating environment in which the infant or toddler is located has also found reconciliation in what the 2017 version of *Te Whāriki* calls a "bioecological model".[3] According to this conceptualisation, the intention is to "understand how the characteristics of the *developing person* ... interact with aspects of the environment ..." (p. 61, emphasis added). This once again brings developmental "being" into alignment with the sociocultural context that alters its route, if not its characteristics. Such theoretical coupling leads to societal obligations in consideration of the unique characteristics and shared interests of infants and toddlers alongside their older peers. Such obligations are further invoked in *Te Whāriki*'s attention to the United Nations Convention on the Rights of the Child (Ministry of Education, 2017, p. 61), which advocates for social justice in consideration of young learners alongside their older peers.

Viewed in tandem with adaptive, ecological, and evolutionary theories, these approaches give rise to new ways of seeing infancy and toddlerhood as unique states of being *and* becoming that warrant specialised attention by pedagogues and policymakers. As McDowall Clark and Baylis (2012) suggest, while a developmental awareness must be part of this approach, it is better put to use as a means of understanding specialised modes of communication than as a way of positioning

---

3   A reassertion of Bronfenbrenner's (1979) ecological model, which appeared prominently in the 1996 version of *Te Whāriki*. Interestingly, no reference is provided for this model in the 2017 version.

the infant or toddler as socially under-developed or un-ready. *Te Whāriki* (Ministry of Education, 2017) has tentatively incorporated this awareness in the text, in statements such as:

> Infants can communicate their needs and, increasingly over time, anticipate events … Infants are rapidly acquiring communication skills, which kaiako support through thoughtful interactions within a language-rich environment. (p. 14)

> Toddlers communicate both verbally and non-verbally and are developing both receptive and productive language skills. (p. 14)

Statements such as these assert the need for specialised pedagogies that pay attention to infants and toddlers as developmentally situated pedagogical partners, who are able to perceive, think, and act on their own terms.

In light of a compelling call for specialisation in infant and toddler pedagogies over recent years, it might seem surprising that *Te Whāriki* (Ministry of Education, 2017) did not opt for a separate curriculum document for infants and toddlers, as Scotland did 7 years earlier (Learning and Teaching Scotland, 2010) and the International Step by Step Association in The Netherlands (Tankersley, 2017) produced during the same year as *Te Whāriki* was "refreshed". In the section that follows, we explore possible reasons for this, based on simultaneous contemporary views concerning "becoming" in the paradox for the infants and toddlers of *Te Whāriki*.

2. Becoming: A stance of flux

The school of Western thought that constitutes the paradox of age has emerged, at least partially, out of increased scepticism concerning the logic of age-related development or progression. According to Eder (1988, cited in Strydom, 1992) such "ontological fallacy" is overthrown by "radically freeing the theory of social evolution from the universal historical and general societal frame" (p. 33) and thus abandoning any such classification. This shift in thinking draws attention to the ways communication and engagement are enacted within societies rather than within "developing individuals". As such, becoming is closely linked to ascribed values and attitudes as opposed to demarcated behaviours (or, as *Te Whāriki* states, "characteristics"), and is described as a socially oriented process of "vergesellschaftung".[4] According to this view, the individual acts in alignment with the nuanced social and cultural codes at their disposal, rather than in alignment with pre-determined and universal sequences of development.

The genesis of this conception lies in the argument that constructions of age bind, and therefore limit, the capacity of children to think beyond their own constraints. Deleuze and Guattari (cited in Holland, 2013) expand this view to the "chaosmos",

---

4 *Vergesellschaftung*: "human social appropriation or socialisation of nature" (Eder, 1988, cited in Strydom, p. 87), but also meaning 'societalisation', adaptation, and integration.

which they describe as a self-organising system that emerges immanently out of matter and is therefore not constructed by code or creed. On this basis it is their contention that, while humans are influenced by social constructs and practices, they are not wholly defined by them. Indeed, these thinkers would argue that humans can and will exceed these domains altogether in creative engagement with the wider cosmos. We see the development of these ideas in postformal thought,[5] which collapses boundaries such as age based on the premise that all experience is fluid, creative, and chaotic (Gidley, 2016). Sumsion (2019) explains the corresponding influence of Deleuze and Guatarri in the development of the Australian *Early Years Learning Framework* (Department of Education, Employment and Workplace Relations, 2009) as a way of marshalling re-conceptualisations of infant "becomings" into early childhood curriculum. Taking this approach, a deliberate attempt has been made to disrupt a developmental classification of certain (age) groups, re-locating the infant as learner within a co-constituted event of becoming:

> In this diffractive encounter the infant is 'read' as an intra-active, affective, agentic and multiplicitous member of the ECEC community and beyond. Here, the fathomless possibilities for understanding and engaging with the infant are brought into conversation with the impossible nature of imperceptibility. (White & Mika, 2019)

In accord with this line of thought, Biesta (2017) argues that levels of "grown-up-ness" should not be determined by age but rather by our relationships in the world. Through our actions, he asserts, we are constantly beginning again. This shift towards the uniqueness of every learning experience for all of us—regardless of age—orients teachers toward a child who is co-constituted with and through others in the world:

> … infantile and grown-up … both options are open for children and for adults—and perhaps we should say that we can only ever know retrospectively whether we have turned out in a particular situation as child-like or adult-like. Our age and the size of our body are no secure indicators for that. (Biesta, 2017, p. 16)

Disruptions to age delineations such as these have become increasingly popular in theories now influencing early childhood education, which were not available when the 1996 version of *Te Whāriki* was written. While somewhat tentative, such views are clearly observable in the 2017 document. For example, the newly introduced theoretical sub-section called "Critical Theories" invites readers to challenge "perceived norms" in the pursuit of social justice goals for equity (Ministry of Education, 2017, p. 62). As with its predecessor, the English version of *Te Whāriki* frequently uses the generic term "children" instead of infants/toddlers/young children when discussing aspects of curriculum. This strengthened positioning perpetuates a stance which seeks, at

---

5 Postformal thought argues for a more conscious cultural evolutionary approach to education (Gidley, 2016).

least partially, to uphold notions of the universal co-constituted child of *Te Whāriki*, one who exists beyond the boundaries of age as competent, capable, and confident irrespective of "developmental" status. Correspondingly, the Māori language version of *Te Whāriki* appears to impose no age delineation in the classification of infants/toddlers/children, using the generic terms "tamariki" (child) and "mokopuna" (grandchild) throughout.

Viewed in isolation from parts of *Te Whāriki* already discussed in the previous section concerning infants and toddlers, it may appear in this conceptualisation that the infant and toddler are absent from curriculum altogether, subsumed into the universal "child" that appears in many parts of the text (as for the Australian curriculum). The universal "child" tends towards an inclusive position on learning as collapsing boundaries and defying developmental constraints. An emerging field at the time of writing resides in posthumanist approaches to understanding childhoods. These approaches collapse all distinctions between human and nature, promulgating a "post-human child" (Murris, 2017). Here, too, infants or toddlers appear to have forfeited their unique status in favour of a broader set of (dis)orienting principles concerning their location in the wider beyond-human world. This world exists beyond a universal human experience of time and space and opens up possibilities for other dimensions of thought that are yet to be granted legitimacy within New Zealand curriculum.

Such an untethered approach, and associated dismissal of age or stage concepts, presents unique opportunities for curriculum to transcend bounded views of learners as "developing" or "progressing" into some more desirable later stage. Instead, all learners are seen as competent on their own terms in the "here-and-now", in partnership with the messy world that constitutes their experience. Several other recently developed early childhood education curricula internationally appear to have aligned themselves with these views. Discussing the Australian *Early Years Learning Framework*, for example, Sumsion (2019) explains the absence of infants and toddlers, who are collapsed into the term "children" in the text. The term "becoming" is explicitly summoned to encompass all children as learners who are "building and shaping their identity through their evolving experiences and relationships which include change and transitions" (Department of Education, Employment and Workplace Relations, 2009, p. 20). Despite this stance, Sumsion suggests that the *Early Years Learning Framework*, like *Te Whāriki* but in different ways, is littered with a series of theoretical "entanglements", not least concerning the uptake of 'becoming' in neo-liberal contexts that are more oriented to notions of 'being'. Sumsion (2019) seeks reconciliation through two routes. The first involves the politicisation of teachers, who can advocate for infants and toddlers in policy and practice even though these children are not spoken of explicitly. The second calls upon teachers to be nimble-footed in their practices to accommodate all children, regardless of age. Sumsion points out that this is a hopeful stance, given the existing low status, qualifications, and recognition of teachers of infants and toddlers in Australia at her time of writing.

Returning to *Te Whāriki*, its stance on the child is moderated by a bicultural perspective that takes into account the embeddedness of the infant and toddler within hapū, iwi, family, and community, as well as early childhood learning contexts. This co-location calls for the treatment of the first years of life as a unique and treasured time while, at the same time, recognising that neither the infant nor the life in which they live exists in isolation from the world (for a fuller discussion of this argument see Mika & White, 2019). The jarring constructs that underpin the paradox of age are upheld within this view—since young learners can only be partially understood on the basis of developmental awareness in isolation from cultural awareness and encounter. Their 'becoming' is therefore embedded in the co-constituted relationships that exist in genealogical, spiritual, and emotional encounters with people, places, and things, in consideration of their special status as infant 'beings'.

This dual emphasis draws attention to the cultural aspirations that orient the necessary presence of infants in *Te Whāriki*. It is here, I conclude, that we find a fuller expression of the paradox of age for New Zealand infants and toddlers, and perhaps also its reconciliation in curriculum.

Reconciliation of the paradox for infants and toddlers in *Te Whāriki*

Reconciling the paradox of age concerning the coexistence of being and becoming and its presence in *Te Whāriki* places a heavy burden on those who work with infants and toddlers in Aotearoa New Zealand. Not only must kaiako work closely with the families and cultures within their communities and these communities' aspirations for success in consideration of the wider world of becoming, but they must concurrently possess a deep and discerning contemporary knowledge of human development. This is especially so for the period of infancy and toddlerhood that marks the first 3 years of life. Importantly, kaiako must work nimbly between family aspirations and developmental theories to ensure one does not dominate over the other by perpetuating universal prescriptions that set limits or by subsuming younger learners into generic "childhood" oblivion or indifference.

> To arouse the teachers imagination the text of *Te Whāriki* must similarly present him/her with various possibilities at the edges. Defiling rationalistic descriptions with the child—many which orient towards adult preferences and standards and deny the child their agency as a consequence—may go some way to forcing an acknowledgement that what lies beyond his/her understanding of the All constitutes that thought as much as the strict argument being carefully articulated in what seems logically obvious in the known domains of child and his or her colonised worlds. (Mika & White, 2019)

Te Whāriki (Ministry of Education, 2017) does not orient readers towards a pedagogy for young children that duplicates education for older peers or promulgates exclusive specialisations based on developmental understandings in isolation of learning. Instead, *Te Whāriki* calls kaiako to account in the earnest contemplation of *this* child (infant or toddler) and their relationship in and with the world for the benefit of all. Kaiako therefore need to have the specialised understandings necessary for appropriate pedagogy in the "here-and-now", while simultaneously working towards unknown futures and yet-to-be realised domains for understanding. This is not a task for unqualified teachers or well-meaning "caregivers", but for our best thinkers as specialised pedagogues. As Gibbons, Stratford, and White have argued, "The development of a specialist qualification should recognize the complexity of the different philosophical approaches to the meaning of well-being" (2017, p. 53). I would add, engagement with the holistic bicultural dimensions of *Te Whāriki* is necessary in order to learn to live (un)comfortably with the paradox that will undoubtedly arise in such contemplations of age.

By its very nature, *Te Whāriki* requires paradoxical thinking concerning age in order to bring older peers, kaiako, whānau, hapū, iwi, community, and policymakers into closer alignment with the fullest expressions of being and becoming conceptualised by the infant and toddler of *Te Whāriki*. Only through specialised yet inclusive biculturally inspired pedagogies of uncertainty that are located in the world can this aspiration reach its fuller potential. In this regard, it seems, there is more work to be done in the fullest appreciation of the paradox of age that is reinforced and, indeed, strengthened in the 2017 edition of *Te Whāriki*. Viewed as both "being" and "becoming" learners, the infants and toddlers of this curriculum call for pedagogical encounters that pay heed to developmental states of being whilst also opening up possibilities for transgression and transformation in and through a changing world. Kaiako must engage with the paradox wholeheartedly if they are to realise these aspirations in consideration of our youngest learners. Fortunately, well-qualified, supported, and informed kaiako in high-quality early childhood services catering for all learners in Aotearoa New Zealand—according to their preferences, talents, aspirations and, yes, ages—are up for the challenge!

References

Biesta, G. J. (2017). *The rediscovery of teaching*. New York, NY: Routledge.

Bowlby, J. (1969/1982). *Attachment and loss: Vol 1 Attachment*. New York, NY: Basic Books.

Bronfenbrenner, U. (1979). *The ecology of human development: Experiments by nature and design*. Cambridge, MA & London, UK: Harvard University Press.

Dalli, C., & White, E. J. (2016). Group-based early childhood education and care for under 2-year-olds: Quality debates, pedagogy and lived experience. In A. Farrell, S. L. Kagan, & E. K. Tisdall (Eds.), *The Sage handbook of early childhood research* (pp. 36–54). London, UK: Sage.

Darwin, C. R. 1877. A biographical sketch of an infant. *Mind. A Quarterly Review of Psychology and Philosophy*, 2(7), 285–294.

Donaldson, M., Grieve, R. & Pratt, C. (1983). *Early childhood development and education: Readings in psychology*. Oxford, UK: Basil Blackwell.

Department of Education, Employment and Workplace Relations. (2009). *Belonging, being and becoming: The Early Years Learning Framework for Australia*. Canberra, ACT: Commonwealth of Australia.

Elkind, D. (1998). Schooling the postmodern child. *Research Bulletin*, 3(1), 1–9.

Farquhar, S., & White, E. J. (2016). *Philosophy and pedagogy of early childhood*. London & New York: Routledge.

Fox, N. A., Leavitt, P., & Nelson, C. A. (2010). How the timing and quality of early experiences influence the development of the brain architecture. *Child Development*, 81(1), 28–40.

Gibbons, A., Stratford, R., & White, E. J. (2017). A 'good life' for infants in early childhood education *and* care? The place of well-being in ECEC curriculum, pedagogy and policy. In E. J. White & C. Dalli (Eds.), *Under-three year-olds in policy and practice* (pp. 41–55). Dordrechdt, The Netherlands: Springer.

Gidley, J. M. (2016). *Postformal education: A philosophy for complex futures*. Cham, Switzerland: Springer.

Hawley, P. (2014). Ontogeny and social dominance: A developmental view of human power patterns. *Evolutionary Psychology*, 12(2), 318–342. http://dx.doi.org/10.1177/147470491401200204

Holland, E. W. (2013). *Deleuze and Guatarri's 'A Thousand Plateaus'*. London, UK: Bloomsbury.

Honneth, A. & Joas, J. (1988). *Social action and human nature*. Cambridge, UK: Cambridge University Press.

Learning and Teaching Scotland. (2010). *Pre-birth to three: Positive outcomes for Scotland's children and families*. National Guidance. Retrieved from https://education.gov.scot/improvement/documents/elc/elc2_prebirthtothree/elc2_prebirthtothreebooklet.pdf

Lee, W., Carr, M., Soutar, B., & Mitchell, L. (2013). *Understanding the Te Whāriki approach: Early years education in practice*. Abingdon, UK: Routledge.

McDowall Clark, R., & Baylis, S. (2012). 'Wasted down there': Policy and practice with the under-threes. *Early Years: An International Research Journal*, 32(2), 229–242. http://dx.doi.org/10.1080/09575146.2011.652939

Mika, C. & White, E.J. (2019). Ngā mokopuna kei te hāereere: Becoming in Aotearoa curriculum –The first 1000 days. In M. Gradovski, E. Eriksen Odegaard, N. Rutanen, J. Sumsion, C. Mika & E.J. White (Eds), *The First 1000 days of early childhood: Becoming*. Singapore: Springer.

Ministry of Education. (1996). *Te whāriki: He whāriki mātauranga mō ngā mokopuna o Aotearoa: Early childhood curriculum*. Wellington: Learning Media.

Ministry of Education. (2017). *Te whāriki: He whāriki mātauranga mō ngā mokopuna o Aotearoa: Early childhood curriculum*. Wellington: Author.

Moss, P. (2006). Structures, understandings and discourses: Possibilities for re-envisioning the early childhood worker. *Contemporary Issues in Early Childhood, 7*(1), 30–41.

Murris, K. (2016). Contesting Early Childhood Series: *The posthuman child: Educational transformation through philosophy with picturebooks*. London, UK: Routledge.

Piaget, J. (1926). *The language and thought of the child*. London, UK: Routledge & Kegan Paul.

Rayna, S., & Laevers, F. (2011). Understanding children from 0 to 3 years of age and its implications for education. What's new on the babies' side? Origins and evolutions. *European Early Childhood Education Research Journal, 19*(2), 161–172. http://dx.doi.org/10.1080/1350293X.2011.574404

Strydom, P. (1992). The ontogenetic fallacy: The immanent critique of Habermas's developmental logical theory of evolution. *Theory, Culture & Society, 9*(3), 65–93. http://dx.doi.org/10.1177/026327692009003004

Sumsion, J. (2019). The Australian Early Years Learning Framework, becoming and children in their first 1000 days. In M. Gradovski, C. Mika, E. Odegaard, N. Rutanen, J. Sumsion, & E. J. White, *The first 1000 days of early childhood: Becoming*. Singapore: Springer.

Tankersley, D. (2016). *A quality framework for early childhood practice in services for children under three years of age*. The Netherlands: International Step by Step Association. Retrieved from: https://www.issa.nl/sites/default/files/pdf/epubs/ISSA_Quality_Framework_0-3/PDF/ISSA_Quality_Framework_0-3_e-version_screen.pdf

Trevarthen, C., & Delafield-Butt, J. (2017). Intersubjectivity in the imagination and feelings of an infant. In E. J. White & C. Dalli (Eds.), *Under-three year olds in policy and practice* (pp. 17–36). Singapore: Springer.

Urban, M. (2018). (D)evaluation of early childhood education and care? A critique of the OECDs International Early Learning Study. *Improving the quality of childhood in Europe vol. 8*. Brussels, Belgium: Alliance for Childhood.

Vygotsky, L. (1934). The problem of age. In *The collected works of L. S. Vygotsky, Volume 5, 1998* (pp. 187–205). (Trans. by A. Blunden, 2008).

White, E.J. & Mika, C. (2019). A geneology of becoming (and being) in the first 1000 days, In, M. Gradovski, E. Eriksen Odegaard, N. Rutanen, J. Sumsion, C. Mika & E.J. White (Eds). *The First 1000 Days of Early Childhood: Becoming*. Singapore: Springer.

White, E. J., & Mika, C. (2013). Coming of age? Infants and toddlers in ECE. In J. Nuttall (Ed.), *Weaving te whāriki: Aotearoa New Zealand's early childhood curriculum framework in theory and practice* (2nd ed., pp. 93–105). Wellington: NZCER Press.

White, J., Hansen, K., Hawkes, K., Redder, B,., Lord, W., & Perks, N. (2018). Key teaching (primary caregiving?) practices during infant transitions to ECEC in Aotearoa New Zealand, *The First years Nga Tau Tuatahi. New Zealand Journal of Infant and Toddler Education, 20*(2), pp. 5–14.

CHAPTER 8

Moving *Te Whāriki* from rhetoric to reality for disabled children and their whānau in early childhood education

Bernadette Macartney

Introduction

This chapter explores the need to more intentionally align and transform thinking and practices within early childhood care and education (ECCE) to realise the aspirations of *Te Whāriki* (Ministry of Education, 1996, 2017) as a mat for *all* to weave and stand on. It turns the focus from change, remediation, and development in the assessment of individual children, toward an assessment of social, cultural, and physical environments, and relationships that teachers and other adults are responsible for creating and sustaining within ECCE. This involves considering why and how disablement and exclusion happen and what forms they take.

Using Disability Studies in Education (DSE) and human rights perspectives, I consider the ideas, practices, and discourses underpinning the language and text of *Te Whāriki*, particularly regarding how inclusion is viewed, and the language and tenor of *Te Whāriki* regarding disabled-labelled children, their whānau,[1] teachers, and teaching (Connor, Gabel, Gallagher & Morton, 2008; Macartney, 2011a). Within the chapter, I outline some of the current barriers to the presence, participation, and learning of disabled children and their whānau in ECCE. These include systemic-structural barriers that constrain inclusion and allow or support exclusion, and barriers that involve how we think and what we do about disability and difference in

---

1 Whānau refers to extended family, family group, a familiar term of address to a number of people—the primary economic unit of traditional Māori society. In the modern context, the term is sometimes used to include friends who may not have any kinship ties to other members (*Māori Dictionary*, https://maoridictionary.co.nz/).

our teaching relationships, practices, and settings. I then examine the *Communication—Mana reo* strand to more closely apply a DSE and human rights analyses and critique to *Te Whāriki*.

Barriers in the education of disabled learners in Aotearoa New Zealand

There are significant, systemic barriers to disabled people's access, participation, and success in education in Aotearoa New Zealand (Independent Monitoring Mechanism on the Rights of Persons with Disabilities, 2016). Inequities start in early childhood education and continue within our school, tertiary, and adult education settings (Wills, Morton, McLean, Stephenson, & Slee, 2014). Inclusive early childhood education, on an equal basis to non-disabled children, can be hard to find and access for disabled children and their families (Gordon-Burns, Gunn, Purdue, & Surtees, 2012). Basic data about the access of disabled children and their whānau to early childhood education settings and the early childhood curriculum are not collected, and therefore not monitored or adequately understood, by the Ministry of Education or any government agency (Macartney, 2016; Murray, 2017). In fact, *no data* are collected by government agencies on the access, participation, experiences, and exclusion of disabled children in ECCE, and there are large gaps in information about disabled children at school, school leavers, and disabled adults in education as well (Independent Monitoring Mechanism on the Rights of Persons with Disabilities, 2016).

Nevertheless, research, anecdotal evidence, human rights and advocacy organisations, and the media continue to highlight the barriers that many disabled children and their whānau experience in accessing and enjoying an inclusive early childhood and school education (IHC, 2008; Independent Monitoring Mechanism on the Rights of Persons with Disabilities, 2016). Two further barriers are explored here due to their special significance: the marketisation of ECCE and variations in teacher agency in relation to disabled learners.

Marketisation of ECCE provision

Market model structures and the commercialisation of ECCE provision in Aotearoa New Zealand have created financial and other disincentives for services to include and teach all children well (Lyons, 2014; Mitchell, 2014). Children who are described as having additional needs, requiring what *Te Whāriki* frames as "additional support" (Ministry of Education, 2017, p. 13), are potentially viewed in terms of their additional cost to a service; this is a view that other children and families are not scrutinised when approaching an ECCE service. The greatest areas of cost in operating an early childhood service are linked to providing the conditions necessary for a quality, *Te Whāriki*-based curriculum for all children. These conditions include teacher qualifications, teacher-to-child ratios, the size of child groups in the service, teachers' pay, other working conditions such as staff non-contact time, and professional leadership and learning opportunities (Dalli, White, Rockel, & Duhn, 2011). There is some evidence that services that invest less in these areas are unlikely to be inclusive (Lyons, 2014).

Reduced ECCE funding from central government, and the erosion of regulations and policy supporting access and quality ECCE, have increased pressure on staff and management (Mitchell, 2014). Working long term within a context of lack of resources and poor support for structural quality makes it hard for services and teachers whose desire is to contribute to and serve their communities well (Radford & Shearsby, 2018).

Teacher agency

Recognising and removing barriers to presence, participation, and learning is a cornerstone of inclusive pedagogies (United Nations Committee on the Rights of Persons with Disabilities, 2016). *Te Whāriki* states that the curriculum:

> ... holds the promise that *all* children will be empowered to learn with and alongside others by engaging in experiences that have meaning for them. This requires kaiako to *actively respond* to the *strengths, interests, abilities and needs of each child* and, at times, provide them with *additional support* in relation to learning, behaviour, development or communication. Offering an inclusive curriculum also involves adapting environments and teaching approaches as necessary and *removing any barriers to participation and learning*. Barriers may be *physical* (for example, the design of the physical environment), *social* (for example, practices that constrain participation) or *conceptual* (beliefs that limit what is considered appropriate for certain children). *Teaching inclusively means that kaiako will work together with families, whānau and community to identify and dismantle such barriers.* (Ministry of Education, 2017, p. 13, emphases added)

Individually and collectively, teachers have the power to exercise agency within their settings to make those settings inclusive of disabled learners. Using and developing professional agency is a core aspect of being an early childhood educator. What teachers believe, think, and do directly shapes experiences and feelings of belonging or not belonging for children and families/whānau. Teachers can consciously use and grow their personal and group agency to influence what happens within daily relationships and environments (Carr, 2001; Macartney, 2011a, 2011b; McIlroy, 2017; Rinaldi, 2006; Ritchie, 2010; Veck, 2009). Teacher confidence and beliefs can affect their capacity and willingness to teach all children well (Macartney & Morton, 2011; McIlroy, 2017; Rivalland & Nuttall, 2010). *Te Whāriki* emphasises that the curriculum is for all children and that, "Kaiako are the key resource in any ECE service. Their primary responsibility is to facilitate children's learning and development through thoughtful and intentional pedagogy. This means they need a wide range of capabilities" (Ministry of Education, 2017, p. 59). However, there is evidence that some teachers and services believe they require (or don't have) 'special' knowledge or skills to teach some children, and/or that the care and education of *some* children is primarily the role and responsibility of others (Purdue, 2004).

Educators draw from values, beliefs, assumptions, and expectations in (co)-constructing the culture, wairua, norms, routines, spaces, and relationships within ECCE settings. The experiences and outcomes of the early childhood curriculum are thereby mediated by teachers. At times, teachers' thoughts and assumptions can act as the biggest barrier to some children's access, learning, participation, and success within our settings (Colvin, Dachyshyn, & Togiaso, 2012; Macartney, 2011a; Purdue, 2004). For this reason, the development and maintenance of inclusive curriculum requires making regular time and space for critical dialogue and reflection. An openness to challenging and changing beliefs and practices is necessary in removing barriers to learning and participation within ECCE settings (Macartney, 2011b; Ministry of Education, 2017; Rinaldi, 2006; Veck, 2009). One body of scholarship—sociocultural interpretations of disability and diversity—provides a resource for teachers who seek to orient their work toward inclusion.

Sociocultural interpretations of disability and diversity

I have argued so far that how the so-called 'problem' of disability is framed and understood leads to very different responses, solutions, and outcomes for disabled people, young and old. It is disappointing, therefore, that disability and ableism are not adequately theorised, visible, or addressed within *Te Whāriki* (Ministry of Education, 1996, 2017). I argue this is the case because *Te Whāriki* lacks a clear and consistent sociocultural and human rights-based approach to disability. The effect of this omission is to *leave space* for exclusionary structures, thinking, and practices to continue un-recognised.

Thinking, attitudes, and approaches that construct disability and difference in terms of individual deficit and deviance from desirable (social and cultural) norms is known as *ableism*. Ableism operates when disabled children and their families are viewed and responded to primarily in terms of what are interpreted as their deficits, differences, special-, or other-ness (Macartney & Morton, 2013). These deficit views contrast with the understanding of diversity and difference as expected, normal, necessary, and welcome aspects of the human, animal, and natural world found in the social model of disability.

The social model of disability

The social model of disability was first articulated by disabled activists, sociologists, and disability organisations in the United Kingdom 50 years ago as a political and theoretical framework to challenge and replace medical, deficit, and individualised thinking and responses to disability, disabled people, and diversity (Barnes, Mercer, & Shakespeare, 1999; Connor et al., 2008; Shakespeare, 2006; Union of the Physically Impaired Against Segregation, 1976). At its core is the impulse to learn about and reflect on how disability is understood and theorised *by disabled people*, whānau, Disability Studies in Education (DSE) scholars, advocates, and allies, in order to develop and transform thinking, curriculum, and society.

The social model rejects the dominant medical–individual model view of disability and disabled people. In particular, it challenges the assumption that disability is a problem, and that the problem is contained within individuals. Instead, the social model locates the problems disabled children and adults experience *within society*, not within individuals who, in a medical–individual model are constructed by and responded to by the dominant culture as different. In other words,

> … it is *society which disables* physically impaired people. Disability is something imposed on top of our impairments, by the way we are unnecessarily isolated and excluded from full participation in society. Disabled people are therefore an *oppressed group* in society. (Union of the Physically Impaired Against Segregation (UPIAS), 1976, in Shakespeare, 2006, p. 198, emphasis added)

The social model has become an international framework for understanding and advancing the rights of disabled people to be equally valued, self-determining, and fully contributing members of society. The catchcry, "Nothing about us without us!" is an important principle of the social model and disability rights movement. Disabled people, their families, and allies are asserting the right to be valued, heard, and in control of their own lives, encapsulated in the United Nations Convention on the Rights of Persons with Disabilities.

United Nations Convention on the Rights of Persons with Disabilities

The social model underpins the United Nations Convention on the Rights of Persons with Disabilities (UNCRPD) (United Nations General Assembly, 2007) to which Aotearoa New Zealand is a signatory. Article 24 of the UNCRPD, on the right to education, outlines governments' and their agencies' responsibilities and obligation to create and maintain a system and conditions that ensure the access of disabled children and young people to an inclusive education. In 2016, the United Nations Committee on the Rights of Persons with Disabilities wrote and officially adopted the *General Comment* on article 24 of the Convention. The *General Comment* clarifies and provides guidance to Convention signatories on the United Nation's interpretation of article 24, the right to education. The Committee describe inclusive education as:

> … a process that transforms culture, policy and practice in all educational environments to accommodate the differing needs of individual students, together

with a commitment to remove the barriers that impede that possibility ... It focuses on the attendance, participation and achievement of all students, especially those who, for different reasons, are excluded or at risk of being marginalized.

Inclusion involves access, permanence and progress to high-quality education without discrimination of any kind, whether within or outside the school system. It seeks to enable communities, systems and structures to combat discrimination, celebrate diversity, promote participation and overcome barriers to learning and participation for all people ... The goal is for all students to learn in inclusive environments. (United Nations Committee on the Rights of Persons with Disabilities, 2016, p. 3)

Ableism and power

The social model of disability, along with sociocultural and human rights frameworks, not only provides a pathway to thinking about and growing inclusive education, but also acknowledges that, ultimately, ableism involves the exercise of power in order to marginalise particular groups of people. These alternative perspectives require teachers to expand their understanding of what constitutes discrimination to include the systemic and cultural exclusion and marginalisation of disabled people, children, and adults within Aotearoa New Zealand's communities and education settings. Disability discrimination, or ableism, is underpinned by the assumption that disabled people, or people who are defined as being disabled, are inferior to non-disabled people. It is through the construction of disabled people as 'other' that discrimination, segregation, and exclusion occur and are justified (Connor et al., 2008; Gabel, 2005).

Ableism operates in the same ways as other forms of discrimination. Oppressive mindsets and associated practices construct and divide groups into those that are assumed to be superior (for example, normal, not special, non-disabled) and inferior (for example, abnormal, special, disabled) to reinforce and (re)produce a hierarchy of human value, power, and privilege. Unmasking ableist assumptions and teaching inclusively therefore requires educators to invite, listen to, learn from, and engage with the perspectives of the people who are most affected and have the absolute right to be heard (United Nations General Assembly, 2007). In order to transform education, non-disabled people need to assume a great deal less about, and listen more, to disabled people and their whānau.

Te Whāriki and ableism

Life in an early childhood service is part of life in the larger community and society. Noticing, interrupting, and replacing sexist and racist narratives is encouraged and articulated in the curriculum as a core part of an early childhood teacher's work (Ministry of Education, 2017). However, I argue that *Te Whāriki* devotes much greater attention and depth of thinking to responding to gender and cultural identity, equity, and diversity than it does to acknowledging and advocating for disabled children's access, identities, and rights. My reading of *Te Whāriki* leads me to conclude that a view of disability as socially and culturally constructed, recognition of disabled people as a marginalised group, and the importance of disabled children developing a positive identity within ECCE are absent, rare, and/or underdeveloped aspects of the curriculum.

For example, in the early section *Language Identity and Culture*, the curriculum states that, "While all children are different and their learning trajectories are influenced by the social and cultural context, there are nevertheless typical characteristics and patterns that can be observed in the years from birth to school entry" (Ministry of Education, 2017, p. 13). This statement can be interpreted as encouraging readers of the curriculum to compare and judge children in relation to a predetermined set of norms—"typical characteristics and patterns". It communicates a hierarchy of value where what is characterised as "typical" (normal) is assumed to be *the* desirable— and only—way of being worth mentioning. This view minimises disabled-labelled children and their experiences within "the social and cultural context" through imposing those norms upon everyone. It dismisses some children's experiences and needs in preference for sameness and normal ways of developing and being.

In the final section of this chapter I turn to a closer examination of *Te Whāriki*, particularly the strand of *Communication—Mana reo*, in the light of the arguments I have outlined so far.

Discourses and approaches to diversity within *Te Whāriki*

As I have argued, understanding disability as a 'problem within an individual' is a barrier to disabled children developing a positive identity, self-image, and agency. *Te Whāriki* states:

> In *Te Whāriki* (all) children are positioned as confident and competent learners from birth ... This curriculum acknowledges that all children have rights to protection and promotion of their health and wellbeing, to equitable access to learning opportunities, to recognition of their language, culture and identity and, increasingly, to agency in their own lives. These rights align closely with the concept of mana. (Ministry of Education, 2017, p. 12)

However, for teachers to be confident that they are enacting the principles and strands of *Te Whāriki* for *every* child, they must be able to notice and transform their cultural (common sense) tendency to equate difference with deficit, and to then define some children in relation to those deficits. An over-emphasis on one aspect or characteristic of any person marks them out as 'not like others'. It runs counter to the holistic and ecological approaches to children, participation, and learning within *Te Whāriki* (Ministry of Education, 1996, 2017). The assumption that a child or group of children are fundamentally different or 'other' leads to exclusion within teaching practices, relationships, and the curriculum. It does not equally recognise and nurture the mana of those children and their whānau. One way this is evident in *Te Whāriki* is through the language of 'additional needs' and 'support'.

'Special needs' and 'additional learning support'

While the principles, strands, and general statements within *Te Whāriki* support, and can provide a framework for, inclusive practices, the curriculum also uses language and terms that contradict these principles, potentially invoking a medical-deficit mindset. The words 'disability' and 'disabled' are not used in any of the iterations of *Te Whāriki* (Ministry of Education, 1993, 1996, 2017). The existence of disability as a positive identity, disability pride, and culture are absent from the curriculum, except for brief references to New Zealand Sign Language and Deaf culture. It is difficult for ECCE to critically engage with social model, DSE, and disability rights perspectives when the language and discourse that support these perspectives are invisible. How do families and disabled children develop positive identities and dispositions, feel valued, and belong if they are not positively and explicitly recognised, visible, or valued within the curriculum? Instead, the curriculum constructs disability as being primarily about individual deficit, deviance, otherness, and need. For example, disabled children have variously been described in *Te Whāriki* as having "special needs" (Ministry of Education, 1993, p. 10; 1996, p. 11), requiring "*significant change to a regular programme and/or additional resources in order to benefit from their learning environment*" (Ministry of Education, 1993, p. 10, emphasis added), and "who require resources *alternative* or *additional* to those *usually provided* within an early childhood education setting" (Ministry of Education, 1996, p. 11, emphases added). In our current curriculum, disabled children are referred to as those who require "*additional learning support*" (Ministry of Education, 2017, pp. 12, 13, 35, 64, emphasis added). I argue that the replacement of the term "special needs" with "additional learning support" in the new curriculum represents a continuum, rather than an interruption, of ableist rhetoric and discourse. This framing raises questions such as: When and with what outcomes might teachers respond to some children's learning, participation, and needs as "additional"? Why is teacher 'support' for some children described as "additional" while for most, presumably 'normal', children teacher support is assumed? I explore these questions in more depth by now turning to the *Communication—Mana reo* strand of *Te Whāriki*.

Communication—Mana reo

Recognising and respecting mana[2] is a central principle, value, and practice within *Te Whāriki*:

> Whakamana means that every child will experience an empowering curriculum that recognises and enhances their mana and supports them to enhance the mana of others ... all children are born with mana inherited from their tipuna ... this means recognising their rights ... to experience equitable opportunities for participation and learning ... (Ministry of Education, 2017, p. 18)

Mana is inextricably linked with identity and the concept of mana forms the basis of every strand within the curriculum. The *Mana reo* strand is about according respect to and nurturing every child and groups' culture, language, and communication, since participation, learning, and development are impeded when a young child is not given adequate access to the language and communication tools that work best for them.

However, *Te Whāriki* conveys mixed messages about the ways it values and promotes the rights and participation of all children, such as sometimes communicating normalising assumptions that obscure some groups' ways of communicating and being. For example, this tension is evident in the ways the curriculum emphasises and privileges oral communication and language/s, written text, and verbal literacy over visual languages and other non-verbal modes of communication. The curriculum notes that a key condition for developing language proficiency is the presence and availability of teachers who are, "able to support the cultural and linguistic diversity of all children" (Ministry of Education, 2017, p. 59). The introduction to the *Mana reo* strand makes the important point that proficiency in language and communication is essential for thinking, making sense of, engaging with, and influencing the world (Ministry of Education, 2017). Yet the lack of attention, detail, and direction about non-dominant or "alternative" (p. 42) forms of language and communication is symptomatic of the curriculum's normative and ableist discursive messaging. My analysis suggests that a disabling mindset is evident within the *Communication—Mana reo* strand through the establishment of a norms-based hierarchy of languages and ways of communicating.

First, reference to New Zealand Sign Language (NZSL) and methods of communication used by "non-verbal" children within the *Mana reo* strand are

---

2 Mana refers to "prestige, authority, control, power, influence, status, spiritual power, charisma—mana is a supernatural force in a person, place or object. *Mana* is the enduring, indestructible power of the *atua* (gods) and is inherited at birth ... The authority of *mana* and *tapu* is inherited and delegated through the senior line from the *atua* as their human agent to act on revealed will. Since authority is a spiritual gift delegated by the *atua*, man remains the agent, never the source of *mana*." Mana tangata refers to "power and status accrued through one's leadership talents, human rights, mana of people" (*Māori Dictionary*, https://maoridictionary.co.nz/).

relegated to a footnote (Ministry of Education, 2017, p. 42). Secondly, these forms of communication are subsumed within the term and norms of "oral language" speakers throughout the main body of the *Mana reo* strand:

> In this document, *'oral language' encompasses any method of communication the child uses as a first language*; this includes New Zealand Sign Language and, for children who are non-verbal, alternative and augmentative communication (AAC). (p. 42, emphasis added)

This statement acts to diminish, rather than enhance, the mana, visibility, and recognition of NZSL and (so-called) alternative communication systems within the curriculum. NZSL has been an official language of New Zealand since 2006.[3] It is a valid language that should be accorded the same status, visibility, and consideration within the curriculum as other languages such as English and te reo Māori. Furthermore, NZSL is visual, not oral. NZSL uses hand and body movements, and positioning, facial expression, lip reading, and touch as the basis of communication.

Every sign language is a dynamic, comprehensive system of communication in its own right. Sign languages have their own grammars and syntax, and are not a direct translation of English or their country of origins' spoken language/s. NZSL connects Deaf and hard of hearing people to the Deaf community and culture and a positive identity. Some children and adults who are not Deaf or hard of hearing, including people who are considered non-verbal, benefit from learning and using NZSL as their primary language and form of communication, or in combination with speaking and/or assistive technology. Including NZSL in the curriculum as an "oral language" (Ministry of Education, 2017, p. 42) contradicts the stated outcome of *all* children (and whānau) having "confidence that *their first language is valued* and increasing ability in the use of at least one language" (p. 42, emphasis added) and of teachers promoting and protecting "the languages and symbols of children's own and others' cultures" (p. 41). Every child's first language and ways of communicating are of equal value and require recognition and nurturing, and should be positioned as such within curriculum frameworks.

Teaching and using augmentative communication involves teachers learning to use assistive technologies and communication systems within their professional setting to support learning and participation. Why and how teachers and services ensure children's access to NZSL, assistive technology, and non-dominant methods of communication is not sufficiently valued, explored, or addressed within the curriculum. A lack of focus and clarity about those children's communication rights makes their access to equitable communication opportunities and language development more precarious and negotiable than others. I argue that the

---

[3] New Zealand Sign Language Act 2006.

complexities of recognising and responding well to multiple languages and modes of communication need to be highlighted and supported across the curriculum, policy, teacher education, professional learning, and resources, not relegated to a footnote.

In my analysis, the *Mana reo* strand offers a fragmented and partial view of children's language and communication needs, development, and rights. The binary created between verbal/oral and non-verbal communication is unhelpful for exploring the complexities of language and communication, especially in young children. For example, in a further footnote under the *Mana reo* strand, it is suggested that "For children who are deaf or hard of hearing, 'hearing' includes watching" (Ministry of Education, 2017, p. 42). As a stand-alone statement, this oversimplifies and minimises the complexities and importance of how young children are using and developing their senses in unique ways in order to make sense, communicate, and participate. Many children and adults use their vision and other senses to perceive information, not just particular groups of children.

A more inclusive framing would be for the *Mana reo* strand to describe language and communication in terms of the multiple ways that children experience and interact with people, places, and things, including their complex use of multiple senses. Privileging oral communication marginalises some groups. Teachers therefore need explicit information and guidance to value, understand, and feel confident about supporting the language and communication of groups who are at risk of being marginalised, so that these groups of children can be educated on an equal basis with others.

Conclusion

Disabled-labelled children and adults' differences or needs are routinely and unconsciously assumed to be their all-defining or most significant characteristic and aspect of their identity. In this chapter I have argued that exclusion can be understood and rationalised as being the result of a person's individual impairments or differences. The social model of disability views such exclusion as the predictable outcome of external structures and arrangements, beliefs, actions, and inactions that privilege particular ways of being, communicating, etc.

Exclusion is a process and outcome of discrimination. It is not caused by the individual's difference or deficit, but by how these differences are constructed and responded to by others. In the first part of the chapter I suggested that disabled children's access to, attendance, and participation in ECCE is often restricted because of inadequate resourcing and arrangements. In the first part of the chapter I also argued, however, that teachers, in collaboration with families and communities, have the power and obligation to challenge and transform discourses that negatively judge and marginalise any group of children and their families. Disabled children (and adults) need to be recognised as a marginalised group. Inclusive education includes, but is much more than, a technical question about the 'how' of teaching. As I have argued in the second half of this chapter, inclusion and inclusive education are fundamentally about human values, rights, equity, and an ethic of belonging (Macartney, 2011b; Ministry of Education, 2017).

Education is not neutral; it is social, political, and ethical. All teachers work in ways that either sustain and/or remove barriers to others' participation and learning. *Te Whāriki*, and the knowledge, philosophy, worldviews, and pedagogies it draws from, are relevant to all children, whānau, and teachers, including disabled children. Teachers have the personal and collective power to decide whether to uncritically keep thinking and behaving in ways that marginalise some children and groups or to become part of creating a better education for everyone.

Recognising and resisting deficit discourses requires early childhood teachers to actively maintain and exercise their professional mana and obligations through critical thinking and advocacy in relationships and interactions with others. Disabled adults, children, their whānau, communities, and often their teachers have a wealth of expertise and knowledge about individual children. The mana and knowledge of children, whānau, teachers, and *Te Whāriki* is rich and needs promoting and protecting. Ensuring equitable access to the curriculum requires clarity about values and advocacy from those involved with disabled children and their whānau. It is inaccurate and disempowering to believe a separate body of knowledge about how to teach certain groups of children, such as those called disabled, is necessary or desirable.

The principles and strands of *Te Whāriki* outline a pedagogical framework for all children, even though my critique indicates a more serious consideration of the conceptual and theoretical framing of the curriculum is necessary. Good teaching includes recognising and valuing diversity in all of its forms. Moving the boundaries of *Te Whāriki* from rhetoric to reality involves recognising disability and disabled people as a valid and positive group and identity in children and society. It also involves teachers systematically noticing, recognising, and removing barriers to the mana, wellbeing, belonging, exploration, communication, and contributions of every child (Gordon-Burns et al., 2012; Macartney, 2011b; Ministry of Education, 2017). This requires teachers to familiarise themselves with, and be guided by, the United Nations Convention on the Rights of Persons with Disabilities (Independent Monitoring Mechanism on the Rights of Persons with Disabilities, 2016; United Nations General Assembly, 2007; UNCRPD, 2016), DSE, and inclusive education research and perspectives (Connor et al., 2008).

For disabled people and their whānau, experiences of ableism are personal and pervasive. Often families are living and acting in isolation from each other. To be transformative and effective, resistance to ableism and to other forms of exclusion requires a collective, cohesive, and deliberate approach. Teachers and policymakers need to lead, learn about, challenge, and advocate for equity and inclusion. Inaction means continuing to defer to normalising narratives that cast some people as unfortunate, special, needy, and not like us, and to understand and respond to them primarily in terms of their perceived differences, problems, and deficits. In order to realise the aspirations of *Te Whāriki* for all children, its dominant narrative about disability and difference as deviation from an ideal norm needs to be consciously rejected and replaced with principles and actions that embed human rights, belonging, and the value and contributions of every person and group in society, including, and perhaps especially, disabled people. Rather than leaving whānau isolated in their struggles to access the belonging, relationships, and participation promised in *Te Whāriki*, we can orient ourselves as allies working alongside children, whānau, and others to face barriers and overcome or find solutions to problems together. This is fundamentally what the principles and strands of *Te Whāriki* intend—and require—us to do.

References

Barnes, C., Mercer, G., & Shakespeare, T. (1999). *Exploring disability: A sociological introduction*. Cambridge, UK: Polity Press.

Carr, M. (2001). *Assessment in early childhood settings: Learning stories*. New York, NY. Sage.

Colvin, G., Dachyshyn, D., & Togiaso, J. (2012). Speaking from the margins to the centre in early childhood education initial teacher education. In D. Gordon-Burns, A. Gunn, K. Purdue, & N. Surtees (Eds.), *Te aotūroa tātaki: Perspectives on inclusion, social justice and equity from Aotearoa New Zealand* (pp. 95–113). Wellington: NZCER Press.

Connor, J., Gabel, S., Gallagher, D., & Morton, M. (2008). Disability Studies and inclusive education—implications for theory, research and practice. *International Journal of Inclusive Education, 12*(5), 441–457.

Dalli, C., White, J., Rockel, J., & Duhn, I. (2011). *Quality early childhood education for under-two-year-olds: What should it look like? A literature review*. Wellington: Ministry of Education.

Gabel, S. (2005). Introduction: Disability studies in education. In S. Gabel (Ed.), *Disability studies in education: Readings in theory and method* (pp. 1–20). New York, NY: Peter Lang.

Gordon-Burns, D., Gunn, A., Purdue, K., & Surtees, N. (Eds.). (2012). *Te aotūroa tātaki: Perspectives on inclusion, social justice and equity from Aotearoa New Zealand*. Wellington: NZCER Press.

IHC. (2008). *IHC complaint under Part 1A of the Human Rights Act, 1993*. Wellington: Author. Retrieved from: https://ihc.org.nz/ihcs-education-complaint

Independent Monitoring Mechanism on the Rights of Persons with Disabilities. (2016, June). *Article 24: The Right to an Inclusive Education E Koekoe Ana te Tūī implementation report*. Wellington: New Zealand Human Rights Commission, Ombudsman, and The New Zealand Convention Coalition.

Lyons, L. (2014). "We know what to say—do we know what to do?" Confronting the disconnection between legislation, policy, and practices for inclusion of young children with disabilities. *Early Childhood Folio, 18*(1), 3–8.

Macartney, B. (2011a). *Disabled by the discourse: Two families' narratives of inclusion, exclusion and resistance in education.* Doctorate of Philosophy in Education, University of Canterbury, Christchurch, New Zealand. Retrieved from: https://ir.canterbury.ac.nz/handle/10092/5307

Macartney, B. (2011b). Teaching through an ethics of belonging, care and obligation as a critical approach to transforming education. *International Journal of Inclusive Education.* First published 16 May 2011 (iFirst). Retrieved from: http://dx.doi.org/10.1080/13603111003686218

Macartney, B. (2016). *Early childhood education and barriers to inclusivity: Working toward a fairer system.* A background paper prepared for the Child Poverty Action Group. https://www.cpag.org.nz/resources-2/background-papers-1/2016-background-papers/

Macartney, B., & Morton, M. (2013). Kinds of participation: Teacher and special education perceptions and practices of 'inclusion' in early childhood and primary school settings. *International Journal of Inclusive Education, 17*(8), 776–792. doi:10.1080/13603116.2011.602529

McIlroy, A. (2017). *"The myth of inability": Exploring children's capability and belonging at primary school through narrative assessment.* Unpublished doctoral thesis, University of Canterbury, Christchurch, New Zealand. Retrieved from: https://ir.canterbury.ac.nz/handle/10092/14939

Ministry of Education. (1993). *Te whāriki: He whāriki mātauranga mō ngā mokopuna o Aotearoa: Draft guidelines for developmentally appropriate programmes in early childhood services.* Wellington: Learning Media.

Ministry of Education. (1996). *Te whāriki: He whāriki mātauranga mō ngā mokopuna o Aotearoa: Early childhood curriculum.* Wellington: Learning Media.

Ministry of Education. (2017). *Te whāriki: He whāriki mātauranga mō ngā mokopuna o Aotearoa: Early childhood curriculum.* Wellington: Author.

Mitchell, L. (2014). Alternatives to the market model: Reclaiming collective democracy in early childhood education and care. *Early Education, 55,* 5–8.

Murray, S. (2017). *Briefing for Hon Nikki Kaye Minister of Education on early childhood education.* Wellington: CCS Disability Action. Retrieved from: https://ccsdisabilityaction.softlinkhosting.co.nz/liberty/opac/search.do

Purdue, K. (2004). *Inclusion and exclusion in early childhood education.* Unpublished doctoral thesis, University of Otago, Dunedin, New Zealand.

Radford, S., & Shearsby, V. (2018). *Discussion paper: Early childhood wellbeing survey.* Unpublished. Greater Christchurch Early Childhood Education Community Futures Network.

Rinaldi, C. (2006). *In dialogue with Reggio Emilia: Listening, researching and responding.* London, UK: Routledge.

Ritchie, J. (2010). Being "sociocultural" in early childhood education practice in Aotearoa. *Early Childhood Folio, 14*(2), 2–7.

Rivalland, C., & Nuttall, J. (2010). Sameness-as-fairness: Early childhood professionals negotiating multiculturalism in childcare. *Early Childhood Folio, 14*(1), 28–32.

Shakespeare, T. (2006). The social model of disability. In L. Davis (Ed.), *The disability studies reader* (2nd ed., pp. 197–204). New York, NY: Routledge. Retrieved from: https://uniteyouthdublin.files.wordpress.com/2015/01/lennard_davis_the_disability_studies_reader_secbookzz-org.pdf

Union of the Physically Impaired Against Segregation (UPIAS). (1976). *UPIAS and the Disability Alliance discuss fundamental principles of disability.* Retrieved from: https://disability-studies.leeds.ac.uk/wp-content/uploads/sites/40/library/UPIAS-fundamental-principles.pdf

United Nations Committee on the Rights of Persons with Disabilities. (2016). *General comment No. 4. Article 24: Right to inclusive education.* Retrieved from: https://www.right-to-education.org/resource/general-comment-4-article-24-right-inclusive-education

United Nations General Assembly. (2006). *United Nations Convention on the Rights of Persons with Disabilities and Optional Protocol.* Geneva: United Nations

Veck, W. (2009). Listening to include. *International Journal of Inclusive Education, 13*(2), 141–155.

Wills, R., Morton, M., McLean, M., Stephenson, M., & Slee, R. (Eds.). (2014). *Tales from school: Learning disability and state education after administrative reform.* Rotterdam, The Netherlands: Sense Publishers.

CHAPTER 9

Te Whāriki, possibility thinking and Learning Stories: Tracking the progress

Margaret Carr, Wendy Lee, Karen Ramsey, Kim Parkinson, Nadine Priebs, and Vera Brown[1]

As global citizens in a rapidly changing and increasingly connected world, children need to be adaptive, creative and resilient. They need to 'learn how to learn' so that they can engage with new contexts, opportunities and challenges with optimism and resourcefulness. For these reasons, *Te Whāriki* emphasises the development of knowledge, skills, attitudes and dispositions that support lifelong learning. (*Te Whāriki*, English version, 2017, p. 7)

Introduction

The above quote frames some thoughts in this chapter about *progress* in early childhood. The learning described in *Te Whāriki* is multi-faceted and complex; knowledge, skills, attitudes, and dispositions are woven and tangled together. But how to address the notion of *progress* without being prescriptive in ways that atomise the knowledge or skills into disconnected small bits that damage and destroy the weavings and entanglements? This chapter contributes to the dialogues and debates that hover over this question. In Part One of this chapter we argue for a notion of progress that protects the entanglement of all the principles and strands in *Te Whāriki*,

---

[1] This chapter is co-authored by the kaiako (Karen, Kim, and Nadine) who did the teaching: noticed, recognised, responded and recorded the Learning Stories in 2013–14 that form the basis of the analysis in the third part of this chapter. The child who did the learning work, Vera, is also a co-author. We acknowledge Vera's family for their contributions to her portfolio, and the permission from Vera and her family, as well as from the kaiako, to publish from it.

using the quote at the beginning of this chapter as leverage for this. We suggest there that *problem-finding and problem-solving*, introduced by Anna Craft (2005, 2008, 2013) as *possibility thinking*, might provide a useful framing. We connect this to the strands of *Te Whāriki*. In Part Two we take up a suggestion from kaiako in the field to add a further dimension for the construction of a learner identity: engagement enthusiasm and élan,[2] described by Mihalyi Csikszentmihalyi (1997) as *flow*, the psychology of engagement with everyday life. Part Three includes examples from a portfolio of learning stories to illustrate progress in these ways. Each section is introduced, and inspired, by part of the quote from *Te Whāriki* that heads up the chapter.

PART ONE: Learning "how to learn": knowledge, skills, attitudes and dispositions that support lifelong learning

In the 1996 version of *Te Whāriki* (Ministry of Education, 1996), the emphasis on outcomes as learning "how to learn", and the weaving together of knowledge and skills with attitudes and dispositions, led to the development of an assessment method that could document this weaving complexity using *stories*. The statement at the beginning of this chapter, from the 2017 version of *Te Whāriki*, emphasises an ambition for the curriculum: the development of knowledge, skills, attitudes, and dispositions that *support lifelong learning*. On p. 63 (Ministry of Education, 2017), that curriculum states that "Narrative forms of assessment, such as learning stories, may make use of a formative assessment sequence: noticing, recognising, responding, recording and revisiting valued learning". These assessments are housed in portfolios. Jay Lemke (2001), in a paper entitled "The long and the short of it", noted the value of a material object as a "tracer" that "carries significant information over time and place and that serves, through local interpretation, to create coherence between distal events" (p. 21). A learner's portfolio does this carrying work; it houses learning stories to provide an ongoing record of the development of learning over time and place. The curriculum also notes that "Portfolios of children's learning are a useful way for kaiako to follow progress and interests" (Ministry of Education, 2017, p. 63). Portfolios enable a looking back in order to look forward; so do Learning Stories. In Aotearoa New Zealand, some primary schools have also introduced Learning Stories, using a 'split screen analysis' to document the learning in curriculum subjects *and* key competencies (see Davis, Wright, Carr, & Peters (2013) for examples and discussions).

---

2 élan is defined as "a combination of style and vigour" in the *Collins English Dictionary* (3rd ed.) (1991), p. 500.

Learning Stories and portfolios enable kaiako, children and whānau to follow progress and interests

> Sociocultural views of learning acknowledge the extent to which learning is entangled with, and made possible through, the material, social, cultural and historical features of the context for learning. (Cowie & Carr, 2016, p. 396)

As *Te Whāriki* (Ministry of Education, 2017, p. 63) points out, "older children will often take their own photographs and dictate the story of their work"; photographs and drawings assist younger learners to read, revisit, and review the latest Learning Story and the portfolio as a whole, especially when the images reflect a series of events that illustrates the sequence of the story.

Learning Stories have four sections:

1. a description of an event, including the context and supports
2. an analysis of the learning with the curriculum in mind (often including a link with a previous Learning Story or a previously observed, but not documented, event)
3. a "What next?" or the collaborative "How might we progress this learning?", and
4. an opportunity for revisiting and reviewing by children, kaiako, and whānau.

These four sections combine to create a *formative* narrative assessment that begins or continues to construct progress. Section 4 invites and enables a collaborative voice on progress. In particular, this last section assumes that portfolios can be taken home, also that they are readily accessible at the early childhood centre. If they are housed near a comfortable couch or armchair at the centre, then children, kaiako and whānau are encouraged to share and comment on the Learning Stories, turn the pages back and forward, and talk about the progress over time. This gives additional life to the learning journey—it gives it an audience. When all four sections work together, the opportunity for children to occasionally dictate the text and/or then share the stories with whānau strengthens their ability to have a say in, and to recognise, their learning journeys. This provides examples of the *Te Whāriki* empowerment principle in practice:

> Perspectives on empowerment are culturally located, hence kaiako need to seek the input of children and their parents and whānau when designing the local curriculum. (Ministry of Education, 2017, p. 18)

Roskill South Kindergarten's Final Report on their Centre of Innovation research (Ramsey, Breen, Sturm, Lee, & Carr, 2006) illustrates what we mean here. In a section entitled 'Revisiting, making sense of an experience', the authors comment on the value of ICT for enabling children to be part of the revisiting—a long tradition at

Roskill South. That Final Report includes comments about recording and revisiting portfolios with the 3- and 4-year-old children in the kindergarten:

> To be able to revisit and see documentation of their previous learning ... it sparks further learning. I think that's still from when we first started using Learning Stories and just listening to children. They know we will listen to what they have to say about what they've done and so they know that when we listen, we write it down, so they know that their stories can be recorded. (Ramsey et al., 2006b, p. 31)

Being adaptive, creative, and resilient: A continuum of strategies

This chapter argues that Anna Craft's construct, *possibility thinking* (Craft, 2005, 2008, 2013), might usefully contribute to a discussion about young children becoming increasingly *adaptive, creative, and resilient* over time. She explains:

> The thesis is that possibility thinking involves a continuum of strategies, with at one end the question "What does this do?" to "What can I do with this?", both of which have the potential to encompass problem finding and problem solving. (Craft, 2005, p. 36)

We suggest that *possibility thinking* and those two associated questions might be a useful way of summarising the complexity of weaving and entanglement that encompass (in the quote from *Te Whāriki* that begins this chapter) the "knowledge, skills, attitudes and dispositions that support life-long learning" with an emphasis on being "adaptive, creative and resilient" (Ministry of Education, 2017, p. 7). We look for the *problem finding* and *problem solving* and a *continuum of strategies* in possibility thinking as one way of theorising longer term processes that describe progression along the five strands of *Te Whāriki*.

Problem finding and problem solving as opportunities for possibility thinking

A review of the Learning Stories published in Carr and Lee (2012) reveals an abundance of opportunities within the *Te Whāriki* curriculum strands for highlighting problem finding and problem solving. They include (from the 2012 publication): being an artist (mosaic work, three-dimensional craftwork with a range of materials), writing, making books, investigating (e.g., fish), curiosity, collaborations, knowledge of Hindu temples, mara tāpu, tā moko, and koru patterning.[3] According to Anna Craft (2013), places that enable possibility thinking will:

> acknowledge the multiple ways in which young people are also expert and empowered, and the many ways in which exciting, meaningful and high quality learning may occur between peers, across ages, between experts and novices, harnessing curiosity and stimulating co-creativity. (p. 130)

---

3   A more recent publication, Carr & Lee (2019), includes Learning Stories from 39 countries that have different early childhood or early years curricula from Aotearoa New Zealand's *Te Whāriki*.

Possibility thinking demands a continuum of strategies and the development over time of learning dispositions, knowledges, and skills.

PART TWO: They need to learn "how to learn" so that they can engage with new contexts, opportunities and challenges with optimism and resourcefulness

In consultations and projects in preparation for the book *Learning Stories: Constructing Learner Identities in Early Education* (Carr & Lee, 2012) four *dimensions of strength* as an ABCD format (Agency, Breadth, Continuities, and Distribution) were proposed to parallel the four principles in *Te Whāriki*. Kaiako then commented to us on the importance of children's courage, determination, and perseverance and recommended that we add an E for engagement, enthusiasm, and élan (Carr & Lee, 2012, pp.137–138). The notion of children as global citizens who engage with challenges "with optimism" in the quote from *Te Whāriki* at the beginning of this chapter, also supports these E attributes, and an E was added to the original ABCD array of dimensions of strength. We will now add it here, too, as a dimension of progress.

Emotion—engagement, enthusiasm and élan: These strategies and qualities underpin children as adaptive, creative, resilient, and optimistic learners. This recognition is a valuable reminder for curriculum decisions—it is also relevant for the future. School-based, neuroscience research from Mary Helen Immordino-Yang has the following to say about meaningful learning in the long term:

> For learning to have a hope of motivating students, of producing deep understanding, or of transferring into real-world skills—all hallmarks of meaningful learning, and all essential to producing informed, skilled, ethical and reflective adults—we need to find ways to leverage the emotional aspects of learning in education. (Immordino-Yang, 2016, p. 18).

PART THREE: *Te Whāriki* emphasises the development of knowledge, skills, attitudes, and dispositions that support lifelong learning

We now analyse for progression a selection of Learning Stories with reference to: (1) the five *Te Whāriki* strands of learning outcome as dimensions of progress, defined for this purpose as *possibility thinking*, problem finding, and problem solving, and (2) the E for *engagement, enthusiasm and élan* as a further dimension of progress.

The Learning Stories are from one assessment portfolio at Roskill South Kindergarten over time. This kindergarten is sited in an ethnically diverse area of a large city, where for many families English is an additional language (for more details on their early research as a Centre of Innovation, see Ramsey, Breen, Sturm, Lee, & Carr, 2005, 2006, and 2007).

In a way, the children here were learning via an apprenticeship model. Anna Craft states that "key elements of apprenticeship models are expertise, guided participation, and authenticity of task for the artist and, therefore, for the pupil, a finding which has emerged from other studies also" (Craft, 2005, p. 142).

These elements were all in place for Vera at Roskill South Kindergarten, where the expertise and guided participation during work and play is shared between children, kaiako, and whānau. In this chapter we describe progress during three self-chosen learning tasks—chosen by Vera when she was a 4-year-old at kindergarten—and analysed in terms of her developing strategies for problem finding and problem solving, also adding the E dimension of engagement, enthusiasm, and élan. These tasks were:

1. Dictating Stories and Making Books
2. Mosaic Work
3. Lunch Preparation.

The problems found were different for each of the three learning tasks, and the strategies for solving them were unique to the tasks and their surrounding resources, environments and pedagogies as well.

Task 1: Dictating Stories and Making Books

Story 1: Adding languages: titles and pictures

Vera draws pictures of her family, and dictates titles for the kaiako to write. These drawings and titles form the first Learning Story for this task.
- This is my daddy. This is Mary.
- This is V.J.
- This is daddy.
- This is mummy.
- This is Mum.

Story 2: Adding technology resources to the storying

Two months later, fourth and fifth language resources are added: the camera and the computer. A Learning Story documents the occasion when one of the kindergarten families had some rabbits to give away, and Vera and her younger brother acquired one each. They were named Max and Ruby. Vera was taught how to use a kindergarten camera, and she enthusiastically approached this new problem to be solved; she had watched other children taking photographs at kindergarten. She took photos of the rabbits at home. These were then downloaded onto a laptop at the kindergarten and printed, with Vera carefully watching each stage of this problem-solving process. She

then glued each photograph onto a page and dictated what was going on in each photo for the teacher to transcribe:
- Daddy making a cage and making the food.
- The cage is finished for Max and Ruby. They have a water bottle. They drink it.
- Ruby eating grass.
- She like carrots and grass.
- Max and Ruby are eating. Eating the food. It's a big leaf.

She next assisted with the binding and then the story was read to the other children at mat time.

Story 3: Ideas in the stories become more complex

Six months later, a Learning Story comments on the growing complexity of Vera's dictated stories. Here is the text:

> It is a common sight to see Vera at the drawing table most mornings as she works on her latest ideas for her book. We have noticed Vera's ideas becoming more complex as she shares her work with us, and this morning when Vera came and asked me to write her story, I reflected on the language she is using and how this has developed over time. As I wrote the words for Vera, I could see connections between this book and previous books she has created. Most of Vera's stories have some drawings and writing around the movie Frozen, and also Rapunzel and sea creatures. What I loved and was astounded by were the use of words such as 'abominable' which was used in the right context, and then the knowledge she shared with me around an 'octopus squirting', a spring that is bouncing, eggs that are hatching chickens, and rocks that are shaking.
>
> **What learning do I think is happening for Vera?**
> … I know that Vera loves to listen to books being read, and through this she has developed a curiosity about the oral language. … through Vera's exploration she is learning that "both the text and the illustrations carry the story, that print can be useful, that books can provide information, and that stories can allow one to enter new worlds." [*Te Whāriki* (Ministry of Education, 1996, p. 79)]
>
> **Vera, as you continue to explore the world of literacy**
> You may be interested in incorporating the use of the iPad. We have an app on the iPad called Book Creator, where you can draw, write your story and even record your story, before printing it.

Vera does not take up the strategy of using the iPad, but as she continues to dictate stories, she is reminded again that the text and the illustrations carry the story. Her whānau write a number of contributions for the portfolio, noting how much they enjoy the stories that Vera brings home and shares with them.

An analysis of progress—Te Whāriki strands, possibility thinking strategies for problem-finding and problem solving, and E as a dimension of progress (Task 1: Dictating Stories and Making Books))

Progress: Belonging and wellbeing

Vera's portfolio of Learning Stories documents the growth in her learning at the kindergarten from age 3 years and 2 months until she begins school on her 5th birthday (a New Zealand tradition). It respects and builds the connection with her family and community from the beginning. The first Learning Story documents her drawing her family, and these drawings begin her portfolio. The family contributes their "aspirations and dreams for Vera's learning journey" to the portfolio, and Vera does too. These whānau contributions to the portfolio continue to strengthen a range of links to home over time—they add a new context for her problem-finding and solving (taking photos at home, for example).

Progress: Exploration, Contribution, Communication, and Possibility Thinking strategies for problem-finding and problem-solving

A comment in Vera's portfolio from home notes her growing disposition to ask questions: "She's asking more questions and not being afraid to even ask a question". Asking questions, being curious, was included as an indicator of possibility thinking in the quote from Craft (2013, p.130), in Part One of this chapter.

Progress: Communication

Problem finding and problem solving is shared between Vera and kaiako, but the problem is chosen by Vera. She dictates a storyline to accompany the drawings, and a kaiako prints her words on the pages, which will be turned into a book. The culture of family and community connection, together with the inclusion of text dictated for a literacy object (a book about the family), begins Vera's kindergarten experience and results in the first entry in her assessment portfolio. Vera is also acquiring skills with new languages/literacies as problem-solving resources. Both the Samoan language and English are spoken at home, and Vera's confidence in speaking mostly English in a new space (the kindergarten) is documented as she dictates her book texts. There are three languages/literacies here, with Vera closely engaged: drawings, spoken language, and the dictated text printed in handwriting on each page and read back to her by the teacher. Over time, further stories are illustrated, dictated, written down, and turned into books—the examples here illustrate the increasing complexity of the sentence structure.

Adding E as a dimension of progress: engagement, enthusiasm, and élan

Here we add a kaiako comment in one of the later Learning Stories that illustrates the affect dimension: *engagement, enthusiasm, and élan* that supported the problem finding and solving.

> Vera, I recently wrote a learning story for you, "An interest deepens", and in this story I made reference to you discovering that text and illustrations carry the story, and that stories can allow one to enter new worlds ... Vera, you often use characters from fairy tales and I can see that this is a passion of yours as you now *create your own fairy tales* using characters from your favourite stories. (Our emphasis)

Task 2: Mosaic Work

Story 1: Completing an abstract mosaic picture, fitting the broken pieces to fill a tile

Resources in this kindergarten include mosaic tile making materials. Learning Stories illustrate Vera's growing initiative as she becomes an expert with these resources—she adds imagination to curiosity in practical and creative ways. Vera completes an abstract mosaic tile, carefully selecting and fitting the broken pieces on offer to fill the square tile.

Story 2: A more complex task—Creating a picture using the mosaic technique

On a later occasion Vera chooses one of her drawings—a "flying dinosaur". With assistance, she traces the drawing onto the tile, then on her own she carefully positions cut black tile shapes for the dinosaur, and other irregularly shaped coloured pieces to fill the background, adding the adhesive and grouting. In a Learning Story for the family, as well as for Vera, one of the kaiako includes the following comment:

> Mosaic is a visual art, and is another language that supports children to communicate their ideas and thoughts.

An analysis of progress—Te Whāriki strands, possibility thinking strategies for problem-finding and problem solving, and E as a dimension of progress (Task 2: Mosaic Work)

Progress: Communication and exploration

The problems Vera finds and sets herself are becoming more complex. Popular resources at this kindergarten include mosaic tile making materials, and the problem-solving includes accessing these materials and managing a sequence of processes to complete this complex task. As the kaiako comments, languages and literacies provide multiple means of representing and expressing ideas, and Vera is exploring possibility thinking in this mode, adding a new problem-solving task—a mosaic tile—to her Making Books strategy work. Examples now include Vera exploring "What does this do?" and "What can I do with this?" when she meets mosaic tiling materials and watches other children using them.

Adding E as a dimension of progress: engagement, enthusiasm, and élan

Vera worked with enthusiasm over 3 days on this more complex self-chosen dinosaur mosaic task over 3 days. It is worthwhile noting that there is a generous physical space set aside at this early childhood centre for "work in progress". This reflects a policy that respects and encourages continuities—the problem-finding in long term self-initiated projects will often increase during the work, and the problem-solving may take some time.

Task 3: Lunch Preparation

Story 1: Lunch preparation—preparing a pizza, following several sequences

When a new routine is introduced to the kindergarten day—children staying for lunch—the children became engaged in, and in charge of, a number of lunch time routines. Vera's portfolio includes a lunch preparation Learning Story, in which she prepares a pizza with others. Each child has a pizza base, and a number of toppings are on offer. Vera chooses pizza sauce as her first topping, then added capsicum, pineapple, and, finally cheese. The Learning Story records that she followed the routine of putting her pizza on a piece of baking paper with her name on it. After cooking, "Then she eats it!"

Story 2: Lunch preparation—from garden to table; sequence includes a written recipe

A Learning Story that includes the collaboration of four children describes a regular event at the kindergarten: picking vegetables from the kindergarten garden. On this occasion it was the carrots and kale that were ready to harvest; the teacher tells them that she looked up some recipe ideas and decided that "carrot and kale muffins looked interesting". The sequence of events that included the four children working together to harvest the vegetables and make the muffin mixture with reference to a recipe (which is included in the Learning Story) is described and photographed. The children each did a taste test, then took turns filling the muffin tins. At lunch time everyone who stayed at the kindergarten for lunch ate a muffin.

Story 3: Lunch preparation—making a cheese sandwich (A group Learning Story was added to Vera's portfolio). Later, Vera makes cheese sandwiches at home for her parents

On a later occasion, cheese sandwiches were on the menu for lunch. Vera made herself a cheese sandwich.

9: *Te Whāriki*, possibility thinking and Learning Stories: Tracking the progress

An analysis of progress—Te Whāriki strands, possibility thinking strategies for problem-finding and problem solving, and E as a dimension of progress (Task 3: Lunch Preparation)

Progress: Wellbeing, belonging, and contribution

Collaborative food preparation is common at this kindergarten. Problem finding and solving as a routine with a sequence included harvesting the vegetables from the garden and following a recipe (assisted by the kaiako). *A Teacher Reflection* at the end of the Group Learning Story about making muffins noted:

> Our lunchtime routine has become a well-established part of our curriculum here at Roskill South Kindergarten. What I saw in the kitchen today was children learning how to grow, harvest, prepare, share and eat fresh and healthy food. Our lunchtime routine engages children's curiosity as well as their taste buds, and is providing positive and memorable food experiences that will form the basis of positive lifelong eating habits.

Communication

The kaiako tells the children that she looked up some recipe ideas [in a recipe book] and she enables the group to refer to the written recipe in order to follow the correct sequence for this problem solving task.

Adding E as a dimension of progress: engagement, enthusiasm, and élan

A whānau analysis and celebration of progress summarises well this dimension of progress. Vera's parents contributed the following comment to the portfolio.

> She told her brother about her lunch and how she made her cheese sandwich by herself and ate it all. She even went for seconds!! She's become a lot more confident and is able to make her parents a sandwich too. We are very pleased with this progress for Vera.

Tracking the learning progress: A conclusion

Vera's kindergarten provided her with many opportunities to complete tasks and projects, which included mastering a challenge and engaging her in possibility thinking. These included collaborative play in a range of contexts and tackling the challenge of coordinating mind and body to achieve the challenges of commando ropes and monkey bars. Early childhood centres provide environments that offer a wide range of curriculum spaces and places for children that include these strategies. These are of course not necessarily the spaces, places, and projects that will be on offer at school and/or later life. However, *Te Whāriki* learning dispositions, including being adaptive, creative and resilient, will be available for the children's learning in new environments, but *only if* the domains of affect that leverage the emotional aspects of learning are present. Vera's examples illustrate opportunities for her growing curiosity and confidence to explore new possibilities—an approach that asks, "What does this do?" and "What can I do with this?"; an inclination to devise and tackle a continuum of strategies for problem-finding and problem-solving. As this chapter illustrates, an apprenticeship with tools and resources and supportive others enabled her to progress the following: story making, art and spatial understandings with pens and mosaics; interest and competence with words and numbers for making books and sequencing the pages; technology skills with a camera; perception of the value of reading a recipe; and the enthusiasm and perseverance with coordinating mind and body as she approached and tackled physical cognitive and emotional challenges.

Portfolios of children's learning in early childhood over time can readily document the ways in which children, kaiako, and whānau co-construct, over time, unique pathways through learning environments as weavings and entanglements of skills, attitudes, and dispositions with domains of knowledge. A portfolio of Learning Stories enables kaiako, children, and whānau to revisit and review the learning over time, and to assist the learners to take this enthusiastic problem-finding and solving into new places. When kaiako "let the uniqueness of the child guide their work" (see the whakataukī in the 2017 *Te Whāriki*—Ministry of Education, 2017, p. 63) and the context is a place of wellbeing, and belonging that encourages an enacted curriculum of exploring, communicating, and contributing to problem finding and problem solving (possibility thinking), then an early childhood education site will be an environment in which children become life-long learners who will "engage with new contexts, opportunities, and challenges with optimism and resourcefulness" (Ministry of Education, 2017, p. 7).

References

Carr, M., & Lee, W. (2012). *Learning stories: Constructing learner identities in early education.* London, UK: Sage.

Carr, M., & Lee, W. (2019). *Learning stories in practice.* London, UK: Sage.

Cowie, B., & Carr, M. (2016). Narrative assessment: A sociocultural view. In M. A. Peters (Ed.), *Encyclopedia of educational philosophy and theory* (pp. 396–400). Singapore: Springer. doi:10.1007/978-981-287-532-7

Craft, A. (2005). *Creativity in schools: Tensions and dilemmas.* London, UK: Routledge.

Craft, A. (2008). Tensions in creativity and education: Enter wisdom and trusteeship? In A. Craft, H. Gardner, & G. Claxton (Eds.), *Creativity, wisdom and trusteeship: Exploring the role of education* (pp. 16–34). Thousand Oaks, CA: Corwin Press.

Craft, A. (2013). Childhood, possibility thinking and wise, humanising educational futures. *International Journal of Educational Research, 61,* 126–134.

Csikszentmihalyi, M. (1997). *Finding flow: The psychology of engagement with everyday life.* New York, NY: HarperCollins.

Davis, K., Wright, J., Carr, M., & Peters, S. (2013). *Key competencies, assessment and learning stories: Talking with teachers and students*. Wellington: NZCER Press.

Immordino-Yang, M. H. (2016). *Emotions, learning, and the brain: Exploring the educational implications of affective neuroscience*. New York, NY: Norton & Co.

Lemke, J. L. (2001). The long and the short of it: Comments on multiple timescale studies of human activity. *Journal of the Learning Sciences, 10*(1), 17–26.

Ministry of Education. (1996). *Te whāriki: He whāriki mātauranga mo ngā mokopuna o Aotearoa: Early childhod curriculum*. Wellington: Learning Media.

Ministry of Education. (2017). *Te whāriki: He whāriki mātauranga mo ngā mokopuna o Aotearoa: Early childhod curriculum*. Wellington: Author.

Ramsey, K., Breen, J., Sturm, J., Lee, W., & Carr, M. (2005). Roskill South Kindergarten: Centre of Innovation. In A. Meade (Ed.), *Catching the waves: Innovation in early childhood education* (pp. 25–30). Wellington: NZCER Press.

Ramsey, K., Breen, J., Sturm, J., Lee, W., & Carr, M. (2006a). Roskill South Kindergarten COI team reflections. In A. Meade (Ed.), *Riding the waves: Innovation in early childhood education* (pp. 38–44). Wellington: NZCER Press.

Ramsey, K., Breen, J., Sturm, J., Lee, W., & Carr, M. (2006b). *Roskill South Kindergarten Centre of Innovation 2003-2006. Final Research Report commissioned by NZ Ministry of Education*. University of Waikato Wilf Malcolm Institute of Educational Research

Ramsey, K., Breen, J., Sturm, J., Lee, W., & Carr, M. (2007). Weaving ICTs into *Te Whāriki* at Roskill South Kindergarten. In A. Meade (Ed.), *Cresting the waves: Innovation in early childhood education* (pp. 29–36). Wellington: NZCER Press.

CHAPTER 10

Click, drag, drop, resize, omit: An activity theory view of how technology is mediating the production of learning in early childhood education

Alexandra C. Gunn and Danneille Reeves

Early childhood assessment information speaks to multiple audiences and is produced for a range of purposes. Foremost, given the formative assessment principles underpinning desired professional practices (Ministry of Education, 2017a), high quality assessment documentation must address children, their whānau, and early childhood kaiako, providing them with insights into a learner's strengths, capabilities, learning dispositions, and learning strategies and trajectories over time. Given the sociocultural underpinnings of the early childhood curriculum *Te Whāriki* (Ministry of Education, 2017a), assessment information must also record the attendant context of learning success and challenge if it is to assist kaiako in their work planning for children's ongoing learning with them, their friends, and their whānau. This is because we understand from a sociocultural view, that learning and development both, are entwined, social, and situated (Rogoff, 2003; Smith, 2013; Vygotsky, 1978). As *Te Whāriki* puts it, learning is located in relationships between "people, places and things" (Ministry of Education, 2017a, p. 21). If we are to understand how these relationships are working in the interests of learning, we must pay attention to how we document them in assessment.

Typically, the context of valued learning is made visible in assessment documentation through photographs and written descriptions of events. In this chapter we pay attention to how learning—in its context—may become represented and by association understood as kaiako modify and arrange evidence gathered for assessment purposes with technological tools (computer hardware and software).

We focus on the *activity* of assessment as evidenced through the construction of narratives about learning while technological tools are mediating that activity. We are interested in how narratives are produced, who and what is in and out of the picture, and how meaning is made about learning along the way.

Viewing teachers' assessment work through activity theory

Within activity theory (AT) we understand that a characteristic feature of humans is that their actions and minds are mediated through tools which develop culturally over time (Engeström, 1999, 2001). Activity is understood as a form of doing directed to an object (Bakke, 2014). The doing is mediated by artefacts or tools, culturally situated and through/with which a person may pursue an object. Objects in this case represent the objective being pursued, as understood by the person or person's working on it (Foot, 2002; Gunn, Hill, Berg, & Haigh, 2016)—in this case, assessment, as coherent accounts of learning are produced as Learning Stories with computers, cameras, software, and the like. One aim of AT is to understand how human consciousness and activity are related (Nardi, 1996)—in this case, the production of assessment information with technological tools, and ultimately understandings of learning that are created. In embarking on this task, to understand how assessment, understandings of learning, and technological tools have become entwined within early childhood practice, we accept that teachers' work has become routinely mediated by technologies: cameras, video, computers, mobile devices, papers, notebooks, pens, and suchlike (Blackwell, Wartella, Lauricella, & Robb, 2015; Davis, Harris & Cunningham, 2019; Mertala, 2017) albeit with some lingering questions over effectiveness of use for teachers and children both (Blackwell, Lauricella, & Wartella, 2014; Dong & Newman, 2018; Edwards, 2016). Furthermore, we also note that over the past 15 years or so, a shift away from paper- and pencil-based methods towards computer-based production of assessment information has occurred (Bolstad, 2004; Wilson, 2011). In some cases this shift has resulted in the cessation of paper-based assessment documentation. This gives rise to problems of equity of access as a potential unintended negative consequence (Cowie & Mitchell, 2015; Kelly & Clarkin-Phillips, 2016).

It is with these concepts in mind and with Danneille's help, I (Alex) have been using an activity theory lens to explore how particular accounts of children's learning may come to be produced as Learning Stories as a teacher interacts with computer-based technologies during so-called non-contact time. Danneille is an experienced early childhood teacher, with dual qualifications for early childhood education and primary teaching, who works in a mixed-age early childhood setting of up to 28 children and six teachers. She has been observed at work and interviewed as part of a broader cross-country study of digital assessment and equity (Gunn, Nuttall, White,

& Wyatt-Smith, 2018). I am intrigued by what the computer and its software might be contributing to the task and am motivated by a longstanding interest in teachers' assessment work and in how principles of assessment—as articulated in *Te Whāriki*— may be actualised through the everyday.

The context of teachers' assessment work in Aotearoa New Zealand at this time

New Zealand has a highly devolved and diverse early childhood sector, but narrative forms of assessment—as Learning Stories—have emerged as a common form of assessment practice in the field (Carr & Lee, 2012; Gunn & de Vocht van Alphen, 2011; Education Review Office, 2007; Stuart, Aitken, Gould, & Meade, 2008). Despite the commonality of approach, evidence of a variable quality of assessment practice has been observed (Education Review Office, 2007, 2015, 2017) and Ministry of Education consultation data associated with the development and introduction of the revised curriculum indicates assessment to be a desired ongoing area of professional development and learning in the field (Ministry of Education, 2017b). These senses of variable practice and desired professional learning and development support are compounded by a growing wider concern over teacher literacy and graduate teachers' sense of preparedness to teach (Education Council, 2016, n.d.; Education Review Office, 2017), and an increased proportion of unqualified kaiako within the system (Ministry of Education, n.d-a.; Ministry of Education, n.d-b.). Furthermore, a sense that the accountability purpose of assessment has come to dominate over the teaching and learning purpose can sometimes prevail. To address such issues, many early childhood services have taken up software solutions to help systematise teachers' assessment efforts and standardise their work.

The software platforms provide a means for entering, organising, writing, and publishing assessment information. That information may then be articulated with learning goals and local/national curriculum priorities, communication with others over intended learning and planning for ongoing learning pathways. Users can employ in-built features such as pre-populated dropdown menus with links to *Te Whāriki* to associate narratives, interpretations of learning, and planning ideas with the national curriculum. Alternatively, users can develop their own dropdown menu links to reflect locally based curriculum priorities or they can ignore such features altogether. Draft versions of assessment documents produced by kaiako can be published to administrators or more senior teachers who can check the acceptability of the documentation and authorise its release or return it to authors for further refinement. Such steps in assessment processes represent a whole new set of labour practices in the field (White, Gunn, Rooney, & Nuttall, 2019). Web-based servers host assessment information that, with permissions granted, can be logged into by kaiako and children's immediate and wider family members using mobile app versions of the software. Asynchronous message board functions and email notifications cue parents and other family members into the fact that a new assessment may be available to read and, if desired, to comment on. Kaiako can respond in turn; such exchanges may come to serve as evidence of kaiako–whānau collaboration over learning priorities and agreed pathways for children's learning.

Beyond these initial uses the platforms are gradually being adapted to allow teachers to use assessment information for their own professional credentialing purposes (for example, professional e-portfolios for registration and certification). Information can be aggregated across individual teachers, particular groups of children, time periods, etc. to provide managers and external audit agencies with evidence of assessment, planning, and curriculum work (Education Review Office, n.d.). Clearly the reach of such platforms is enormous and having an increasing effect upon teachers' work. Bakke (2014) describes such platforms as transparent, arguing that people work through rather than on them, unconsciously. People don't see or aren't conscious of the mediating role of the tool. This position recognises the ubiquitous nature of human–computer interactions in daily life, including in early childhood education (Archard & Archard, 2016; Blackwell et al., 2015; Bolstad, 2004; Davis, Harris & Cunningham, 2019; Mertala, 2017). Thus, it is timely to take a closer look at teachers' meaning making about learning in the context of *Te Whāriki*, as they pursue the assessment activity with such platforms and technological tools. Next we turn to a case study of Danneille's work when using such a platform to produce assessment documentation about children's learning.

Inputting information and working with and through software to construct stories about learning

We are living in an increasingly visual culture and new questions are arising for early childhood practice as a consequence (White, 2016). Photograph and video making have become common practice, especially in support of early childhood assessment. This is not to say that the act of photograph taking or video making is non-problematic (Mitchell, 2011; Sturken & Cartwright, 2009) but the availability and range of digital tools in early childhood education is increasing, and unless a particular stance is taken by a service to the contrary, daily use seems largely inevitable (Archard & Archard; Blackwell et al, 2015; Bolstad, 2004). Key to the photograph's inclusion in assessment is the way it supports access to assessment information for parents, and family members who are not present (Cowie & Mitchell, 2015), including those who may need to rely more on pictures rather than words for meaning (Kelly & Clarkin-Phillips, 2016).

10: Click, drag, drop, resize, omit: An activity theory view of how technology is mediating the production of learning in early childhood education

Photos and videos are also lauded for their readability by children who may use these to recall events and discuss learning over, with teachers (Reese, Gunn, Bateman, & Carr, 2019). The photograph supports meaning making, playing a role in the formation and sustaining of a coherent narrative about learning. Representing more than an objective seeing or simply the photograph taker's perspective, photos aid meaning making by illustrating how important relationships, places, and things contribute to and sustain valued learning. In this way photographs are more than simply representation (Sturken & Cartwright, 2009) because they provide a means of understanding something about how an individual or group of individuals is experiencing the world (Pacini-Ketchabaw, Kind & Kocher, 2017).

In the broader study of the ways in which digital tools are informing and changing teachers' work in early childhood education, I (Alex) was observing Danneille's work in producing assessment documentation using computer software. Both paper and pen notes and video footage of Danneille's non-contact time were recorded during a workshadowing protocol. Later when discussing the video footage and recalling the work in a semi-structured research interview, Danneille and I noticed that the uploading, downloading, and management of photographs within this process took a very long time (about 20 minutes of the available hour allocated to producing the Learning Story she was working on that day). Furthermore, we observed that individual photos were being selected, unselected, omitted, and sequenced in a range of ways within the developing narrative as Danneille worked iteratively between photographs and written text to produce her account. This raised our awareness of the fact she might create any one of a number of possible different stories about children's learning using the evidence to hand. Our observations of the arranging and modification of images and text led us to recognise the key role the photos were having in helping to construct the story that would eventually be told. We began to wonder about how the inclusion, editing, omission, and sequencing of photos actually mattered to the assessment. In one instance, where photos were deleted, they removed people from the narrative altogether—what did this say about what would ultimately be understood about the conditions for valued learning? And how may this have altered our and others' potential understandings of what and who may have acted in support of the valued learning in the future?

Danneille was concerned to represent the learning as it actually occurred, including a recognition of *Te Whāriki*'s sense of learning as situated and contingent with the range of people and things involved, in place (Ministry of Education, 2017a, p. 21). We could see that, as she worked to produce a coherent account, her actions with the computer and software were revealing particular decisions about the evidence necessary for inclusion, the sequencing of content, word selection, etc. required to tell the story. Practices of clicking, dragging, resizing, deleting, and rotating images and text were abundant in the activity. Only by slowing down and analysing the process closely as the story was being made, could we perceive the effects of such practices on what would come to represent the valued learning—we had seen Bakke's (2014) transparency of the tools playing out and into the assessment activity.

Having had the chance to reflect on this more, we do not think the play of the tools within Danneille's meaning making is inconsequential. Furthermore, as Danneille's assessment work with technological tools is typical of many early childhood teachers everyday practices (Education Review Office, 2007), it raises questions for us all. Our data illustrate how the evidence of most documented assessment work in early childhood education, produced with Bakke's (2014) so-called transparent technological tools, can be turned very quickly in a myriad of ways in the process of human and tool use, to support the construction of potentially very differing stories about children's learning. Next, to explore this in more detail we examine two Learning Stories that Danneille produced through these processes. The first example is a Learning Story concerning Logan,[1] literacy practices (Logan's current learning focus[2]), and a particular mix of people and things. The second example is a group Learning Story about children at gym, focussing on an individual's changed capabilities in relation to gross motor challenges over time.

Making Name Tags is a group Learning Story featuring three children whose interests converged over the activity of making name tags to wear. I (Alex) had been work-shadowing Danneille and had observed and made notes of the activity as it occurred. Described by Danneille as being about Logan, the assessment involves Danneille, Logan, Mika, and Blair, in a particular place, using specific types of things. The Learning Story resulted in a plan by Danneille to shape the ongoing learning environment for them all in literacy-oriented ways.

The narrative records that Mika requested resources with which to make a name tag. Danneille writes that she suspects the interest to have been sparked by Mika's recent experience of student teachers at the centre—they routinely wore name tags for identification purposes. Felt tip pens, cardboard, tape for fixing the finished tags to Mika's shirt-top, and a basket containing children's actual name tags were retrieved from shelves nearby and brought to a table. Logan, who'd heard Mika make the request and observed the beginnings of the activity, quickly indicated a desire to join, and did so. Danneille assisted Logan and Mika with their task. After overhearing

---

1. As the chapter is principally concerned with Danneille's work practices and the way technologies are playing into assessment, we elected to use pseudonyms to refer to children throughout.
2. Danneille had explained during the work-shadowing protocol that, at regular intervals across the year, kaiako and parents decided together a learning focus for each child that kaiako could then plan for and document progress over time. The learning focus was noted in a clear file folder accessible to all kaiako in the centre.

Logan say their name in a discussion with Danneille about letters, a third child, Blair, joined the activity also.

Throughout the play the children worked alongside each other, sometimes with the direct support of Danneille, until each had a name tag to wear. Danneille took photos during the play for later use in the Learning Story she had in mind to create. Eventually 11 photographs were selected for inclusion in the documented assessment. Each child is shown working on their own label, Logan and Mika are pictured side-by-side twice—once writing and once wearing their name tags—and there are close up photos of Blair and Logan's completed name-tags/writing, and close ups of Logan and Blair each writing.

In the words of the Learning Story Danneille describes the care Logan took when forming letters. Also mentioned is the fact that Logan and Blair use a pincer grip when holding the pen; a skill noted for its future utility for writing development. Danneille sums up the Learning Story by recognising all three children's growing awareness of symbols and text, indicating that this will be supported on an ongoing way through planning. Danneille records an intention to provide a text-rich learning environment inclusive of media that will support the children to engage with text in ways that have meaning for them.

Once the story was published using the platform and available to view, Mika's parent had written a comment on the software's message board, saying how much Mika missed being at the centre (they were then on holiday). The parent recalled how Mika had wanted to wear a name tag on a recent family outing; Danneille's response recognises the family's absence and eagerness for their return.

Gym is a group Learning Story that foregrounds seven children's play with gross motor resources and equipment in a local gymnasium that they regularly visit. When printed out, the Learning Story comprises four pages of photographs (25 in total) and written text. The narrative spans two different visits to the gym, beginning with a comment by Danneille about her not having been at the gym for a while and being keen therefore to find out what the children have been up to while there. Having asked on the way to the gym what Lennie, Idra, and Han would like to do once they arrive and hearing an enthusiastic list of activities in response, the narrative describes how Danneille and the teachers set out equipment for the gym visit associated with the first of these (jumping and climbing).

The first sequences of photographs show various children standing atop a set of large foam stairs, jumping off these, and landing and on a large hexagonal foam shape (a 'crash pad'). Each of the Learning Story's seven focus children is represented in motion by the series of photographs. Descriptions of what the photographs are depicting include comments such as, "Han and Idra are dare-devils when jumping off the stairs onto the crash pad", "Lennie and Phoenix are gaining confidence jumping from the stairs", "Frankie and Aiden are experimenting with other ways to get from the stairs to the crash pad" (in this case climbing rather than jumping). West is at the gym for the first time. A photo shows West in mid-leap; an associated comment notes that West is "confident to jump to the crash pad".

Next the Learning Story includes documentation of the following week's visit to the gym, representing the 'pool noodles' play that Lennie, Idra, and Han had previously suggested. Children and teachers are pictured batting balls with pool noodles, striking, sword fighting, etc. After this section of the Learning Story a final comment about next week's forthcoming gym visit indicates likely activity choices—the last items on the list of things Lennie, Idra, and Han said they'd like to be doing at the gym: ropes and swings.

Constructing learning with images and text

When Danneille and I watched the video of her at work producing Learning Stories using photographs and text within a software platform, we noted the labour being invested in photograph management and manipulation, including how pictures were edited, sequenced, and omitted according to decisions Danneille was making about their usefulness to the assessment activity she was engaging in at the time. The stories Danneille worked on were not pre-determined beyond the broad-scale foci of, in these examples, literacy or gross motor play, before she sat to work on them with the computer, software, and other tools. They emerged in the interplay between the manipulation of photographs, typed words, cross-referencing of data sources, and the affordances of the software for manipulating these within a narrative sequence until Dannielle was satisfied with the account being produced. Close analysis of Dannielle's movements and actions (picking things up, downloading photos, clicking, dragging, resizing, reading, comparing, thinking, etc), what she wrote, and how she altered words and pictures on the computer screen, reveal how these actions together produced the text that became accepted as the documented account of valued learning from these events. Danneille was looking through the tools, and towards the finished assessment document, her gaze firmly on the production of a coherent narrative about valued learning (literacy or gross motor play related). The actions of clicking, resizing, sequencing, cross-referencing and so forth seemed to be playing recursively back into the sense making about learning that Danneille was doing at the time. Subsequently, the decisions made in those moments about what to include—or not—and how, were shaping what might be understood as and about valued learning then as well as in the future.

The Learning Story about Logan (and Blair and Mika—involving Danneille, in a place, with resources) was for Danneille, at the time she was producing the story, first and foremost about children's literacy learning. However, it also stands as a good example of how one's interpretive processes may draw from photographs (and other text) in a Learning Story to comprehend much more than what a writer may have intended. Danneille recognised the play initiated by Mika to be worthy of documenting because it came to involve Logan, and Danneille had remembered, she explained in interview, Logan's literacy related learning focus, part of which Danneille construed writing as being central to. The photographs privilege Logan's (and Blair's) writing ability but the value of literacy learning is extended to all three children via Danneille's documented planning intention of providing a text-rich literacy environment for all.

There are other valued Learning Stories, however, that can be told with the evidence at hand. We can see for instance that Logan and Blair's accomplishments were contingent with a particular mix of people and things. It was Mika recalling the experience of having student teachers in the centre that initiated the play; and it was Danneille's quick responses that supported the play to occur. Their shared historical experience (Danneille and Mika with the name-tag wearing student teachers) pre-empted the name tag making event. Furthermore, having a place to make the tags (a clear table to work on) and having the appropriate resources handy (card, pens, tape, actual name-tags to copy letters from) was critical to (Mika), Logan, and Blair's literacy accomplishments that day.

The co-location of the resources the children used with a space to work in is clearly visible in the photos. This mattered for what was able to occur. Despite Danneille being motivated by a chance to document evidence in support of Logan's literacy focus, the role Mika played in initiating this authentic literacy experience is also reflected in the assessment evidence. The fact that Blair's involvement was prompted by overhearing Logan and Dannielle's conversation is also visible (in the words Danneille wrote).

Reading both the pictures and words from multiple perspectives in this way, to take a wider account of the people, place, and things interacting here, makes other valued learning able to be perceived and recognised. So while in one sense a lead story about Logan helped drive Danneille's decisions about what to document and to include in the documented assessment, and the technological tools allowed this story to be told, an astute kaiako paying attention to the attendant context of valued learning as depicted in photographs has a wealth of additional information to use for planning and making sense of learning. Ongoing questions raised for us in the Logan, Blair, and Mika example include: What stories weren't told? What evidence was omitted and why? What does this Learning Story tell us about how Logan, Blair, and Mika are using other people's interests to scaffold their own? If it is true that Mika's interest was spurred on through previous observations of student teachers wearing name tags, as Danneille suspected, do we think differently of Mika as a learner, given this as an example of Mika drawing from past events to shape the present? What else do we know of Mika acting as a resource for others' play? How far does Blair and Logan's involvement in play as a result of observation of their peers extend and who does it extend to?

The gym story provides quite a different narrative account involving a lead-story about a group's visits to the gym over several weeks and mini-stories about individuals' gross motor play as well. For Danneille the Learning Story served a purpose in catching her up with what had changed at gym since the last time she'd been there with children. It also provided a chance to document change in relation to each child's unique capabilities with the large motor play (jumping, leaping, climbing, etc.) and their participation in group activity with the large foam noodles. The single assessment functioned for the group and Danneille in multiple ways. Subsequently it was included in each featured child's learning portfolio as well as a record of whole group curriculum.

Many tens of photos were taken by Danneille at the gym visits. From these she collated and created sequences of photos about individual children. The pictures themselves were not necessarily taken sequentially, although some were (and others are) presented as if they were. For example, the images show various children in the background of a sequence of three pictures that depict a person standing atop a set of foam stairs, jumping from them, and landing. That these pictures were selected and others omitted in this instance is fairly inconsequential to accomplishment of the lead-story, but the bringing together of pictures and words in this way reflects Danneille's production of the story as she manipulated and sequenced words and photos with technological tools. The words accompanying the photographs foreground a preferred interpretation of what's being depicted, suggesting that a close examination of the photos is unwarranted. It is the accomplishment of each child as leaper and jumper that's showcased in the play between text and photo, in order that these might be distinguished amongst the hurly burly of an excited, frenzied, busy morning of a jumping, running, sliding, shouting, rambunctious visit to the gym. In this gym Learning Story the effect is to accomplish, on a static two-dimensional page, the equivalent of a film-maker's edited wide-lens landscape view of events, punctuated by several instances of close-up zoomed-in action, followed by another wide-angled view and an imagining of gym events likely to eventuate in the week to come. In this example the technological tools seem most definitely looked *through*—assisting Danneille's work towards the assessment object and, in this process, production of a coherent narrative account of valued learning collectively (changed capacity with gross motor play) that showcased individual's achievements along the way.

Together these two examples of a teacher's assessment work show how, with the use of technological tools, the interplay of photos and texts works in multiple ways to shape the stories of learning that may be told and interpreted with early childhood assessment evidence. Photographs can lead the narrative as well as represent it; they can also make evidence available to expand the interpretations of valued learning that are possible. Thus, extended analyses of evidence that has already been gathered may be made more of, and, for a wider range of children, used to improve the manageability of assessment work in early childhood education. This close look at evidence can lead to more thorough and complex meaning making about learning as it relates with many people, places, and things in the early childhood environment.

Through this project we have come to appreciate how technological tools may be mediating kaiako sense-making even more than we have recognised already. The fact that the technological tools make pictures and words so mobile, editable, and omissible within a narrative, coupled with the ubiquitous nature of technologies in everyday life, underscores the transparency of the tools in our assessment work. We argue for kaiako to be much more aware of the possible and different stories that may be told through their arrangement, inclusion, omission, and manipulation of photos and words in children's documented assessments. Finally, we urge kaiako to remain clear about the fact that the stories they end up telling through documented assessments are simply a snapshot of the much more dynamic and situated formative assessment practice that they engage in with children every day. However, paying close attention to the arrangement of evidence in a documented assessment, and re-reading that assessment evidence for a fuller appreciation of how the people and things in place contribute to what's been made possible, may provide many more fruitful opportunities for planning and teaching from assessment than previously recognised. We encourage others to look more closely, as we have done, at how pursuit of the assessment object is mediated in human-tool interaction along the way.

References

Archard S. & Archard S. (2016). Jessica connects: A case study focussing on one child's use of information and communication technology (ICT) in an early childhood education setting. In V. Sharma & A. Brink (eds.), *Childhood through the looking glass* (pp.129–139). Oxford, UK: Inter-Disciplinary Press.

Bakke, S. (2014). Immediacy in user interfaces: An activity theoretical approach. In M. Kurosu (ed.), *Human-computer interaction, Part 1* (pp.14–22). Cham, Switzerland: Springer International Publishing.

Blackwell, C. K., Wartella, E., Lauricella, A. R. & Robb, M. B. (2015). *Technology in the lives of educators and early childhood programs: Trends in access, use, and professional development from 2012–2014.* Washington, DC: NAEYC, Fred Rogers Centre and CMHD.

Blackwell, C. K., Lauricella, A. R. & Wartella, E. (2014). Factors influencing digital technology use in early childhood education. *Computers and Education, 77,* 82–90.

Bolstad, R. (2004). *The role and potential of ICT in early childhood education. A review of New Zealand and international literature*. Wellington: New Zealand Council for Educational Research.

Carr, M. & Lee, W. (2012). *Learning Stories: Constructing learner identities in early education*. London, UK: Sage.

Cowie, B. & Mitchell, L. (2015). Equity as family/whānau opportunities for participation in formative assessment. *Assessment Matters, 8*, 119–141.

Davis, N., Harris, L., & Cunningham, U. (2019). Professional ecologies shaping technology adoption in early childhood education with multilingual children. *British Journal of Educational Technology, 50*(3), 1320–1339.

Dong, C. M. & Newman, L. (2018). Enacting pedagogy in ICT-enabled classrooms: Conversations with teachers in Shanghai. *Technology, Pedagogy and Education, 27*(4), 499–511.

Education Council. (n.d.). *Our Vision: Initial Teacher Education 2021*. Retrieved from https://teachingcouncil.nz/content/future-focused-initial-teacher-education

Education Council. (2016). *Strategic options for developing future oriented initial teacher education*. Retrieved from https://teachingcouncil.nz/content/future-focused-initial-teacher-education

Education Review Office. (n.d.). *Designing, implementing and evaluating curriculum in early learning services: What is important and what works?* Retrieved from https://www.ero.govt.nz/publications/early-learning-curriculum/designing-implementing-and-evaluating-curriculum-in-early-learning-services-what-is-important-and-what-works/

Education Review Office. (2007). *The quality of assessment in early childhood education. National Report*. Wellington: Author.

Education Review Office. (2015). *Continuity of learning: transitions from early childhood services to schools. National Report*. Wellington: Author.

Education Review Office. (2017). *Newly graduated teachers: Preparation and confidence to teach. National Report*. Wellington: Author.

Edwards, S. (2016). New concepts of play and the problem of technology, digital media and popular-culture integration with play-based learning in early childhood education. *Technology, Pedagogy and Education, 25*(4), 513–532.

Engeström, Y. (1999). Activity theory and individual and social transformation. In Y. Engeström, R. Miettinen & R. Punamäki (Eds.), *Perspectives on activity theory* (pp. 19–38). Cambridge, UK: Cambridge University Press.

Engeström, Y. (2001). Expansive learning at work: Toward an activity theoretical reconceptualization. *Journal of Education and Work, 14*(1), 133–156.

Foot, K. A. (2002). Pursuing an evolving object: A case study in object formation and identification. *Mind, Culture, and Activity, 9*(2), 132–149.

Gunn, A. C. & de Vocht, L. (2011). Seeking social justice and equity through narrative assessment in early childhood education. *International Journal of Equity and Innovation in Early Childhood, 9*(1), 31–43.

Gunn, A. C., Hill, M. F., Berg, D. & Haigh, M. (2016). The changing work of teacher educators in Aotearoa New Zealand: A view through activity theory. *Asia–Pacific Journal of Teacher Education, 44*(4), 306–319.

Gunn, A. C., Nuttall, J., White, E. J., & Wyatt-Smith, C. (2018). *Early childhood teachers' use of digital assessment tools to plan opportunities for counter-oppressive learning: Research proposal*. Dunedin:

University of Otago.

Kelly, J. & Clarkin-Phillips, J. (2016). Letter from the Waikato, *Early Education, 59,* 4–5.

Mertala, P. (2017). Wag the dog–The nature and foundations of preschool educators' positive ICT pedagogical beliefs. *Computers in Human Behaviour, 69,* 197–206.

Ministry of Education (n.d.-a). *Time series data: Number of teaching staff by qualification status (2011-2017).* Retrieved from https://www.educationcounts.govt.nz/statistics/early-childhood-education/staffing

Ministry of Education. (n.d.-b). *The national picture: What does the ECE census 2017 tell us about ECE teaching staff?* Available from https://www.educationcounts.govt.nz/__data/assets/pdf_file/0003/184557/ECE-Summary-page-Teaching-staff.pdf

Ministry of Education. (2017a). *Te whāriki: He whāriki mātauranga mō ngā mokopuna o Aotearoa: early childhood curriculum.* Wellington: Author.

Ministry of Education, (2017b). *Update of Te Whāriki: Report on the engagement process.* Wellington: Author. Retrieved from https://www.education.govt.nz/assets/Documents/Early-Childhood/ONLINE-Te-Whariki-Update-Long-v21A.PDF

Mitchell, C. (2011). *Doing visual research.* London, UK: Sage.

Nardi, B. (1996). Studying context: A comparison of activity theory, situated action models and distributed cognition. In B. Nardi (Ed.), *Context and consciousness: Activity theory and human-computer interaction.* (pp. 69–102). Cambridge, MA: The MIT Press.

Pacini-Ketchabaw, V., Kind, S. & Kocher, L. M. (2017). *Encounters with materials in early childhood education.* New York and London: Routledge

Reese, E., Gunn, A. C., Bateman, A. & Carr, M. (2019). Teacher-child talk about learning stories in New Zealand: A strategy for eliciting children's complex language. *Early Years Journal.* doi:10.1080/09575146.2019.1621804

Rogoff, B. (2003) *The cultural nature of human development.* Oxford & New York: Oxford University Press.

Smith, A. B. (2013). *Understanding children and childhood: A New Zealand perspective* (5th ed.). Wellington: Bridget Williams Books.

Stuart, D. Aitken, H., Gould, K. & Meade, A. (2008). *Evaluation of the implementation of 'Kei Tua o te Pae Assessment for Learning: Early Childhood Exemplars': Impact evaluation of the Kei Tua o te Pae 2006 professional development.* Wellington: Ministry of Education.

Sturken, M. & Cartwright, L. (2009). *Practices of looking.* New York, NY: Oxford University Press.

Vygotsky, L. S. (1978). *Mind in society. The development of higher psychological processes.* Cambridge, MA & London, UK: Harvard University Press.

White, E. J. (2016). A philosophy of seeing: The work of the eye/'I' in early years educational practice. *Journal of Philosophy of Education, 50*(3), 474–489.

White, J., Gunn, A. Rooney, T. & Nuttall, J. (2019, June). *Digitally cast eyes: Assessing young learners through digital assessment technologies.* Association for Visual Pedagogies International Conference, Ocular becomings in dangerous times: The politics of 'seeing'. RMIT University, Melbourne.

Wilson, V. (2011). *Web bound: How does the use of ICT support the involvement of children, their families/whānau and their teachers in assessment for learning?* Unpublished master's thesis, University of Canterbury, Christchurch. Retrieved from https://ir.canterbury.ac.nz/handle/10092/5567

CHAPTER 11

Back to the future: Curriculum and the pedagogue in the age of Communities of Learning | Kāhui Ako

Andrew Gibbons and Sandy Farquhar

Introduction

Analysis of the relationship between the early childhood and the school curriculum featured in the first two editions of *Weaving Te Whāriki* (Nuttall, 2003: Nuttall, 2013). This chapter extends the analysis further, following the update of the early childhood curriculum, *Te Whāriki*, in 2017 (Ministry of Education, 2017). The aim of the chapter is to promote critical dialogue regarding the nature of curriculum for early childhood centre communities. The chapter begins with a theorisation of curriculum and the role of the pedagogue. It then addresses selected continuities and differences between the 2017 update to *Te Whāriki* and the school curriculum. Applying contemporary research about children's experiences of centre-to-school transitions, the chapter explores cross-sector conceptualisations of the curriculum as a continuous and linear pathway. The final section evaluates the impact of government policy initiatives that promote greater continuity in pathways from early childhood through to primary and secondary school. Taking Communities of Learning | Kāhui Ako as a specific case, the chapter explores some tensions and challenges in conceptualising the curriculum as a continuous pathway.

The purpose of this book is to support productive and engaging dialogue about curriculum. The focus in this chapter is to explore the ways in which curriculum dialogue weaves together *Te Whāriki* and *The New Zealand Curriculum* (NZC) (Ministry of Education, 2017; 2007). The two documents are explicitly designed to work together, so it is helpful to have an understanding of their deeper conceptual design. Although intended to work together, they are not designed with the same concept and purpose of curriculum in mind. This chapter engages critically with the ways in which the documents work together, a critique grounded in the notion of dialogue and in the question from the Ministry of Education (2017a): "What do you know about the connections between early childhood and school curriculum documents as a platform for professional conversations and curriculum continuity for children?"

This question highlights the importance of deep engagement in the curriculum through a focus on professional conversations. In their centre and school communities, teachers are expected to be active professionals who engage in dialogue about the curriculum, including the two documents form the basis of that ongoing dialogue. In this chapter we provide just a few of the many possible professional conversations to engage in with colleagues across education sectors and through which we can question the meaning, nature, and purpose of curriculum. In particular, we explore the idea of continuity as an important provocation. It demands that we consider the nature and purpose of the two curriculum documents in terms of how they work, both separately and together, to inform teachers. The point here is not to suggest that continuity is either good or bad, but that it is a curriculum concept that we need to make sense of in relation to daily practices and experiences in early childhood centre communities.

The chapter examines some possibilities and challenges for dialogue through the concept of curriculum. When we talk about curriculum, what do we mean? The concept of transition is critiqued as the central challenge to the idea of curriculum continuity. Transition is a key area of tension because how we conceive of it and how it is experienced have implications for professional conversations about curriculum. To complete the chapter, we explore one example of the ways in which curriculum dialogue is challenged by contrasting perspectives of curriculum, through analysis of the Communities of Learning | Kāhui Ako. We examine the phenomenon of Communities of Learning for early childhood education curriculum and for the transition from early childhood education to primary schooling, with a particular focus on the measurement of achievement and curriculum continuity.

Communities of Learning were introduced in 2014 as part of the New Zealand Government's *Investing in Educational Success* initiative, aimed at raising teaching quality and enabling education providers to work together to share teaching and leadership resources (Ministry of Education, 2016). The Communities of Learning were initially called Communities of Schools. They were later renamed as Communities of *Learning* to connect the pathway between early learning and school, promoting "the potential for a seamless transition from one part of the education sector to the next" (Ministry of Education, 2017c, p. 21). Communities of Learning have formed around school communities. A 2017 Ministry (2017c) report indicates that only 2% of the nation's early childhood centres belong to a Community of Learning, although the report also notes more recent growth in terms of early childhood education community involvement.

Communities of Learning exemplify many conceptual challenges for sustained curriculum dialogue and contribute to the ongoing discussion of the relationship between *Te Whāriki* (Ministry of Education, 2017b) and the wider education sector. In particular, the focus on Communities of Learning reveals deep and enduring beliefs around transition, achievement, measurement, and more. These beliefs broadly inform many curriculum debates. For instance, beliefs about transition, achievement and measurement have informed debates on the use of international tools for the measurement of a child's early childhood learning (see Moss & Urban, 2019). Exploring these beliefs, we argue, is an important dimension of a 'ground-up' and collective professional practice (see, for instance, Dalli, 2008; Dalli, 2010; Dalli, Miller, & Urban, 2012).

This chapter draws on a critical reading of policy texts and the social and political contexts in which these texts emerge and influence individuals and communities. We advocate for an approach that encourages careful and critical reflection on the discourses that inform curriculum, guided in particular by Mac Naughton's views on critical reflection:

> that there are always far more questions than there are answers, that I cannot pretend that there are no power effects related to my actions as a teacher and that there are rarely, if ever, simple solutions to the incredibly complex task of teaching. (Mac Naughton, 2005, p. 15).

Discourse, according to Foucault (1981), occurs at the nexus of power/knowledge—where texts and narratives embody meaning from institutional practices and power through social relations. The idea of discourse is drawn on here to explore the language that inscribes our understanding of curriculum, with particular focus on the language of transitions and the Communities of Learning. A Foucauldian approach enables engagement with policy texts, unavoidably grounded in narrative and metaphor, to reveal some of the ways subjects (children, teachers, parents, and so on) are acting/being acted upon. Discourse implies the presence of a subject.

For Ricoeur (1976), it is through discourse that we understand our world and our selves in the world. Discourse informs what can be said, when it can be said, who can say it, and with what authority it may be said. Discourse is ever evolving, shaping knowledge and social practices by which societies maintain structure, coherence, and relationships. Ricoeur's philosophy forms part of a hermeneutic tradition that looks at the way we think, understand, and interpret ourselves through texts. For Ricoeur, the task of hermeneutics is not to discover an unmediated and essential reality, but to continue to mediate reality through new, creative interpretations, and to recognise a world of many meanings. With this spirit of complexity, there is no clear definition of curriculum; our enactment of curriculum is always political and always subjective. The purpose of this chapter is therefore to provide a platform for ongoing critical dialogues to inform early childhood curriculum. We touch on just some possible curriculum conversations, keeping in mind that these conversations will vary from community to community, and will tend to be ongoing and complex with many possible foci and directions.

Theorising curriculum

The different ways we understand and theorise curriculum have significant implications for centre and school communities in terms of expertise in teaching and learning. There are also implications in terms of dialogue between centre communities and primary schools regarding, for instance, each child's transition from one setting to another. Theorising the relationship between early childhood and school curricula involves ongoing questioning of, making sense of, and engaging reflectively with, the curriculum in various communities. Curriculum involves more than just formulating plans and designing practices to implement given policy-driven strategies like achievement challenges. Curriculum theory can invite and support a depth of discussion into the meaning, purpose, and experience of curriculum.

A good place to start with a general theorising of curriculum is with the question "What is curriculum?". Egan (2003) poses this question to show why curriculum conversations are challenged by the very definition of the word "curriculum". For instance, people who regard a curriculum as a specific list of things to learn—a subject or specified content knowledge— would probably find it challenging to regard *Te Whāriki* (Ministry of Education, 2017b) as a curriculum since it lacks such specificities. Rather, it invites significant interpretation and adaptation to local contexts. In other words, *Te Whāriki* may not look like a curriculum at all to some interpreters since it does not specify in detail which knowledge or learning outcomes to teach children. On the other hand, while widely considered to be an open and broad document (see Mutch, 2013), we consider the curriculum for schools, *The New Zealand Curriculum* (NZC) (Ministry of Education, 2007), more clearly and specifically predetermines learning through the articulation of achievement objectives and progress indicators. In other words, the two curriculum documents employ and guide different discourses of what constitutes 'the curriculum' and, for instance, what counts as 'progress' and 'achievement'.

In his work on the nature of curriculum, Egan (2003) traces the historical development of ideas about curriculum from their Latin origins as a course to be run, through a later focus on things to be studied (i.e., content), and a subsequent recognition of the individual learner as an important variable in the co-construction of knowledge. Egan's conclusion is that the curriculum for early childhood education necessarily addresses the *how* as well as the *what* of teaching and learning. This approach is most evident in the development of ideas like pedagogical content knowledge, which go beyond knowledge of subject matter per se to the dimension of subject knowledge *for teaching*, embodying "the most powerful ways of representing and formulating the subject [content] that makes it comprehensible for others" (Shulman, 1986, p. 9).

Including the *how* of teaching means teaching is not separate from the curriculum or simply a delivery mechanism for a pre-existing curriculum; it is integral to the curriculum. This distinction has been a key driver in the development of *Te Whāriki*; importantly, this perspective characterises the difference between teacher-as-technician and teacher-as-pedagogue (Moss, 2006). Curriculum for the teacher-as-technician focuses on achievement of prescribed learning outcomes, relying on the language of evidence and measurement. It valorises standardised knowledge, specified outcomes, and measurement data to determine learning within limited school-subject areas. Biesta's (2007) critique of this technical evidence-based model of teaching and learning is based on its distance from professional considerations and its effective removal of the teacher from teaching. His concern is that education requires more than just technical solutions; it requires sensitivity to difference, to context, and to values and beliefs. It is not just about *what* to teach or *how* to teach—but rather *what*, *how*, and *why*. The *why* of teaching gets lost for the technician, whereas it is central for the pedagogue.

Te Whāriki (Ministry of Education, 2017b) requires an understanding of curriculum as being more than measurable subject knowledge, and of the role of the teacher as more than a transmitter of measurable subject knowledge. This position does not reject the idea that curriculum involves knowledge in particular subjects (e.g., reading, writing, mathematics), but asserts that there is much more to explore and reflect on when it comes to dialogue about curriculum. This is particularly the case when curriculum is defined as a totality of experiences, as it is in *Te Whāriki*. For the teacher-as-pedagogue, that extension of the notion of curriculum involves exploration of content, pedagogy, care, and relationships as "interconnected facets of life that cannot be envisaged separately" (Moss, 2006, p. 32).

Te Whāriki and *The New Zealand Curriculum*

On the topic of the relationship between early childhood education and school, the Ministry of Education (2017a) expects that schools and centres have a knowledge of all relevant curriculum documents and practices, and engage in constant communication about curriculum. The Ministry (2017c) emphasises that curriculum documents provide guidance for ongoing curriculum dialogue. This focus resonates with the idea of the teacher engaged in theorising curriculum in depth and understanding dialogue as being central to the *how* and *why* of curriculum. In this section, we look at some of the elements of each document that form the basis for professional curriculum conversations.

The first element is the use of visual metaphor, keeping in mind that visual metaphors are powerful elements of each curriculum discourse. Both curricula draw on visual metaphors: the nautilus in *NZC* and the whāriki (or woven mat) in *Te Whāriki*. Nature metaphors are common in education. Botanical metaphors are used to signify unfolding growth; natality metaphors signify giving birth to ideas and nurturing talent; and elements of nature (earth, wind, and fire) are used to describe education in terms of a foundation or grounding in something, "lighting a fire" or "fanning the flames". These metaphors influence how we think and feel about the world (Lakoff & Johnson, 2003) and, in particular, the place of early childhood and school curricula in the world. The nautilus in *NZC* is associated with the physical sciences, implying growth and developmental progression. This metaphor is instructive when considering the curriculum in terms of stages of achievement across the traditional learning areas. In outlining the purpose and scope of the curriculum, *NZC* (Ministry of Education, 2007, p. 6) states that it sets "the direction" for learning.

Te Whāriki's woven mat metaphor, in contrast, invites thinking about the holistic and complex weave of curriculum, where the curriculum "provides a basis for each setting to weave a local curriculum that reflects its own distinctive character and values" (Ministry of Education, 2017b, p. 7). The woven mat (whāriki) symbolises the processes of weaving different strands into a whole through understanding the ways in which threads come together in particular ways. The whāriki also invites an awareness of the curriculum as always socially and culturally mediated. The metaphors of *NZC* and *Te Whāriki* symbolise different discourses regarding the nature and purpose of not just curriculum but also learning, teaching, schooling, and education (one symbolising a learner's developmental journey, the other an interaction between different dimensions of a community of learners). However, the metaphors that both *NZC* and *Te Whāriki* use are at the same time both expressive of nature so, in this sense, suggestive of some deeper commonalities to explore critically. Indeed, *Te Whāriki* suggests that the two curricula are based on similar principles, with similar approaches to valued learning:

> In *Te Whāriki*, learning dispositions and working theories are seen to be closely interrelated. The same is true of the key competencies and learning areas in *The New Zealand Curriculum*. In both cases the approach to learning recognises the need for a 'split screen' pedagogy that maintains a dual focus on the 'how' and the 'what' of learning (Ministry of Education, 2017b, p. 52).

11: Back to the future: Curriculum and the pedagogue in the age of Communities of Learning | Kāhui Ako

Similarities are emphasised in an extended matrix, spanning five pages of *Te Whāriki* (pp. 53–77), which maps its strands and learning outcomes with key competencies, learning areas, and values in *NZC*. The matrix includes a column headed "the weaving" that attempts to draw together the threads from the two curricula to show the degree of alignment (see also Peters & Paki, 2013).

The New Zealand Curriculum addresses the connection with *Te Whāriki* in principle by recognising the aim of offering all students a broad education that "makes links within and across learning areas, provides for coherent transitions, and opens up pathways to further learning" (Ministry of Education, 2007, p. 9). *NZC* outlines the respective tasks of early childhood, secondary, and tertiary education in providing students with positive transition experiences and a clear sense of continuity and direction (p. 41). It draws on *Te Whāriki*'s five curriculum strands, aligning them with the key competencies of *NZC*. These competencies were developed out of OECD research into the essential life and work skills that students need to acquire in their schooling (Hipkins, 2018). Hipkins notes that initial work on the key competencies drew on the metaphor and symbol of the mat and weaving, consistent with *Te Whāriki*. In the published version of *NZC* this symbol was replaced by a set of nested arrows that appear more consistent with the idea of a set direction or pathway. However, McDowell and Hipkins (2017, 2018) re-employ the weaving metaphor to guide the integration of key competencies into curriculum dialogue and practice.

Rather than mapping directly onto the learning areas and key competencies of *NZC*, the strands and principles of *Te Whāriki* invite open-ended questions about learning. *Te Whāriki* invites the teacher-as-pedagogue to engage in dialogue about what it means, for instance, to learn a language and to explore what language is and how it is used—a more complex experience than what could be captured by pre-defined learning outcomes. *Te Whāriki* highlights the centrality of shared expertise in curriculum, with the child, the family and whānau, and the community each having an essential contribution to dialogue about curriculum. This is reflected in the curriculum through a commitment to realising social justice, equity, rights, and participation. *Te Whāriki* has a strong legacy in this area. Curriculum is considered as a totality within a framework of inclusion, diversity, and rights, involving the critical responsibility of removing barriers to participation that lead to exclusion or marginalisation of individuals and groups. Curriculum, for instance, requires that teachers understand the entirety of their planned and unplanned engagement within the centre community as contributing to the rights of the child (Taylor & Te One, 2016). So how does this approach to curriculum guide an understanding of transition from early childhood education to primary school?

Curriculum coherence and transitions

Te Whāriki acknowledges the many transitions children make in their lives and, consistent with the strands and principles, recognises transitions as complex, interconnected, and occurring in many dimensions of the lives of infants, toddlers, and young children. As such, curriculum always has a relationship with transitions. Transition is facilitated by settings that are "thoughtfully planned", that "recognise what children bring with them", and that acknowledge the early childhood education setting as "part of their wider world and inclusive of their parents and whanau" (Ministry of Education, 2017b, p. 31). In addition, *Te Whāriki* explains that transition from early childhood education to school is supported when the school "fosters a child's relationships with teachers and other children and affirms their identity", when it "builds on the learning experiences that the child brings with them", when it "considers the child's whole experience of school", and when it is "welcoming of family and whānau" (p. 41). These emphases resonate with the *how* and *why* of the curriculum. Transition is therefore much more than simply getting "ready" for school, and requires professional conversations within and between early childhood education and school communities. Given its complexity, it is perhaps understandable that transition is regarded as an ongoing challenge for education in Aotearoa New Zealand (see, for instance, NZEI Te Riu Roa, 2014).

Transition involves moving from one discrete reality to another, with change occurring through time; it is not a process of elision or merging so that two realities become one. In other words, borders are crossed rather than removed. Peters and Sandberg (2017) describe a series of action research projects in New Zealand in which teachers from early childhood education and school engaged in reciprocal exploration of this boundary space between sectors to create borderlands instead of sharp divides:

> Teachers in the project examined each other's curricula, spent time observing in the other sector and discussed these observations with each other to gain an understanding of what had been seen. Based on these understandings, they explored ways of sharing information and planning. Regular meetings included discussions that highlighted the constraints within each sector, as well as the similarities in personal teacher philosophies about learning and their goals for the children. Where before there had been some tensions regarding different approaches in the other sector, new understandings were developed about why these existed, and the teachers focused on supporting the children's learning journeys collaboratively. (Peters & Sandberg, 2017, p. 227)

Borderlands preserve the integrity of both spaces while allowing a negotiated passage between the two. In similar fashion, the idea of transition as a 'bridge', as crossing a threshold between one reality and another, requires communication from both sides, resulting in changing perspectives and a sense of shared purpose. Again, the integrity of the 'banks' on either side is preserved while still allowing safe passage. The territorial metaphor is extended further with the idea of 'rites of passage' as special recognition of an individual moving from one reality to another. Rather than blurring the boundaries, differences are marked and celebrated through acts and ceremonies accompanying life transitions.

The border metaphor (borderlands, bridges, and rites of passage) invites teachers to preserve and celebrate the unique character of each sector, with potential for collaboration across sectors to support children's learning as they move from the familiar to the unknown. Coherence in transition may be achieved not by making education sectors the same, but by establishing appropriate accommodative practices in the borderlands. Indeed, in both policy and academic analysis the value and importance of a diverse range of early childhood education services is recognised (Shuker & Cherrington, 2016) as well as diverse philosophies and curriculum approaches. These philosophies and approaches are expected to draw from curriculum frameworks in ways that ensure philosophy and practice reflect the local community's values and beliefs. For curriculum dialogue this means that the idea of smooth transitions could be seen as somewhat problematic; the task of teachers as pedagogues rather than as technicians is to be open to all kinds of terrains and journeys, some bumpy, some smooth, some long, some short—but all of which are a shared dialogical journey.

That journey is significantly influenced by government initiatives that focus on educational transitions—initiatives like Investing in Educational Success and the Communities of Learning | Kāhui Ako. In the next section we apply the idea of curriculum dialogue to Communities of Learning. The Communities of Learning are significant to curriculum because of the expectations for continuity and coherence between early childhood and primary school experiences, and for seamless pathways through the learning journey. Ministry of Education (2016; n.d.) guidelines for Communities of Learning clearly influence how centre communities make sense of curriculum, especially in terms of learning pathways and achievement.

Communities of Learning and curriculum dialogue

According to the Education Review Office (ERO), Communities of Learning provide a sense of collegiality and community, an opportunity to build trusting relationships between institutions, increased opportunities for student learning and success, and a seamless learning pathway from early childhood through to higher education (Education Review Office, 2017). These intentions for collectivity and collegiality appear to resonate closely with *Te Whāriki* and would arguably align with the early childhood curriculum in rich and valued ways. However, we argue that in the first

3 years of government guidance for Communities of Learning an emphasis on achievement (Education Review Office, 2017) has created a significantly narrower understanding of curriculum and limited the scope for dialogue.

Communities of Learning focus on teachers and teaching, and in particular on teaching practices that impact on achievement, "lifting the quality of leadership and teaching so that best practice becomes universal" (Ministry of Education, 2017c, p. 2). Each Community of Learning must establish an achievement challenge, approved by the Ministry: "a set of objectives formulated in response to careful analysis of local needs" that lead to an "achievement plan" (p. 8). Participants in Communities of Learning, including early childhood centres, are expected to embed their achievement challenges as charter targets, making "tracking the impact of instructional practice more visible" (Education Review Office, 2017, p. 21). Embedding involves writing such targets into a centre philosophy and policies.

Communities of Learning undertake "deliberate and systematic analysis of data to identify priorities for improvement" (Education Review Office, 2017, p. 13). Data are a critical element of the Communities of Learning and have significant implications for curriculum. The Ministry of Education (2017c) reports that effective Communities of Learning are using "data to identify achievement challenges, and to monitor and evaluate how well the actions they are taking are working" (p. 1). Data is regarded as central to the programme because success is best understood and measured in terms of achievement—symptomatic of the developmental discourse symbolised in the metaphor of the nautilus.

Early evaluations of Communities of Learning indicate a high level of confidence and collaboration, strong leadership, good foundations for working towards the achievement challenges, and a predominant focus, as required, on achievement challenges for which there is national data: reading, writing, mathematics, and NCEA outcomes (Ministry of Education, 2017c). The majority of Communities of Learning leaders and across-schools teachers[1] see improving student transitions as a core goal, although less than a third of Communities of Learning had actually met with an early childhood centre community (Ministry of Education, 2017c). In contrast, almost all Communities of Learning see their focus as improving achievement and better collaboration, although they were less clear about how to achieve collaboration and "what it would look like in practice" (Ministry of Education, 2017c, p. 28).

The ERO report on the Communities of Learning provides evidence that early childhood centres have had very limited involvement in developing the Communities of Learning's mission, achievement aims, responsibilities, and innovations in practice

---

1 Across-schools teachers (also known as across-community teachers) are responsible for pedagogical leadership in a designated area. They guide teachers within a COL in inquiry into pedagogical practices (Ministry of Education, 2016).

(Education Review Office, 2017). ERO explains this disparity as, in part, a result of the absence of early childhood education in the original IES initiative. Nevertheless, the imbalance is exacerbated by school communities' exclusion of early childhood education centres for purportedly logistical reasons, such as there being too many centres and unpredictable parental use of centres (Education Review Office, 2017). Certainly, there is a clear expectation and advocacy for early childhood education involvement (Education Review Office, 2017) and evidence to this effect in the most recent round of applications (Ministry of Education, 2017c). The Ministry of Education (n.d.) sees early childhood education as integral to the child's learning journey. It sees a *potential* role for centres (rather than an essential or critical role) in supporting Communities of Learning to better meet the needs of children transitioning to school, through a shared understanding of differences in curriculum, including pedagogy.

Although it is eminently sensible for educational programmes to focus on better learning and higher achievement, the idea of measurable achievement gains is problematic, highlighting tensions between *Te Whāriki* and *NZC* (Ministry of Education, 2017; 2007). The task of weaving the two curricular approaches together within a Community of Learning is complex when different ideas about achievement and measurement inform the respective sectors (see, for instance, Biesta, 2009; Goodley, 2018). As noted above, the Ministry of Education suggests that early childhood education can contribute to the setting of achievement challenges and how those challenges are met, although for achievement challenges to be acceptable to Communities of Learning policy they must be determined through what can be measured in particular ways.

The practices of transition from early childhood to school are necessarily shaped by the curriculum approaches of both settings, by the relationship between the two curriculum documents and their associated discourses, and by the efforts and expectations of key players in various educational communities. The Communities of Learning programme plays a significant role in transition practices as the Ministry of Education, through the Communities of Learning programme and its achievement targets, shapes the priorities and practices of schools and centres. The Ministry (n.d.) is explicit that making links between *Te Whāriki* and *NZC* will "help build shared understanding of what is valued learning, what progress could look like and how Kāhui Ako [Communities of Learning] can design a local curriculum with parents and whānau to meet the needs of their children" (Ministry of Education, n.d., p. 2). For early childhood centres, a key conversation is whether externally determined achievement targets meet the needs of their children and their communities. If early childhood education teachers and centre communities have a marginal or peripheral voice in the Communities of Learning or any future whole system curriculum intervention, the challenge is to raise awareness of the essential contributions that cross-sector dialogue has for the child's educational transitions. It is essential to be aware of and address this challenge in order to not lose the "hard-won understanding that early childhood is a phase of development in its own right, and should not be defined and thought about merely in terms of the future 'goal' of readiness for school" (Early Childhood Action, 2012, p. 8). Perhaps most importantly, the challenge is to keep in play the idea that the two curriculum documents employ and promote different discourses and that these discourses should not be conflated in attempts to create a coherent and singular educational pathway for the learner.

A disconnect between the previous school curriculum and *Te Whāriki* (Mutch, 2003) was ameliorated to some degree with the introduction of key competencies in the 2007 revision (Mutch & Trim, 2013). The key competencies allow the two curricula to work together at the same time as retaining their specific characters. However, the focus on achievement pathways may signal a return to earlier curriculum disconnection with the possibility of a regime of pre-specified achievement pathways and standardised approaches to assessment via measurement. Conceptually, programmes like Communities of Learning may promote the idea of the learning journey as a single and coherent pathway. Greater coherence may be desirable, but it can also limit opportunities for different ways of thinking about educational experiences and educational aims. In addition, the idea of continuity between early learning and primary schooling can be code for minimising the significance of the transition process, with the educational journey conceptualised as a weaving together of experiences into one seamless pathway. The "allure of coherence" requires critical dialogue to support the "difficulties in navigating the gaps that appear when character and coherence diverge" (Gibbons, 2011, p. 13).

Concluding thoughts

Te Whāriki guides the early childhood sector with the culturally significant metaphor of a woven mat, its strands and principles serving their various textural functions in the fabric of the mat. Under the current Communities of Learning directions, and the significant absence of early childhood education voices in Communities of Learning, the intricacy of the woven mat, with its significance for the early childhood sector, may be corralled into a narrower curriculum pathway. Having drawn on decades of advocacy for early childhood education as a whole-of-community practice, *Te Whāriki* speaks clearly to a community of diverse learners in a sector with a rich history and a shared process of developing an open-ended, child-focussed curriculum. The new Communities of Learning present a very different focus—centrally steered by the Ministry of Education, characterised by notions of measurement and achievement, and directing the practices of schools and early childhood centres in prescribing and measuring learning targets to be endorsed by the Ministry. Early childhood education and schooling are two fundamentally different sectors in terms of historical development and curriculum definition and style. There is, then, a deep conceptual and structural challenge to be engaged with here.

As with many educational policy initiatives, Communities of Learning may not be around for very long. Nevertheless, we are concerned about the limited theorising and the lack of consultation across sectors that have characterised the development of Communities of Learning and continue to underpin their existence, and which may remain in place after they are gone. For early childhood educators, the pedagogical call is for negotiation and dialogue among various parties about the nature of curriculum and learning, and for a vision of multiple pathways and achievement criteria appropriate to diverse settings and reflective of their communities. This requires advocacy for new Communities of Learning that are open ended and underpinned by engagement in pedagogical debate about the purposes and processes of education. Our hope is that these new Communities can be critical in their interpretation of political imperatives, formative in their approaches to assessment of children's work, and generative of new and unforeseen knowledge.

References

Biesta, G. (2007). Why "what works" won't work: Evidence-based practice and the democratic deficit in educational research. *Educational Theory (57)*1, 1–22. http://dx.doi.org/10.1111/j.1741-5446.2006.00241.x

Biesta, G. (2009). Good education in an age of measurement: On the need to reconnect with the question of purpose in education. *Educational Assessment, Evaluation and Accountability*, 21(1), 33–46.

Dalli, C. (2008). Pedagogy, knowledge and collaboration: Towards a ground-up perspective on professionalism. *European Early Childhood Education Research Journal*, 16(2), 175–185.

Dalli, C. (2010). Towards the re-emergence of a critical ecology of the early childhood profession in New Zealand. *Contemporary Issues in Early Childhood*, 11(1), 61–74. http://dx.doi.org/10.2304/ciec.2010.11.1.61

Dalli, C., Miller, L., & Urban, M. (2012). *Early childhood grows up: Towards a critical ecology of the profession*. In L. Miller, C. Dalli, & M. Urban (Eds.), *Early childhood grows up: Towards a critical ecology of the profession* (pp. 3–19). London, UK: Springer.

Early Childhood Action. (2012). *Unhurried pathways: A new framework for early childhood*. Winchester, UK: Author.

Education Review Office. (2017). *Communities of learning | Kāhui Ako in action: What we know so far*. Wellington: Author.

Egan, K. (2003). What is curriculum? *Journal for the Canadian Association of Curriculum Studies*, 1(1), 9–16.

Foucault, M. (1981). The order of discourse. In E. Young (Ed.), *Untying the text: A post-structuralist reader* (pp. 51–78). Henley-on-Thames, UK: Routledge & Keegan Paul.

Gibbons, A. (2011). The incoherence of curriculum: Questions concerning early childhood teacher educators. *Australasian Journal of Early Childhood, 36*(1), 8–15.

Goodley, C. (2018). Reflecting on being an effective teacher in an age of measurement. *Reflective Practice, 19*(2), 167–178.

Hipkins, R. (2017). *Weaving a coherent curriculum: How the idea of 'capabilities' can help*. Wellington: New Zealand Council for Educational Research.

Hipkins, R. (2018). *How the key competencies were developed: The evidence base*. Wellington: New Zealand Council for Educational Research.

Lakoff, G., & Johnson, M. (2003 [1980]). *Metaphors we live by*. Chicago, IL: University of Chicago Press.

Mac Naughton, G. (2005). *Doing Foucault in early childhood studies: Applying poststructural ideas*. London, UK: Routledge.

McDowell, S., & Hipkins, R. (2018). *How the key competencies evolved over time: Insights from the research*. Wellington: New Zealand Council for Educational Research.

Ministry of Education. (2007). *The New Zealand curriculum*. Wellington: Learning Media.

Ministry of Education. (2016). *Community of learning: Guide for schools and kura*. Retrieved from http://www.education.govt.nz/assets/Documents/col/Communities-of-Learning-Guide-for-Schools-and-Kura-web-enabled.pdf

Ministry of Education. (2017a). *What we have in common: Curriculum connections (transitions in ECE)*. Retrieved from http://www.education.govt.nz/early-childhood/teaching-and-learning/transitions-in-early-learning/what-we-have-in-common-curriculum-connections/

Ministry of Education. (2017b). *Te whāriki: He whāriki mātauranga mō ngā mokopuna o Aotearoa:Early childhood curriculum*. Wellington: Author.

Ministry of Education. (2017c). *Uptake and early implementation: Communities of learning | Kāhui Ako*. Retrieved from https://www.educationcounts.govt.nz/publications/schooling/181545

Ministry of Education. (n.d.). *Supporting early learning representation*. Retrieved from https://www.education.govt.nz/assets/Documents/col/Supporting-early-learning-representation.pdf

Moss, P. (2006). Structures, understandings and discourses: Possibilities for re-envisioning the early childhood worker. *Contemporary Issues in Early Childhood (7)*1, 30–41. http://dx.doi.org/10.2304/ciec.2006.7.1.30

Moss, P., & Urban, M. (2019). The Organisation for Economic Co-operation and Development's International Early Learning Study: What's going on. *Contemporary Issues in Early Childhood, 20*(2), 207–212. https://doi.org/10.1177/1463949118803269

Mutch, C. (2003). One context, two outcomes: A comparison of *Te Whāriki* and the New Zealand curriculum framework. In J. Nuttall (Ed.), *Weaving Te Whāriki. Aotearoa New Zealand's early childhood curriculum framework in theory and practice* (pp. 111–129). Wellington: NZCER Press.

Mutch, C., & Trim, B. (2013). Improvement, accountability and sustainability: A comparison of developments in the early childhood and schooling sectors. In J. Nuttall (Ed.), *Weaving Te Whāriki. Aotearoa New Zealand's early childhood curriculum framework in theory and practice* (2nd ed., pp. 71–91). Wellington: NZCER Press.

Nuttall, J. (Ed.) (2003). *Weaving Te Whāriki:Aotearoa New Zealand's early childhood document in theory and practice*. Wellington: NZCER Press.

Nuttall, J. (Ed.) (2013). *Weaving Te Whāriki: Aotearoa New Zealand's early childhood document in theory and practice* (2nd ed.). Wellington: NZCER Press

NZEI Te Riu Roa. (2014). *A case study on the provision of early childhood education. Submission to the Productivity Commission Inquiry: More effective social services*. Wellington: Author. Retrieved from https://www.productivity.govt.nz/assets/Submission-Documents/d80b212239/Sub-040-New-Zealand-Educational-Institute-Te-Riu-Roa.pdf

Peters, S., & Paki, V. (2013). *Te Whāriki*: Weaving multiple perspectives on transitions. In J. Nuttall (Ed.), *Weaving Te Whāriki. Aotearoa New Zealand's early childhood curriculum framework in theory and practice* (2nd ed., pp. 197–213). Wellington: NZCER Press.

Peters, S., & Sandberg, G. (2017). Bridges, borderlands and rites of passage. In N. Ballam, B. Perry, & A. Garpelin (Eds.) *POET—Pedagogies of educational transitions European and Antipodean research* (pp. 223–237). Dordrecht, The Netherlands: Springer.

Ricoeur, P. (1976). *Interpretation theory: Discourse and the surplus of meaning*. Fort Worth, TX: Texas Christian University Press.

Shuker, M.J., & Cherrington, S. (2016). Diversity in New Zealand early childhood education: Challenges and opportunities. *International Journal of Early Years Education, 24*(2), 172–187.

Shulman, L. (1986). Those who understand: Knowledge growth in teaching. *Educational Researcher (15)*2, 4–14.

Taylor, N., & Te One, S. (2016). Children's rights in Aotearoa/New Zealand. In C. Dalli & A. Meade (Eds.), *Research, policy and advocacy in the early years: Writing inspired by the achievements of Professor Anne Smith* (pp. 48–58). Wellington: NZCER Press.

PART 3

Te Whāriki in international contexts

CHAPTER 12

Re-reading and re-activating *Te Whāriki* through a posthuman childhood studies lens

Marek Tesar and Sonja Arndt

Introduction

This chapter offers a re-reading of the revised *Te Whāriki* using a posthuman childhood studies lens. Posthuman childhood studies, as part of critical theories, shifts and blurs boundaries, and asks questions about human nature, and the relationships of children with other beings, matters, objects, energies, and our planet more generally. This lens calls on us to rethink the kinds of childhoods that might be constructed through *Te Whāriki*. Seminal posthuman theorist Rosi Braidotti (2013) bases her posthuman thinking on studies in philosophy, science and technology, and philosophies of the subject, and provides a useful starting point for rethinking children as complicatedly relational beings entangled in and with their worlds. She notes that posthumanism is a "navigational tool" for exploring "ways of engaging affirmatively with the present" (p. 5), for example in the contemporary time of the Anthropocene, in our "globally linked and technologically mediated societies" (p. 5). When *Te Whāriki* was revised in 2017, the Minister of Education stated in the Foreword that it reflects "changes in the early learning context, including the diversity of New Zealand society today, contemporary theories and pedagogies" (Ministry of Education, 2017, p. 2). The importance of viewing *Te Whāriki* through a posthuman childhood studies lens is that it positions the curriculum framework within one of these 'contemporary theories and pedagogies'. Most importantly, a posthuman childhood studies lens offers new and more specific articulations and understandings of children and their childhoods as interdependent and intra-related with more-than-human worlds, things, and beings.

This re-reading also responds to the sections in the revised *Te Whāriki* that indicate its reflection of critical and emerging research and theory. Applying a posthuman lens adds another dimension to the "critical theoretical lenses" (Ministry of Education, 2017, p. 62) through which children and childhoods are conceptualised in contemporary research, and which "challenge[s] disparities, injustices, inequalities and perceived norms" (p. 62). As such, this [re-]reading of *Te Whāriki* through a childhood studies posthuman lens positions the document within "emerging research and theory" (p. 62), which, according to the revised document, appears to be somewhat narrowly limited to neuro-scientific developments. Therefore, this chapter seeks to expand the notion of critical and emerging theories and in doing so offer opportunities for conceptualising children and childhoods through recent critical research and theoretical developments in studies of the subject, interrelationalities, and worldly interconnectedness.

The chapter further recognises the breadth and richness of critical engagements with early childhood education (ECE) and the study of young children and their childhoods in Aotearoa New Zealand over the past 20 or so years. Many of Aotearoa's thinkers and teacher educators have engaged with and utilised critical, poststructural, and posthuman approaches in their scholarship. Re-readings of *Te Whāriki* through diverse approaches to critical theories make a considerable contribution to broadening conceptions and understandings of very young children, blurring binaries, questioning assumptions and pedagogies (as argued, for example, by Gunn, 2015). This chapter focuses on how some of these conceptions might arise and shift, when we re-read *Te Whāriki* through a posthuman childhood studies lens.

Beyond responding to the positionings of the document within theory and research, the importance and urgency of taking a posthuman childhood studies lens lies in two pedagogical points. First, it picks up on *Te Whāriki*'s goal in Strand 2, *Belonging— Mana whenua*, which emphasises the importance of children's engagements and encounters with "people, places and things" (Ministry of Education, 2017, p. 24). A posthuman re-reading of this goal elevates the relationships with places and things, beyond the human, as a crucial aspect that may challenge dominant human-centric perceptions (Duhn, 2014; Taylor, Pacini-Ketchabaw, & Blaise, 2012). This point importantly recognises the strand of *Belonging*, particularly through its focus on a bicultural relationship with the land "based on whakapapa, respect and aroha" (Ministry of Education, 2017, p. 31) and time (Rameka, 2016, 2018). Secondly, and relatedly, this re-reading responds to contemporary concerns with devastations and a lack of response to the environmental interconnectedness of humans and non-humans in a local and global sense in the time of the Anthropocene (the current geological age, an epoch in which human activity has become the dominant influence on both the environment and climate). Malone (2015) argues for a stronger focus on understanding sustainability where:

> the broader focus of sustainable development is one of the ways the global community can meet the natural, social and economic needs of humans within the planetary boundaries and resource limits—so that human and planetary development can be both sustainable, and be sustained. (p. 410)

Considering the urgency of contemporary anthropocentric concerns has critical implications for how we approach *Te Whāriki*'s constructions of childhoods and practices within early childhood settings (Tesar & Arndt, 2018). Latour (2014), for example, laments the lack of preparedness within the general population for recognising the deeply related ways in which we are all connected, especially in terms of local and global crises. Connecting children in their early years with both local and wider global concerns requires not only deeply scientific studies, but also a shifting attitude, to recognise that "[t]here is no distant place anymore" (p. 2), and that we, and our orientations and practices, are all implicated and responsible. Such a thinking is a deeply moral, ethical, and often difficult undertaking, and a pressing one. Re-reading *Te Whāriki* through a posthuman childhood studies lens reinforces such interconnectednesses and responsibilities, calling for a perpetual questioning and critical engagement and re-engagement with conceptions of children as simultaneously with, in, and as, people, places, and things.

Taking a childhood studies (new sociology of childhood) approach as a point of departure (see James, Jenks, & Prout, 1998), helps us to outline shifts that are further enabled by a posthuman childhood studies positioning. A childhood studies approach is an interdisciplinary approach to studying diverse conceptions of children and childhoods that draws on predominantly human- (child-)centric thought and influences. Adopting a posthuman lens in the study of childhoods helps us to explore more-than-human understandings within *Te Whāriki*, and the images of children and their childhoods that it constructs. Such a re-reading of the curriculum framework fosters an ongoing critical engagement and questioning of what curriculum means for "children as 21st century citizens, learning how to learn in a fast changing and globally connected world" (Ministry of Education, 2017, p. 2).

Childhood studies as a point of departure

Framing a posthuman focus within, with a childhood studies lens, grounds the rethinking of how childhood is conceptualised and situated within children's lives, education, and worlds, in an existing body of work. Since the 1980s, a childhood studies approach has evolved as a shift from a biological understanding of children as immature, to the idea that childhood is a construct and children are social actors. Most notably, a childhood studies approach challenges the historical and developmental notion that a young child is ontologically incomplete. Instead, in a childhood studies approach, children are argued as actively involved social agents in their own lives (James, Jenks, & Prout, 1998; James & Prout, 1997).

A childhood studies approach seeks to dismantle fixed structural ideas around children and childhoods, and ideas of how children contribute as members of society. Childhood studies emerges from a range of humanities and social science disciplines (for example, human geography, architecture, law, social work, and philosophy). Historically, it advances the idea that childhoods are neither definable nor linear. Rather, it posits childhoods as complex interactions of individual experiences with ideologies and localities. This reflects shifts over time, as views on childhood have changed from the concept of childhood as non-existent up to the Middle Ages (Ariès, 1962; Cunningham, 2005), to the view of children as "evil or savage" where "all people are born in original sin" (Tesar, Rodriguez, & Kupferman, 2016, p. 170). Tesar et al. (2016) note views about childhood that perpetuate the dependence of children on adults, characterising "childhood as empty" for example, "as blank slates" as Locke did, requiring "knowledge supplied by the family and the society ... [to] ultimately become productive parts of the social fabric" (p. 170). While in another influential view, which deeply affects ECE, "Rousseau inverted the wild state of nature" depicting "the child as living in a perfected state of nature" where children are seen as "possessing essential goodness" (p. 170). That childhoods require input, management, and protection by adults is deeply steeped in these and many other philosophical perspectives that have not only shaped historical and contemporary education (May, 2013; Mitchell, 2010), but also parenting.

A childhood studies lens is strongly aligned with a focus on children's rights. In Aotearoa New Zealand, Smith (2013) was instrumental in elevating children as social actors in research and practices that focus on children's rights and active participation in their own childhoods. A rights-based approach seeks to protect children and their childhoods from harm. It recognises that children develop skills throughout life, and thus renders them also vulnerable and lacking the competence or skills which simultaneously opens up pathways to govern and mould them in keeping with the interests of the governing agencies. Acting in the best interests of a child is a contested concept that arises from this approach, which childhood studies research disrupts with questions, by asking: "Whose best interest is really being considered?" And, further: "According to whose definition is it the best interest, and from whose (cultural, powerful, educational, and so on) perspective?"

Inserting a posthuman focus into a childhood studies approach reflects the views on children's development, subjectivities, and lives, as complex and in constant evolution. Complicating this view, recent calls by Konstantoni and Emejulu (2017, p. 7) aim for "new and revised theorisations" to further recognise and to "illuminate, challenge and expand scholarship and debate about children and childhoods in different spaces and places across the globe". This emphasises the need for openness to the uncertainty that arises in re-viewing contemporary constructions and pedagogies, highlighting the concept of intersectionality as an important reminder to integrate such notions as children's differences based on race, sexual orientation, gender, and culture into the ways in which we think of children and their childhoods. Taking up the call for revised theorisations of children and childhoods builds on the historical developments of philosophical and theoretical shifts in relation to the child subject, identity, education, and global relationality. This interdisciplinarity and call for intersectionality affirms the importance of ongoing thought and re-reading of *Te Whāriki*, in relation to contemporary theory and research, such as through a posthuman childhood studies lens.

Te Whāriki's situation of children and their learning within their social and cultural surroundings is an ideal entry point for a revised theorisation, allowing complex articulations of the deeply relational entanglements of children and their contexts that a posthuman lens offers. In relation to children and childhoods, the key arguments, as Malone (2016) and others such as Taylor (2011) have argued, are not only to debunk and challenge representations of childhoods that portray children as dependent, lacking competency, and that normalise them in their development, but to break down the nature–culture binaries that separate human children and childhoods from non-human others.

A childhood studies approach, then, involves pedagogies, research, and activism around childhood and children that avoid essentialising. Skelton's (2015) curation of work by childhood studies scholars shows that the diverse set of thoughts, principles, theories, and approaches within a childhood studies framework focuses on sociological concerns and the structural impacts that affect children's rights and agency, in particular through regulatory policy, and local and societal influences on children and their childhoods. This is evident in *Te Whāriki*, where young children's development is viewed as "shaped by cultural expectations about what they should be capable of doing and when and where it is appropriate to demonstrate those capabilities" (Ministry of Education, 2017, p. 13).

This re-reading of *Te Whāriki* takes the above shifts and developments within childhood studies as a point of departure, to move beyond the pure humanist, sociological conceptions of a childhood studies lens (Duhn, 2015). It involves reading and re-reading, engaging with the multiple relationships in which children are enmeshed, thinking with the posthuman theory arising from the work of Braidotti

(2013), Barad (2003, 2015), Bennett (2010), and others, to shift to a posthuman childhood studies lens. In doing so, we return to the two points of importance and urgency of taking a posthuman lens by blurring the boundaries of human and non-human; nature-culture; and conceptions of people, places and things; and of children's worldly interrelationships and dependencies in relation to global environmental sustainability.

Te Whāriki's child and people, places, and things

Like its original version, the revised *Te Whāriki* constructs children and childhoods as agentic, holistic, and as immersed in their local cultural context. Its states that children are "competent and confident learners and communicators" who are "healthy in mind, body and spirit" and who are "secure in their sense of belonging and in the knowledge that they make a valued contribution to society" (Ministry of Education, 2017, p. 5). This inclusive orientation may be interpreted and applied in multiple ways, and, in one sense, this is likely its intention. It is an ideal opening to a deeper and ongoing posthuman childhood studies interpretation and re-interpretation, which questions and blurs conceptions of, for example, learners, mind, body, and spirit, and of contributing in valued ways to society.

Critical engagements with constructions of the child in the 1996 *Te Whāriki* have already problematised its aspirations for children, seeing indications of a cosmopolitan, global child, as Duhn (2006) suggests, that is "embedded in New Zealand's … neo-liberal visions of the future global subject" (p. 191). Governed by *Te Whāriki*, such neoliberal subjects—the children—are seen as embodiments of policy and government interests in global markets and competition, where they are viewed, for example, as "the lifelong learner, the flexible worker, the autonomous decision maker" (p. 195). Concerns with a relatively rapid shift to a neoliberal commodification of childhoods has further been highlighted by Cederman (2008), provoking questioning through her suggestions that the *Te Whāriki* child is constructed as an "'ideal child' or child.com, a consumerist child 'drowning' in a sea of technology" (p. 191). The concerns with a corporatisation of ECE continue, as exemplified in the more recent rise and fall of corporate ECE, which is seen as detracting from programmes' focus on children and children's learning needs, and teachers' ability to attend to them (Kamenarac, 2019; Mitchell, 2014). In our re-reading, we follow a process that Barad (2014) calls a process of diffraction, where we turn and re-turn to topics and ideas; that is, we read and re-read, all the time making new meaning of previous and new thoughts on the curriculum framework. As such, we cannot ignore the political, cultural, and environmental structures that continue to provoke such critical engagements as Duhn's, Cederman's and Mitchell's referred to here, as indeed they and others continue to affect contemporary constructions of children and childhoods through a posthuman lens.

Re-reading infants, toddlers, and young children

Te Whāriki's structuring of sections for "infants, toddlers, and young children" reflects a model of thinking where children's age determines their capabilities and expectations. Traditional developmental psychology strongly influenced this thinking, based on universal definitions of developmental stages and milestones, omitting understandings of the influences of culture and society, of individual subjectivities and differences (Bloch, Swadener, & Cannella, 2014, 2018). The limitations of developmentally focused early childhood practices have been critiqued since the early 1990s, highlighting also the omission of the complex influences of ideology, globalisation, and technology (Bloch et al., 2014, 2018). Such a view denies the strong focus, within a childhood studies approach, of children as social actors immersed in complex cultural contexts, the importance of children's voice, or of their participation and decision making in matters relevant to their childhoods (James et al., 1998).

While the curriculum framework partially appears to sit uncomfortably within the presentation of developmental, linear progressions of what infants, toddlers, or young children should be able to do, it also complicates the developmental focus on distinct age groups, as its holistic and empowering aspiration that children are "competent and confident learners" (Ministry of Education, 2017, p. 2) reflects a more open construction of infants, toddlers, and young children (pp. 13–15). Language that alludes to possibly universalising characteristics and expectations to follow "a predictable sequence" (Ministry of Education, 2017, p. 13), and that further "assessment, planning, intervention and support" (p. 13) might be required, if children deviate from such predicted developmental norms further adds to the contradiction. A close reading of the attributes, interests, and capabilities of each of the named groups of infants, toddlers, and young children reveals an intention to include culture, diversity, agency, and embeddedness in the local and worldly context as influential on children's competence, confidence, and contributions to society. Our re-reading arises from this uneasiness. Adding a posthuman reading aims not to solve, but to elevate the messiness of Aotearoa New Zealand childhoods, as entangled not only human, but also material, temporal, and worldly interconnected matter, determinations, and forces. In relation to "people, places and things" (Ministry of Education, 2017, p. 32), such an entanglement is illustrated in the strand of *Belonging—Mana whenua* and constructions of the bicultural child.

Re-reading the bicultural child

The bicultural weaving of *Te Whāriki* uniquely constructs childhoods as already complex and, in a sense, unknowable. Through the promotion of bicultural practices within early childhood settings, and in whakataukī throughout the document, children are represented as taonga; that is, as treasured and as valued. That children are taonga is further promoted in the interweavings of the developmental conception of the child with a belief in the empowerment of the child, through the notion of mana, a complex term invoking both power and status. A uniquely Aotearoa New Zealand construction is thus built on children's cultural groundedness, where they are seen as "secure in their sense of belonging" (Ministry of Education, 2017, p. 51). In constructing particular childhoods, we tend to approach such a cultural immersion from our own historical, cultural, and personal perspectives, as Stewart (2018) both claims and cautions. A posthuman childhood studies reading of *Te Whāriki*'s constructions of the child in relation to people, places, and things, elevates the focus beyond human complications; for example, of historical and contemporary power relations, linguistic and practical interpretations, and marginalisations, as raised by Stewart. Raising the importance of places affirms a strong bicultural emphasis on relationships with Papatūānuku (the earth), which is closely related to a raised focus also on matter and materialities; for example, through the influences and interrelationships of humans with forces and energies of nature, as Barad (2003, 2015) asserts. (Re)inserting conceptualisations of matter in relation to the child shifts our thinking beyond the visible, measurable, and conceivable. It perhaps offers inroads into complex articulations of what might be seen as children's healthy "mind ... and spirit" and their "sense of belonging" (Ministry of Education, 2017, p. 5), and perhaps also of a complex metaphysical understanding of what it means in Aotearoa New Zealand to be bicultural, in a worlded way (Mika, 2017). These insights offer us a further opening to reconceptualise the "valued contributions" (Ministry of Education, 2017, p. 5) that children might make to society, through an affirmative re-activation of *Te Whāriki* through a posthuman lens.

Re-activating *Te Whāriki*'s child through a posthuman childhood studies lens

Re-activating *Te Whāriki* through a posthuman lens pushes us to consider constructions and treatments of children and childhoods that move beyond the human. This is not to deny the existence of the human, nor of the importance of the many critical humanist theories emerging in recent years (Braidotti, 2013, 2019). Rather, it invites a blurring of the boundaries of what might be constructed as child or childhood, beyond any singular constructions or age groups, to encompass the multiplicities of nuanced entanglements of contemporary childhoods with things, matters, and contexts. It thus pushes us to move beyond what have become seen as "conventional humanist qualitative" ways of thinking (St. Pierre, 2014, p. 2), to rethink what might emerge from "the ruins" (p. 2) of developmental theories and studies, by re-activating *Te Whāriki* posthumanly.

Posthumanism, Braidotti (2013) claims, is an imagining of life with and beyond the human. It is a "qualitative shift in our thinking about what exactly is the basic unit of common reference for our species, our polity and our relationship to the other inhabitants of this planet" (p. 2). A posthuman perspective therefore already complicates the nature–culture binaries, not to do without the human, but to elevate all that is, alongside, and closely interrelated with, the humans. Already, when we view constructions of children within *Te Whāriki*'s framings, we are drawn to consider children's interconnectedness with beyond-the-human places and things, or 'other inhabitants of this planet'. The posthuman childhood studies elaboration of relationships and determinants of life has the effect of more overtly decentring the child, and opening up the conception of, for example, the provision of an early childhood curriculum to consider the possibilities offered by localised 'other inhabitants of this planet'. That is other life, other beings, or things in the environment, the atmosphere, the Earth, and beyond. Children and their childhoods, then, are constructed as one part of a greater than human assemblage.

Bennett (2010) adds to this conception the possibility that non-human things and matter can act agentically, or have vibrancy, in our relational contexts. She offers a useful explanation of assemblages, as "ad hoc groupings of diverse elements, of vibrant materials of all sorts. Assemblages are living, throbbing confederations that are able to function despite the persistent presence of energies that confound them from within" (pp. 23–24).

Through this conceptual stance, re-activating *Te Whāriki* through a posthuman childhood studies lens adds a useful articulation of children and childhoods within something that is vibrant and complicated. The "living, throbbing confederation" of *Te Whāriki*'s social, cultural, and posthuman assemblage relates children and their childhoods beyond human relationships, imaginings, and actions. It contends that, as an assemblage, not only do all beings, things, and children mutually and reciprocally affect and influence each other, but they intra-act in ways beyond human awareness or predictability. Barad's (2003) scientific work introduces us to the notion of intra-action, where the encounters between things, beings, and forces are constantly, actively reconfigured as a result of relationships with each other. Children's encounters and contributions to their worlds arise from and are shaped by and within these relationships, which Braidotti (2013) calls an "ontological relationality" (p. 100). From this perspective, children's intrinsic dependencies arise from *within relationships which already exist.*

Re-activating conceptions of people, places, and things

Reconceptualising children's relationships with people, places, and things is central to a posthuman childhood studies lens. Through *Te Whāriki*, the principle of *Relationships—Ngā hononga* positions children as learning "through responsive and reciprocal relationships with people, places and things" (Ministry of Education, 2017, p. 21). It provokes teachers to allow children to do so by trying "out their ideas and refin[ing] their working theories" (p. 21). Re-activating this notion by conceiving it in ways that shift beyond a human-centric view opens up to Haraway's (2007) ideas of relationships with the "significant otherness" (p. 8) of other species. In addition, it invites us to challenge the idea of seeing matter merely as "passive stuff, as raw, brute, or inert" (Bennett, 2010, p. vii), for example, in pedagogical considerations and teaching decisions (Arndt & Tesar, 2019). And, further, it invites us to provoke instead a certain "estrangement" as Bennett (2010) calls this space, where a "vital materiality" (p. vii) might occur. This view opens up possibilities of how matter itself might be vibrant, how it can be active, and how *things* can *act on* and *be acted on*, by others (human or non-human) within children's lives and worlds, within their early childhood settings and beyond.

Re-activating children's contributions in the Anthropocene

Pedagogically, *Te Whāriki* aims to be a "basis for weaving with children, parents and whānau" (Ministry of Education, 2017, p. 8) for each ECE setting to develop a local curriculum that considers "the aspirations and learning priorities of hapū, iwi and community" (p. 8). What emerges as the curriculum within each setting, therefore, is intended to be unique and emergent on the basis of local specificities, opening up conceptualisations of curriculum to relational interdependencies that may be unintended, but nevertheless present (Ritchie, 2015; Tesar & Arndt, 2018). The curriculum framework elevates children's capacity to participate actively in decision making about their own childhoods, as has been outlined in many studies with and by children (Malone, 2016). In what seems to be a questioning of its age-based delineation of children (as either infants, toddlers, or young children), *Te Whāriki* (Ministry of Education, 2017) itself suggests that "in an empowering environment, children have agency to create and act on their own ideas, develop knowledge and skills" (p. 18). It suggests that children are empowered when such agency occurs "in areas that interest them and" that they are "increasingly" able "to make decisions and judgments on matters that relate to them" (p. 18). Through a posthuman childhood studies lens, children and adults are not seen as binary opposites, but as human subjects that intra-act with the world in always relational ways, implicating all inhabitants of the planet, including other than human subjects and objects. A posthuman childhood studies reading, then, reconceptualises children's intra-relationalities beyond human subjects and culture. Ceder (2018) explains intra-relationality as deriving from Barad's notion of intra-action, as shifting our views towards accepting multiple truths and ongoing becomings. In this sense, it helps us to see children's relationships with worldly, anthropocentric concerns as open and unpredictable, rather than as particular, separate truths, individuals, or things, or even as distant and not relevant.

Through a posthuman reading, when children seen as intra-relationally entangled with and alongside the other matter, things, and energies with which they co-inhere in their surroundings (Arndt & Tesar, 2016), "people, places and things" become implicated by the acts and agency not only of the human, but of the things, materials, and matter acting within assemblages (Bennett, 2010). Instead of children's voices and agency being downplayed through considerations as "unknowing, irrational and immature" (Murris, 2013, p. 249), a posthuman approach instead elevates it, not above, but enmeshed with and arising from the intra-acting relationships in which they exist.

As we have argued throughout the chapter, a childhood studies lens provides us with a valuable entry point for re-reading *Te Whāriki* from a posthuman childhood studies perspective. Alerting teachers, family members, and other adults to the power of children's voice, *Te Whāriki* (Ministry of Education, 2017) asks, "[i]n what ways do kaiako support children to contribute to curriculum decision making"? (p. 40). Valuing teachers' reflection and consideration of this point, such questioning provokes conceptions of children as powerful, knowledgeable, and capable of determining what should happen in their day in early childhood settings. It pushes the reader, teachers, and others involved with children to consider the act of determining curriculum as emergent, alive, and open, and as an assemblage involving human and more-than-human acts and relationalities.

This re-reading and re-activation of *Te Whāriki* places the curriculum framework and its conceptions of children and childhoods firmly in relation with such processes of what happens in children's worlds. It highlights their intrinsic connections with what happens locally, in Aotearoa New Zealand, and with the ways in which we read and orient ourselves towards the principles, strands, goals, and learning outcomes of *Te Whāriki* in relation to children and their childhoods, their representation, agency, voice, relationships, and worldly interconnectedness. Recognising children's inextricable connections within global concerns and local and global relationships is an urgent first step that responds to Latour's (2014) concerns with a lack of preparedness to deal with them. New dimensions of ethical and moral decision making become elevated when we invoke posthuman conceptions of childhoods, children, and their other-than-human relationalities, bringing to the fore the nuances and specificities of encounters with people, places, and things by which these concerns are knowingly and unknowingly affected.

Concluding comments: Perpetually re-activating *Te Whāriki*

Our intention in this chapter has been to offer a provocation not only for our re-reading, but for ongoing re-readings and constant re-engagements in thoughtful reconceptualisations of *Te Whāriki*'s possible intent, meaning, and positioning in relation to contemporary and emerging research and theories. This re-reading of *Te Whāriki* aims to act as an opening to potentialities, for continuing reconceptualisations of children and childhoods, contemporary theory and research, and practice. Diffractive reading and re-reading *Te Whāriki* through a posthuman childhood studies lens activates and questions conceptions of children's realities, lives, and relationships. It reveals and elevates intricate entanglements within constructions of childhoods in *Te Whāriki*, by elaborating on the meanings of "people, places and things" (Ministry of Education, 2017, p. 12), and by recognising explicit material agency that implicates human ways of being and interdependencies with worldly concerns, as arising in contemporary environmental and sustainability concerns.

The perpetual evolution of a childhood studies lens pushes us not only to re-read *Te Whāriki* in a different way, but to re-activate it in constantly new, and often speculative, ways. A posthuman childhood studies lens calls for a constant process of diffraction, turning and re-turning, reading and re-reading, building on new conceptualisations, senses, and energies. In this chapter we have offered merely another starting point, as each child–thing–being, each context, and each intra-relationship evolves, again and again.

References

Ariès, P. (1962). *Centuries of childhood*. London, UK: Cape.

Arndt, S., & Tesar, M. (2016). A more-than-social movement: The post-human condition of quality in the early years. *Contemporary Issues in Early Childhood, 17*(1), 16–25. doi:10.1177/1463949115627896

Arndt, S., & Tesar, M. (2019). Posthuman encounters in New Zealand early childhood teacher education. In A. Bayley & C. A. Taylor (Eds.), *Posthumanism and higher education: Reimagining pedagogy, practice and research* (pp. 85–102). Cham, Switzerland: Palgrave Macmillan.

Barad, K. (2003). Posthumanist performativity: Toward an understanding of how matter comes to matter. *Signs: Journal of Women in Culture and Society, 28*(3), 801–831. doi:10.1086/345321

Barad, K. (2014). Diffracting diffraction: Cutting together-apart. *Parallax, 20*(3), 168–187. doi:10.1080/13534645.2014.927623

Barad, K. (2015). Transmaterialities: Trans*/matter/realities and queer political imaginings. *GLQ: A Journal of Lesbian and Gay Studies, 21*(2–3), 387–422. doi:10.1215/10642684-2843239

Bennett, J. (2010). *Vibrant matter: A political ecology of things*. Durham, NC: Duke University Press.

Bloch, M., Swadener, B., & Cannella, G. S. (2014). Introduction: Exploring reconceptualist histories and possibilities. In M. Bloch, B. Swadener, & G. S. Cannella (Eds.), *Reconceptualising early childhood care and education: A reader. Critical questions, new imaginaries and social activism* (pp. 1–18). New York, NY: Peter Lang.

Bloch, M., Swadener, B. B., & Cannella, G. S. (2018). Introduction: Reconceptualist histories and possibilities. In M. Bloch, B. B. Swadener, & G. S. Cannella (Eds.), *Reconceptualizing early childhood education and care: A reader. Critical questions, new imaginaries and social activism* (2nd ed., pp. 1–17). New York, NY: Peter Lang.

Braidotti, R. (2013). *The posthuman*. Cambridge, UK: Polity Press.

Braidotti, R. (2019). Preface: The posthuman as exuberant excess. In F. Ferrando (Ed.), *Philosophical posthumanism* (pp. xi–xvii). London, UK: Bloomsbury.

Ceder, S. (2018). *Towards a posthuman theory of educational relationality*. London, UK: Routledge.

Cederman, K. (2008). Not weaving but drowning? The child.com in New Zealand early childhood pedagogies. *International Journal of Early Childhood, 40*(2), 119–130.

Cunningham, H. (2005). *Children and childhood in Western society since 1500*. New York, NY: Longman.

Duhn, I. (2006). The making of global citizens: Traces of cosmopolitanism in the New Zealand early childhood curriculum, Te Whāriki. *Contemporary Issues in Early Childhood, 7*(3), 191–202.

Duhn, I. (2015). Making agency matter: Rethinking infant and toddler agency in educational discourse. *Discourse: Studies in the Cultural Politics of Education, 36*(6), 920–931. doi:10.1080/01596306.2014.918535

Gunn, A. C. (2015). The potential of queer theorising in early childhood education: Disrupting heteronormativity and practising for inclusion. In A. C. Gunn & L. A. Smith (Eds.), *Sexual cultures in Aotearoa New Zealand education* (pp. 21–34). Dunedin: Otago University Press.

Haraway, D. (2007). *When species meet*. Minneapolis, MN: University of Minnesota Press.

James, A., Jenks, C., & Prout, A. (1998). *Theorizing childhood*. Cambridge, UK: Polity Press.

James, A., & Prout, A. (1997). Preface to second edition. In A. James & A. Prout (Eds.), *Constructing and reconstructing childhood: Contemporary issues in the sociological study of childhood* (2nd ed., pp. ix–xvii). London, UK: RoutledgeFalmer.

Kamenarac, O. (2019). *Discursive constructions of teachers' professional identities in early childhood policies and practice in Aotearoa New Zealand: Complexities and contradictions*. Unpublished doctoral thesis, University of Waikato, Hamilton, New Zealand.

Konstantoni, K., & Emejulu, A. (2017). When intersectionality met childhood studies: The dilemmas of a travelling concept. *Children's Geographies, 15*(1), 6–22. doi:10.1080/14733285.2016.1249824

Latour, B. (2014). Agency at the time of the anthropocene. *New Literary History, 45*(1), 1–18. doi:10.1353/nlh.2014.0003

Malone, K. (2015), Children's rights and the crisis of rapid urbanization: Exploring the United Nations Post 2015 Sustainable Development Agenda and the potential role for UNICEF's Child Friendly Cities Initiative. *The International Journal of Children's Rights, 23*, 405–424.

Malone, K. (2016). Posthumanist approaches to theorising children's human–nature relations. In K. Nairn, P. Kraftl, & T. Skelton (Eds.), *Space, place and environment* (3rd ed., pp. 1–22). Singapore: Springer.

May, H. (2013). *The discovery of early childhood* (2nd ed.). Wellington: NZCER Press.

Mika, C. (2017). *Indigenous education and the metaphysics of presence: A worlded philosophy*. London, UK: Routledge.

Ministry of Education. (2017). *Te whāriki: He whāriki mātauranga mō ngā mokopuna o Aotearoa: Early childhood curriculum*. Wellington: Author.

Mitchell, L. (2010). Constructions of childhood in early childhood education policy debate in New Zealand. *Contemporary Issues in Early Childhood, 11*(4), 328–341.

Mitchell, L. (2014, 2 December). Linda Mitchell: Put children's education before shareholders. *The New Zealand Herald*. Retrieved from: http://www.nzherald.co.nz/nz/news/article.cfm?c_id=1&objectid=11367139

Murris, K. (2013). The epistemic challenge of hearing children's voices. *Studies in Philosophy and Education, 32*(3), 245–259.

Rameka, L. (2016). Kia whakatōmuri te haere whakamua: 'I walk backwards into the future with my eyes fixed on my past'. *Contemporary Issues in Early Childhood, 17*(4), 387–398. doi:10.1177/1463949116677923

Rameka, L. (2018). A Māori perspective of being and belonging. *Contemporary Issues in Early Childhood, 19*(4), 367–378. https://doi.org/10.1177/1463949118808099

Ritchie, J. (2015). Social, cultural, and ecological justice in the age of the Anthropocene: A New Zealand early childhood care and education perspective. *Journal of Pedagogy, 6*(2), 41–56.

Skelton, T. (2015). *Geographies of children and young people* (vols. I–XII). Singapore: Springer.

Smith, A. B. (2013). *Understanding children and childhood: A New Zealand perspective* (5th ed.). Wellington: Bridget Williams Books.

St. Pierre, E. A. (2014). A brief and personal history of post-qualitative research: Toward "post-inquiry". *Journal of Curriculum Theorizing, 30*(2), 2–19.

Stewart, G. (2018). Rebooting biculturalism in education in Aotearoa–New Zealand. *New Zealand Journal of Teachers' Work, 15*(1), 8–11.

Taylor, A. (2011). Reconceptualizing the 'nature' of childhood. *Childhood, 18*(4), 420–433. doi:10.1177/0907568211404951

Taylor, A., Pacini-Ketchabaw, V., & Blaise, M. (2012). Children's relation to the more-than-human world. *Contemporary Issues in Early Childhood, 13*(2), 81–85. doi:10.2304/ciec.2012.13.2.81

Tesar, M., & Arndt, S. (2018). Posthuman childhoods: Questions concerning quality. In M. Bloch, B. Swadener, & G. Cannella (Eds.), *Reconceptualizing early childhood education and care: Foundational debates, new imaginaries, and social action/activism* (2nd ed., pp. 113–129). New York, NY: Peter Lang.

Tesar, M., Rodriguez, S., & Kupferman, D. (2016). Philosophy and pedagogy of childhood, adolescence and youth. *Global Studies of Childhood, 6*(2), 169–176. doi: 10.1177/2043610616647623

CHAPTER 13

The theoretical foundations of *Te Whāriki* and the *Early Years Learning Framework*: Enduring and living or capturing fossilised practices?

Marilyn Fleer

Introduction

This chapter presents a critical comparison of the theoretical lenses that inform *Te Whāriki* (Ministry of Education, 2017) in Aotearoa New Zealand and the *Early Years Learning Framework* (*EYLF*) (Department of Education, Employment and Workplace Relations, 2009) in Australia. Specifically, the analysis presented will foreground the theories that have informed each curriculum, the challenges that this brings, and how the teacher/educator is positioned.

The literature has always celebrated *Te Whāriki* as a substantial early childhood curriculum of great importance (Blaiklock, 2017; Hedges, Peterson, & Wajskop, 2018), and its influence can be seen early on in Australia (see A. Roantree, ACT Department of Education and Community Services, personal communication, 2000; Wilks, Nyland, Chancellor, & Elliot, 2008), Denmark (Olsen, 1996, cited in Carr & May, 2000), Germany (Keesing-Styles, 2002) and Norway (Sobstad, 1997, cited in Carr & May, 2000). Although curriculum writers look for different things when analysing curricula (McLachlan, Fleer, & Edwards, 2018), there has been sufficient sustained interest in *Te Whāriki* for international researchers to ask why this document has been so enduring, as well as wondering if the core values and principles are retained in the updated 2017 version (Ministry of Education, 2017).

The original 1993 draft version of *Te Whāriki* only remained in circulation for 3 years, and the substantial reference list never made it into production for the 1996 curriculum (Hedges, 2011). But a streamlined reference list has re-emerged in the revised 2017 document, like a shadow from the past.

The many voices of the early childhood community and the diversity of views of child development and practice appear to be reflected within the revised version (Ministry of Education, 2017). The original *Te Whāriki* (Ministry of Education, 1996) grew out of a particular cultural and political context (see Duhn, 2006; McLachlan 2011; Mitchell, 2011; Ritchie, 2011; Te One & Ewens, Chapter 2 this volume) and provided a new theoretical direction for early childhood education for the whole of Aotearoa New Zealand (McLachlan, 2011; Rameka, 2011; Ritchie, 2008, 2011; Ritchie & Buzzelli, 2012; White, 2011). The revised 2017 version of *Te Whāriki* continues to foreground its original theoretical roots but has expanded its use of the concept of working theories (see Hedges, 2010; 2011; Hedges & Cullen, 2005). It also foregrounds kaupapa Māori theory, Bronfenbrenner's bioecological theory, Pasifika approaches/worldviews, and critical theories.

Over many years, the community has been exposed to a curriculum of some sophistication, incorporating broadly based concepts. This has meant that an ongoing dialogue around the particularities had to take place within the field if implementation of its intent was to be successful (see Cullen, 1996; Dalli, 2011). But also, dialogue was needed to grow the foundational concepts, as practices evolved through further research and the professional learning of teachers (Hedges & Cooper, 2018). It is through dialogue that a curriculum becomes a living document and reaches out into the professional community, giving new perspectives to practice, such that "individuals and centres develop their own curriculum pattern through a process of talk, reflection, planning, evaluation and assessment" (Carr & May, 2000, p. 59). This dialogue has been actively fostered through many innovations, including research programmes and resources (Meade, 2007), as well as ongoing professional development of Aotearoa New Zealand's teachers. However, as noted by Duhn (2006), "*Te Whaariki's* effectiveness as a progressive curriculum depends on teachers' interpretation of it" (p. 196), and on opportunities for engaging in collaborative research and professional learning (see Hedges, 2011) to afford deeper understanding (Hedges, 2014; Hedges & Cooper, 2018). As was noted for the 1996 version, and as is still relevant for the 2017 document, Cullen (2008) has stated that:

> Because *Te Whāriki* is principled rather than prescriptive it relies heavily on teacher qualities to guide teaching practices. Hence it attracts an ideological commitment from teachers, rather than a primary focus on programmes that are grounded in evidence of children's learning. (p. 10)

Even as the revised version is introduced into practice, it is important to be mindful of longstanding comments, such as suggested by Duhn (2006), that "As a teaching tool, *Te Whaariki* has been widely accepted without much criticism or even

13: The theoretical foundations of *Te Whāriki* and the *Early Years Learning Framework*:
Enduring and living or capturing fossilised practices?

critical engagement" (p. 191). Alvestad, Duncan, and Berge (2009) have argued that a reliance on the "Principles and Strands can run the risk of teachers simply repeating and reinforcing their traditional practice" (p. 12). Yet recently, it has been suggested that much of the reputational foundations that form the basis of *Te Whāriki* could be flawed, as it is claimed that "insufficient attention to empirical information about children's learning and in some cases, appear to be based on opinion rather than evidence" (Blaiklock, 2017, p. 38). What is the empirical basis for the 2017 document? This is difficult to determine, because the reference list, like many curricula around the world, does not provide full detail of its evidence base. Rather it says that its evidence base is theoretically informed.

Historically, strong critiques have been made by scholars in Aotearoa New Zealand. Yet, these researchers also point to the importance of empirical support needed for the implementation of curriculum, but particularly for such a sophisticated curriculum framework as *Te Whāriki* (Alvestad, Duncan, & Berge, 2009; Hedges, Peterson, & Wajskop, 2018; McLaughlin, 2011).

This has resonance for curriculum development in Australia, where Sumsion et al. (2009) have argued that the *Early Years Learning Framework* (*EYLF*), with its streamlined form, also requires continued dialogue and ongoing expansion of the central concepts through research and theoretical scholarship. The *EYLF* is also a principled curriculum framework.

Researchers in Aotearoa New Zealand have highlighted not just the importance of teacher knowledge, but also the multi-theoretical foundations used (Hedges, 2011; Hedges & Cooper, 2018), whereby significant gains in practice have resulted from innovative and world-leading policies for supporting ongoing practice (see Alvestad et al., 2009).

Whilst it is not possible to examine the evidence base of *Te Whāriki*, an exploration of the foundational theories informing it is possible. Therefore the question is asked: What theoretical foundations have informed the 2017 *Te Whāriki*? What is learned is discussed in relation to the theories informing the *EYLF* in order to better understand the theoretical basis of each document. This chapter does not position one curriculum framework above another, but rather seeks to learn from the experiences of Aotearoa New Zealand as Australia moves towards revisions in the future. Through highlighting the theories used to frame these curricula, both countries benefit.

Methodological note

The analysis undertaken and reported in this chapter treats curriculum documents, and the curriculum writers' papers and other authors' work, as data. A search of available writings on *Te Whāriki* was undertaken, and from this pool, articles related to both the longstanding and recent thinking of authors from Aotearoa New Zealand were selected. In particular, papers that presented a Māori perspective, those that discussed theoretical underpinnings, and those that detailed the curriculum's developmental processes were examined more closely. Some articles duplicated what had been said elsewhere and were not used. The 1993 draft, the 1996 and the 2017 curricula were carefully considered in the context of the theories that informed these versions. Since the revised document has only been in circulation since 2017, longstanding references are heavily drawn upon to support the broad critique and to show the historical chronology of key ideas and research that emerged over time.

I acknowledge that as a researcher from outside Aotearoa New Zealand it will never be possible for me to fully understand the context in which *Te Whāriki* evolved, or indeed to appreciate the importance of one article above another from an insider's perspective. Yet I have followed the literature on *Te Whāriki* closely. As a result, some articles that are important, or weighted more highly by particular scholars within Aotearoa New Zealand, may not appear to an outsider to hold the same significance. Nevertheless, ethnographic research has demonstrated over the years that an outsider's perspective may offer some new insights compared to those who live in a culture, and who may no longer see aspects of the fabric of their existence or historical background.

A static document within a dynamic research context

It is the authors and the academy who give life to broadly framed curriculum documents, expanding and re-theorising *Te Whāriki* through their published work. This is also pertinent to the *EYLF*. The dynamics between a static document and an ever-growing research context, are represented below in Figure 13.1 as *spheres of control*, where government sanctioning determines the final product (government control) but where the academy continues to engage in dialogue about the intent and directions of the original curriculum (academy control). The external sphere of the academy in partnership with practice is what keeps the document as a living curriculum. The central circle depicts a static and unchanging document, while the outer circle shows an expansive zone that continues to change with research, practice, and theoretical scholarship. With this expansive reading of curricula across both countries as living documents, it becomes possible to see why the 1996 *Te Whāriki* evolved into the 2017 *Te Whāriki*. Like Aotearoa New Zealand, Australia has kept in circulation the 2009 curriculum even though the evidence base continues to grow beyond the original development of the curriculum. But what were the original foundations that have endured in *Te Whāriki*, and why do they matter? Are there synergies with the nature of curriculum development in Australia? These questions are explored further below.

13: The theoretical foundations of *Te Whāriki* and the *Early Years Learning Framework*: Enduring and living or capturing fossilised practices?

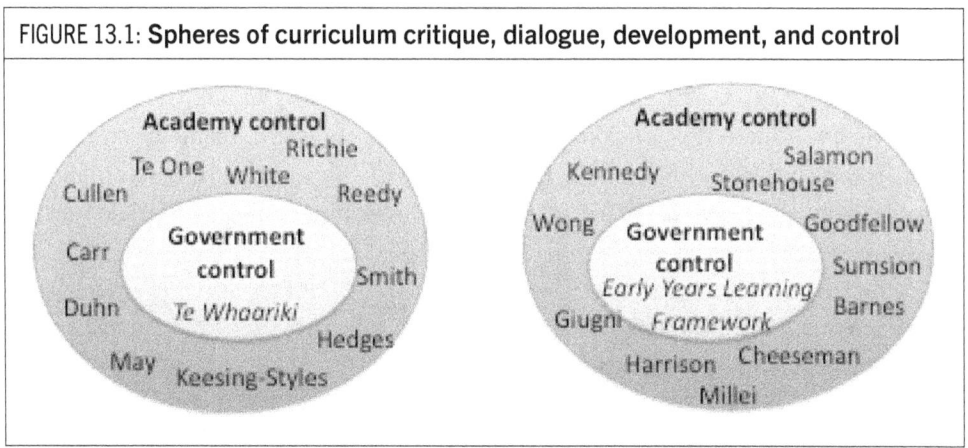

FIGURE 13.1: **Spheres of curriculum critique, dialogue, development, and control**

Curriculum longevity or has it passed its use-by date?

In order to achieve the goals of this chapter, it is important to return to the original conceptualisation of *Te Whāriki* and to learn why scholars thought the curriculum was so important. Longstanding commentary in Aotearoa New Zealand suggests that,

> *Te Whāriki* marked a milestone for early childhood education in Aotearoa/New Zealand. Not only was it the first national curriculum for the sector, but it was also the first national curriculum to 'represent and reflect Māori politics and pedagogy' (Te One, 2003, p. 24 cited in Duhn, 2006, p. 195)

The *EYLF* in Australia was also the first national curriculum for early childhood professionals. Prior to this a diversity of curricula were used across most states and territories. *Te Whāriki* was developed much earlier than the *EYLF*, yet in Aotearoa New Zealand the 1996 document took until 2017 before it was revised. So why was this so? Will Australia face this curriculum longevity? Most curricula around the world only have a shelf life of about 5 years before there is a period of renewal (McLachlan et al., 2018). Why did it take 20 years for a revised curriculum to emerge? The answer lies in the theoretical genealogy of the original draft.

Theoretical genealogy

Back in 2007 White et al. wrote that "The eclectic theoretical underpinnings of *Te Whaariki* reflect Aotearoa New Zealand's diverse society" (p. 94) and in 2000 Carr and May acknowledged that the theoretical roots of the 1996 curriculum were informed not only by local and cultural informants, but also by sociocultural and ecological theoretical frameworks. They assembled 10 pages of "annotated footnotes and references from the national and international literature" (Carr & May, 2000, pp. 60–61). Examples include: Bronfenbrenner, 1979; Claxton, 1990; Donaldson, 1978; Donaldson, Grieve, &

Pratt, 1983; Gardner, 1983; Paley, 1990; Piaget & Inhelder, 1969; Schweinhart, Barnes, & Weikart, 1993; Tizard, 1986; Vygotsky, 1978; and Wells, 1987. These references support the claim made later by the authors that 1996 *Te Whāriki* was genuinely located within the international literature as a voice guiding, framing, and legitimising the curriculum (see Carr & May, 1993a, 1993b, 1994, 1996, 1997, 2000). Interestingly, an examination of footnotes within the 1996 *Te Whāriki* suggest that developmentally appropriate practice (Bredekamp, 1987) was also influential. For example:

> The Early childhood curriculum—
> - Humanly appropriate experiences
> - Nationally appropriate experiences
> - Culturally appropriate experiences
> - Developmentally appropriate experiences
> - Individually appropriate experiences
> - Educationally appropriate experiences.
>
> (Ministry of Education, 1993, n.p.)

Yet others have suggested that the primary perspective of 1996 *Te Whāriki* is socio-cultural, as observed by Cullen (2001) when she stated that "*Te Whaariki*, the early childhood education curriculum, has come to be viewed as a socio-cultural curriculum" (Cullen, 2001, p. 1); and as noted by Ritchie in 2002:

> The theoretical base to the document can be situated within the wider arena of socio-cultural educational theory, as espoused by Wertsch (1995a), Rogoff (1990, 1995, 1998) and others. (Ritchie, 2002, p. 32)

Similarly, Hedges (2010) states that the draft and 1996 "curriculum draws on multiple theoretical perspectives but has been recently interpreted largely from a socio-cultural perspective ..." (p. 300). In the original draft, references to the work of Vygotsky can be found in the extended footnote at the back of the document. What can be learned from a study of the original genealogy of the theoretical foundations of the draft and 1996 curricula? *Te Whāriki* was internationally unique because it went beyond Developmentally Appropriate Practice conventions and brought to life other theoretical frames to guide curriculum development. With this theoretical backdrop, what theoretical remnants remain in the 2017 curriculum?

Different to previous iterations of curriculum development in Aotearoa New Zealand, the 2017 version of *Te Whāriki* has three pages devoted to the theories and approaches that underpin the curriculum. What is the same is that Bronfenbrenner, Vygotsky, and kaupapa Māori are explicitly mentioned. No longer is it necessary to trace the theoretical foundations from the draft to the 1996 version or to examine the footnotes or to read how scholars discuss *Te Whāriki* when identifying what underpins

13: The theoretical foundations of *Te Whāriki* and the *Early Years Learning Framework*: Enduring and living or capturing fossilised practices?

the document. The foundations are explicitly discussed (see Table 13.1) as models, approaches, and theories. Specifically, it is argued that the principles within *Te Whāriki* "are a synthesis of traditional Māori thinking and sociocultural theorising…" (Ministry of Education, 2017, p. 60) that foreground empowerment/whakamana, holistic development/kotahitanga, family and community/whānau tangata, and relationships/ngā hononga. Table 13.1 briefly summarises the interpretations of theory found in the 2017 *Te Whāriki*.

TABLE 13.1: **Diversity of theories informing practice in Aotearoa New Zealand**

FOUNDATIONAL THEORY	INTERPRETATIONS OF THEORY FOR INFORMING PRACTICE
Bioecological model	Drawn from Urie Bronfenbrenner's "ecological systems model", it is argued in *Te Whāriki* (Ministry of Education, 2017) that the "nested contexts and relationships of family, community, and wider local, national and global influences" explain the process of wellbeing and development of the child (p. 60). *Teachers/Kaiako are challenged* to "recognise that children's worlds are rapidly changing and connected across time" (Ministry of Education, 2017, p. 61). Its focus is on the "reciprocal individual–environmental influences that drive learning and development" (p. 61).
Sociocultural theories	Recognising the theories of child development developed by Lev Vygotsky and elaborated by Jerome Bruner, *Te Whāriki* (Ministry of Education, 2017) foregrounds learning, developmental, and environmental factors. In this framing, thinking and language come from everyday life, and where the nature of individual and social action develops in relation to the child's culture. *Teachers/kaiako have a key role* in developing children's learning, recognising the importance of cultural materials, artefacts and tools, signs and societal symbols, and having deep knowledge of language and child development.
Kaupapa Māori theory	Situated within land, culture, history, kaupapa Māori theory is derived from Māori ways of knowing and being. Māori knowledge, language, and culture in the curriculum support "Māori to achieve educational success as Māori" (Ministry of Education, 2017, p. 61). It would appear that teachers/kaiako are enablers of language and culture driven by whānau, hapu, and iwi understandings.
Pasifika approaches	Pasifika approaches in Aotearoa New Zealand draw upon "different ethnic-specific ways of knowing and being" (Ministry of Education, 2017, p. 62) but where the values of respect and reciprocity position children as treasures and the hope of the future. It would appear that teaching is a shared cultural practice of all members of the aiga / extended family.
Critical theories	Critical theories in *Te Whāriki* foreground the examination of social conditions, global influences, and equity of opportunity in relation to children's learning and development. Teachers have a key role in promoting "equitable practices with children, parents and whānau" (Ministry of Education, 2017, p. 62).

(cont'd)

Emerging research and theory	Foregrounded in *Te Whāriki* is a growing body of research that has examined the development of infant brains as they biologically mature. Central here is how the interaction between neuroscience and the studies of gene-environment interaction have highlighted how genes switch on or off in relation to how a child enters into and experiences their environment.
	It is suggested in *Te Whāriki* that studies of this interaction are "providing evidence for how children's biological foundations interact with specific aspects of the environment during development and how brain development can be nurtured by high-quality early learning environments" (Ministry of Education, 2017, p. 62). This matters for the role of the teacher.

When the content of Table 13.1 is considered in the context of the genealogy of *Te Whāriki*, new understandings emerge about what now matters in Aotearoa New Zealand. What is different is that voice is given strongly to Pasifika approaches, critical theories, and neuroscience and gene activation research. This suggests that theoretical plurality is actively promoted and made visible in *Te Whāriki*, rather than covertly embedded. Further evidence of this plurality in 2017 *Te Whāriki* can be seen in how the role of the teacher differs depending upon the theoretical lens used to guide early childhood practices for supporting children's learning and development. The role of the teachers/kaiako is captured in Table 13.1.

Theoretical plurality made visible or covertly embedded?

Regardless of how theory is positioned within curriculum—explicit or covert—it is the early childhood teacher who must operationalise the document. How are they to make sense of theoretical plurality? Questions posed include, should I adopt one theory of child development? Are there many theories of child development that need to be used to guide practice? Should the theories be merged? The issue of theory has also been prevalent in the longstanding writing about the 1996 version. For instance, Nuttall (2003) signals how socio-cultural theory (Wertsch, 1995a) becomes merged with constructivist theory when naming these as one theoretical approach:

> The socio-cultural constructivist bases of *Te Whāriki* mean that it is up to teachers ... (Nuttall, 2003, p. 3)

Further, Ritchie (2002), in drawing upon the uniqueness of the Māori perspective in the 1996 *Te Whāriki*, also highlighted some of the original tensions when she stated that early childhood teachers would be "working at the level of family/whānau rather than being solely child-focused" (Ritchie, 2002, p. 36), where the latter (child-focused) approach was historically more constructivist-driven. Ritchie acknowledges the importance of the collective rather than concentrating always on the individual. The tension between a developmental perspective and a cultural-

13: The theoretical foundations of *Te Whāriki* and the *Early Years Learning Framework*: Enduring and living or capturing fossilised practices?

historical (Vygotsky, 1998) or socio-cultural (Wertsch, 1995b) view was played out early, as noted by Nuttall (2003) when she described the range of theories invoked by a group of teachers in her doctoral research:

> References to theories of development included: 'So that's cooperative play' (stage theories); a comment about a child's 'phobia' (psychodynamic theory); and 'I'd like to put [on the planning sheet] … gender awareness. Non-gender specific roles' (gender theory). Some general principles in early childhood curriculum implementation were also discussed; 'Yes, but it's quite different from primary or secondary where they are set curriculum' (curriculum theory); 'areas' of play (based on Piagetian, free-play approaches); 'core curriculum'; and the general issue of striking a balance between 'teacher directed' (behaviourist) approaches, and 'ideas emerging from the children' (constructivist approaches). At another meeting, the same group referred to theories of applied behaviour analysis, including discussing the kinds of 'treats' they might offer as 'rewards' to compliant children. (Nuttall, 2003, p. 9)

And, as Duhn (2006) also wrote about in relation to the 1996 version:

> *Te Whaariki*'s reputation as a progressive early childhood curriculum rests particularly on its ability to accommodate diverse perspectives. For example, *Te Whaariki* promotes both universal and socioculturally specific approaches to early years education through its commitment to key theorists from developmental psychology as well as from sociocultural perspectives. (Duhn, 2006, p. 196)

The 1996 *Te Whāriki* paved the way for moving the discourse of early childhood education from a universal perspective of "developmental" (Dahlberg, Moss, & Pence, 1999). But as Hedges (2010) originally noted teachers can have difficulties in "appropriating a new theoretical discourse (sociocultural theory), when they have been embedded in another (developmental psychology) that mediates understanding of the new theory" (p. 308). This difficulty was not specific to Aotearoa New Zealand. It emerged over the same period in Australia (see Fleer, 2010; Fleer & Richardson, 2004). In Australia, the *EYLF* actively advocates for using a broad range of theories, and according to Giugni (2011) this invites deliberate theoretical musing when drawing upon the *EYLF*:

> I deliberately explored my practice first and then turned to the *EYLF* to begin mapping: firstly mapping my practices against the *EYLF* and secondly mapping the *EYLF* against my practice. This afforded me the opportunity to look for the 'leakages' (Deleuze, 1993) that trickled out between the dominant discourses of early childhood that produce the *EYLF* and those I was enacting in my practice. (Giugni, 2011, p. 13)

Theoretical complexity has been designed into the *EYLF* and is evident in the 2017 *Te Whāriki* in Aotearoa New Zealand. The complexity of *Te Whāriki* and of the *EYLF* arises because of the range of theoretical perspectives that are presented in one document. Back in 1996, and again in 2001 and 2008, Cullen argued that many teachers originally did not have the necessary theoretical knowledge to fully appreciate the complexity of *Te Whāriki*, and therefore to make use of the document as intended by its authors. Because *Te Whāriki* was written to take account both of local voices and of the international literature, some discordance can be found, such as when the importance of the individual and the importance of the collective are considered. The disjunction between individual and collective could, however, be viewed as an important professional learning opportunity for examining what Duhn (2006) has called the "meadows in between". The *EYLF* also affords this challenge, one that the authors have embraced as important for helping professionalise the field (see Sumsion & Wong, 2011). White (2011) nicely captures the ongoing challenges faced by the field, through positioning the curriculum as a contested document when she says:

> Taking the view of curriculum as a constant ideological battle between order and certainty versus dissensus and disruption makes it possible to engage with and highlight practices and their underlying orientations that are lodged somewhere within the living curriculum. (p. 2)

The shift in curriculum design in Aotearoa New Zealand has signalled a movement away from focusing only on the child and their interests to considering culture as the focus. For instance, from a cultural-historical perspective (Vygotsky, 1987), curriculum is underpinned by the view that children learn with and use the community's tools for thinking and learning. As such, the community's tools become the focus, not just what is of interest to the child (see also Hedges, 2010). One of the interesting features of *Te Whāriki* is the way in which the authors have retained a more community-oriented view of the child's interest through incorporating wellbeing/mana atua, belonging/mana whenua, contribution/mana tangata, communication/mana reo, and exploration/mana aotūroa.

As has been shown by Hedges (2011) and White (2011), teachers are now in a stronger position to manage the diversity of theories that inform curriculum and curriculum implementation, and the huge investment in research and professional learning in Aotearoa New Zealand (McLachlan, 2011) has had a significant impact on teacher engagement with new theories and practices (e.g., Meade, 2007). Table 13.1 is illustrative of this theoretical diversity, but in ways that recognises that when using a particular lens, the role of the teacher will be different. This is an important development in the revision of *Te Whāriki* in Aotearoa New Zealand. The role of the teacher in relation to the theoretical lens adopted is explicitly captured in the 2017 curriculum, whilst it is absent in the *EYLF*.

13: The theoretical foundations of *Te Whāriki* and the *Early Years Learning Framework*:
Enduring and living or capturing fossilised practices?

Theoretical plurality in early childhood curriculum in Australia

Like *Te Whāriki* in Aotearoa New Zealand, the *EYLF* explicitly advocates "Different theories about early childhood [in order to] inform approaches to children's learning and development" (Department of Education, Employment and Workplace Relations, 2009, p. 11). In Australia, educators draw upon a diverse range of theories to inform their work (Sumsion et al., 2009), including critical and poststructural perspectives, as well as developmental, cultural-historical and socio-behavioural theories of children's development (see Salamon, 2011) to open up multiple possibilities (see also Goodfellow, 2009).

The diversity of theories that are acknowledged in the *EYLF* is shown in Table 13.2 (with some text drawn from Department of Education, Employment and Workplace Relations, 2009, p. 11). What is immediately evident from this summary is the broad spectrum of theories now used within the field and in the academy. Blaise (2009) has coined the term "postdevelopmental", which is useful in an analysis of the *EYLF*. A deliberate aim in the *EYLF is* to foreground both developmental and post-developmental theories. As a result of the writers making explicit these theories in the document, the field has engaged in discussion, professional learning, resource development, reading of publications, and explanations of what these theories might mean for planning children's learning and development. Giugni (2011) suggests that the *EYLF* "call[s] for early childhood educators to engage with theory in their everyday practice" (p. 11) and that it challenges them to explicitly choose theories "as a way to talk about practice in new ways" (p. 13). This is directly in line with Ritchie (2008), who suggests that the original *Te Whāriki* is a tool to engage teachers in new ways with their practices.

TABLE 13.2: **Diversity of theories informing practice in Australia**

FOUNDATIONAL THEORY	INTERPRETATIONS OF THEORY FOR INFORMING PRACTICE
Developmental theories	The focus is on describing and understanding the process of change, usually framed around age or stages of predetermined development. Traditional child development domains are usually foregrounded (e.g., social-emotional, cognitive, language, physical).
	"[in a] developmental discourse of early childhood education, the teacher is positioned as someone who sets up developmentally appropriate experiences and provides children with choices and the opportunity to take some authority over their learning. The teacher is a facilitator of children's learning through play. However, within a feminist post-structuralist disclosure, the early childhood teacher is positioned as an interventionist; a teacher 'who takes a proactive and explicit political stance with children against social inequities' (Ryan & Oshner, 1999, p. 15)." (Ortlipp, Arthur, & Woodrow, 2011, p. 57)

Socio-behaviourist theories	"Focus on the role of experience as shaping behaviour." (Department of Education, Employment and Workplace Relations, 2009, p. 11)
Sociocultural or cultural-historical theories	*Sociocultural* is the label usually applied when drawing upon North American research and scholarship (e.g., Wertsch, 1995b); cultural-historical is the term used when drawing upon Russian scholarship and research (e.g., Vygotsky, 1987). "Processes of change foreground cultural development through children's social situation of development in families and other community interactions and relationships." (Department of Education, Employment and Workplace Relations, 2009, p. 11) Ortlipp et al. (2011) state that "Early childhood teachers who see themselves as someone who 'scaffolds' children's learning, someone who works with children within their 'zone of proximal development' and leads children's learning rather than following it can be seen to be taking up socio-cultural discourses of education and the subject positions made available within those discourses." (pp. 57–58)
Critical theories	"Invite teachers to challenge assumptions about curriculum, and consider how their decisions may affect children differently." (Department of Education, Employment and Workplace Relations, 2009, p. 11)
Post-structuralist theories	These theories offer insights into issues of power, equity, and social justice in early childhood settings. Millei and Sumsion (2011) give the example that in earlier drafts of the *Early Years Learning Framework* (citing Department of Education, Employment and Workplace Relations, 2008, p. 8) "the document [creates] a 'space for politics and power relations, [problematising through the curriculum] where children are excluded on the basis of gender, age, size, skin colour, proficiency with English, class, ethnicity, sexuality and more' (p. 8). It [the *Early Years Learning Framework*] prescribes that the role of the educator is to 'work with children to challenge power assumptions and create play experiences that promote equity, fairness and justice" (p. 8). (Millei & Sumsion, 2011, p. 74)

These theories are incorporated within the document to serve as tools to help early childhood educators in their thinking about and planning for child development and learning, and can be loosely divided into developmental and post-developmental theories. Developmental theories include those theories that use age as a central criterion for defining development (e.g., milestones), where the child's development is usually understood as divided into particular domains (social-emotional, language, physical, etc), and where the process of maturation drives a child's development. It is generally acknowledged in Australia that this view of child development is limiting and out of date. Extensive critique and discussion of this theory were undertaken within the field quite some time ago, and these arguments are well known to most.

Post-developmental theories now appear to be of interest to the field (see Fleer, 2013), but are probably less well understood. Post-developmental theories include a sociocultural (Wertsch, 1995a, 1995b) or cultural-historical (Vygotsky, 1998) view of child development (see Peers, 2011), critical theory, and poststructuralist theory.

13: The theoretical foundations of *Te Whāriki* and the *Early Years Learning Framework*: Enduring and living or capturing fossilised practices?

Sociocultural theory is generally well known within the field, but critical theory and poststructuralist theory are only known to some. For instance, in a study by Fleer (2013) of 239 early childhood teachers from the south-eastern part of Australia, it was found that of those who predominantly followed one theory of child development to support their view of play, 65% of these drew upon sociocultural or cultural-historical theory, 12% used Piaget's theorising to guide their work, 12% used poststructuralist theory, 8% drew upon socio-behaviourist theory, and 3% used behaviourism. However, it was interesting that, of the total number of respondents, 34% drew upon multiple theories as advocated in the *EYLF*; indeed, among those who strongly advocated for one theory, 10 respondents indicated that they had leanings towards other theories for other aspects of their work.

When these figures are compared with Nuttall's (2003) earlier work in Aotearoa New Zealand, and with the discussions put forward by Duhn (2006) and Ritchie (2008), it can be argued that even though teachers in Australia have not had a national curriculum to guide their practices over the past 20 years, there is a familiarity with contemporary theories of child development, auguring well for the uptake of the *EYLF*. Furthermore, the *EYLF*, with its focus on a diversity of child development theories, has acted as a catalyst for teachers to re-engage in discussions about theory. Here we see a parallel in Aotearoa New Zealand, where teachers engage with a diversity of theories.

At national forums during the development of the *EYLF*, the authors of the framework publicly stated they did not espouse one particular model of child development to inform curriculum design; rather, a diversity of theories was supported. This is in line with what has emerged from the implementation of *Te Whāriki* over the past 20 years. The *EYLF*, as a poststructuralist document, does not claim to support one theoretical approach and resists a singular regime of theoretical truth (Sumsion et al., 2009); by default it supports a poststructuralist stance. Earlier versions of the document support this claim (see Millei & Sumsion, 2011; Sumsion & Wong, 2011). For instance, in a thoughtful deconstruction of the *EYLF* (interrogating the concept of "belonging"), Sumsion and Wong (2011) state that:

> It takes as its starting point the premise that the questions asked of curriculum and the contexts of curricular development and implementation are fundamental to curriculum scholarship—a view held by 'mainstream' (for example, Dillon, 2009) and critical (for example, Popkewitz, 2009; Apple, 2010) curriculum theorists alike. For the former, key questions of curriculum centre on 'who, whom, what, where, when, why, how, what results' (Dillon, 2009, p. 347). For the latter, questions of rationalities, discourses and silences are key. Hence curriculum theorists ask: Which discourses 'count'? What rationalities underpin these discourses? Where/what are the silences? What are their effects and implications? (Sumsion & Wong, 2011, p. 28)

Sumsion and Wong go on to suggest that during the curriculum development phase,

> A significant feature of that context was a requirement for the use of unrelentingly positive language in documents such as the EYLF. Such requirements leave little official space for the language of problematisation and critique. (2011, p. 38)

The shaping of *Te Whāriki* had similar beginnings (see Te One and Ewens, Chapter 2 this volume), leaving the job of critique until after the curriculum development phase (e.g., White, 2011). In Australia, we have self-critique of the *EYLF*, but as yet no discussion on its revision has been mooted by the field or by government.

Conclusion

As we have seen in both Australia and Aotearoa New Zealand, poststructuralist theory, post-colonial theory, and critical theory provide important tools for reflecting on practice and on curriculum development. They are useful tools for progressing and questioning knowledge generation within practice and within the academy. But these tools do not in and of themselves provide the field with a theory of child development. They have a different role, as has been concisely argued by Ritchie:

> Generating these shared spaces represents a movement beyond colonised binaries of coloniser/colonised subjectivities, yet at the same time operates in a place which remains deeply mindful of the pain and trauma still reflected profoundly in the negative social statistics of Māori (Ministry of Health, 2006) that is the ongoing legacy of colonisation. (Ritchie, 2008, p. 208)

When curriculum is viewed as an instrument of government for producing particular kinds of children (Duhn, 2006), or as a site for the problematisation and contestation of existing discourses and teacher identities (Ortlipp et al., 2011), post-developmental concepts become powerful tools for disrupting taken-for-granted practices. Here we see the spaces or "meadows" (Duhn, 2006) of dialogue emerging.

Both *Te Whāriki* and the *EYLF* support a diversity of views surrounding theories about children's development. Both include sociocultural/cultural-historical and critical theories for informing child development. Cultural-historical theory provides a theory of child development within each framework, and this allows teachers in Australia to actively replace longstanding developmental theories with a cultural-historical view of children's development. In Aotearoa New Zealand critique has occurred over 20 years, enriching both practice and research—where the role of the teacher is clearly different when a different theoretical lens is adopted by the teacher. In Australia, the role of the educator and the theoretical challenge of knowing what certain theories allow or do not allow, is still in the process of ongoing dialogue. But, teachers in Australia have as part of their toolkit poststructuralist theory for affording important new directions. It is the post curriculum development period in which authors in both countries continue to be in the "meadows in between" (Duhn, 2006), expanding the dialogue and leaving it to the field to go further than what is presented in each of the published curricula (White, 2011). Consequently, the changes in the 2017 curriculum are more about sharpening up the theoretical underpinnings than a substantial reworking of the document.

Is it possible that the curriculum developers in Aotearoa New Zealand took the safe option and did not substantially re-theorise the curriculum on purpose? Did they leave it to the academic community and to teachers to continue to refine, expand, and re-theorise *Te Whāriki?* Perhaps they sought to position scholars and teachers with agency to work on a living document. Or were there time constraints for realising a new vision? Could the risk of being safe mean fossilised practices may emerge in the field? Is it possible that there was a real fear of losing what was so treasured and enduring if the re-developed document turned into something completely new. Maybe the risk was too great. Nevertheless, the 2017 revised *Te Whāriki* will continue to act as a tool for guiding practices into the future—but only time will tell if the theories within *Te Whāriki* positions teachers as developing a living curriculum, or if the curriculum embeds fossilised practices within sedimentary layers dusted by time.

References

Alvestad, M., Duncan, J., & Berge, A. (2009). New Zealand early childhood education teachers talk about *Te Whāriki*. *New Zealand Journal of Teachers' Work, 6*(1), 3–19.

Blaise, M. (2009). "What a girl wants, what a girl needs!": Responding to sex, gender and sexuality in the early childhood classroom. *Journal of Research in Childhood Education, 33*(4), 450–461.

Blaiklock, K. (2017). What are children learning in early childhood education in New Zealand? *Australasian Journal of Early Childhood, 38*(2), 51–56.

Bredekamp, S. (Ed.). (1987). *Developmentally appropriate practice in early childhood programs serving children from birth through age 8*. Washington, DC: National Association for the Education of Young Children.

Bronfenbrenner, U. (1979). *The ecology of human development*. Cambridge, MA: Harvard University Press.

Carr, M. (2001). A sociocultural approach to learning orientation in an early childhood setting. *International Journal of Qualitative Studies in Education, 14*(4), 525–542.

Carr, M., & May, H. (1993a). Choosing a model: Reflecting on the development process of *Te Whaariki*, National early childhood curriculum guidelines in New Zealand. *International Journal of Early Years Education, 1*(3), 7–22.

Carr, M., & May, H. (1993b, February). *The role of government in early childhood curriculum in New Zealand*. Paper presented at the New Zealand Council for Educational Research invitational seminar, What is the Government's Role in Early Childhood Education?, Wellington.

Carr, M., & May, H. (1994). Weaving patterns: Developing national early childhood curriculum guidelines in Aotearoa–New Zealand. *Australian Journal of Early Childhood Education, 19*(1), 25–33.

Carr, M., & May, H. (1996). *Te Whāriki*, making a difference for the under fives?: The new national early childhood curricula. *Delta: Policy and Practice in Education, 48*(1), 101–112.

Carr, M., & May, H. (1997). Making a difference for the under-fives?: The early implementation of *Te Whaariki*, the New Zealand national early childhood curriculum. *International Journal of Early Years Education, 5*(3), 225–236.

Carr, M., & May, H. (2000). *Te Whāriki*: Curriculum voices. In H. Penn (Ed.), *Early childhood services: Theory, policy and practice* (pp. 53–73). Buckingham, UK: Open University Press.

Claxton, G. (1990). *Teaching to learn*. London, UK: Cassell.

Cullen, J. (1996). The challenge of *Te Whāriki* for future developments in early childhood education. *Delta: Policy and Practice in Education, 48*(1), 113–125.

Cullen, J. (2001, September). *Assessment dilemmas in a socio-cultural curriculum*. Keynote address to TRCC course on Assessment in Early Childhood, Wellington.

Cullen, J. (2008, December). *Outcomes of early childhood education: Do we know, can we tell, and does it matter?* Jean Herbison Lecture, presented at the New Zealand Australian Research Conference, Palmerston North.

Dahlberg, G., Moss, P., & Pence, A. (1999). *Beyond quality in early childhood education and care: Postmodern perspectives*. London, UK: Falmer Press.

Dalli, C. (2011). A curriculum of open possibilities: A New Zealand kindergarten teacher's view of professional practice. *Early Years: An International Journal of Research and Development, 31*(3), 229–243.

Department of Education, Employment and Workplace Relations. (2008). *Early years learning framework consultation*. Retrieved from http://www.vcaa.viceduau/vcaa/earlyyears/COAG_EYL_Framework20081113.pdf

Department of Education, Employment and Workplace Relations. (2009). *Early years learning framework*. Canberra, ACT: Commonwealth of Australia.

Deleuze, G. (1993). *The fold: Leibniz and the baroque*. Minneapolis, MN: University of Minnesota Press.

Donaldson, M. (1978). *Children's minds*. London, UK: Fontana/Collins.

Donaldson, M., Grieve, R., & Pratt, C. (Eds.). (1983). *Early childhood development and education*. Oxford, UK: Blackwell.

Duhn, I. (2006). The making of global citizens: Traces of cosmopolitanism in the New Zealand early childhood curriculum, *Te whaariki*. *Contemporary Issues in Early Childhood, 7*(3), 191–202.

Fleer, M. (2010). *Early learning and development: Cultural-historical concepts in play*. Cambridge, UK: Cambridge University Press.

Fleer, M. (2013). Re-theorising *play activities*: Making room for diverse *cultural expressions* of play. In O. F. Lillemyr, S. Dockett, & B. Perry (Eds.), *Perspectives on play and learning: Theory and research on early years' education*. (pp. 175–192). Charlotte, NC: Information Age Publishing.

Fleer, M., & Richardson, C. (2004). Moving from a constructivist-developmental framework for planning to a socio-cultural approach: Foregrounding the tension between individual and community. *Journal of Australian Research in Early Childhood Education, 10*(2), 70–87.

Gardner, H. (1983). *Frames of mind*. New York, NY: Basic Books.

Giugni, M. (2011). "Becoming worldly with": An encounter with the *Early years learning framework*. *Contemporary Issues in Early Childhood, 12*(1), 11–27.

Goodfellow, J. (2009). *The early years learning framework: Getting started*. Research in Practice series. Canberra, ACT: Early Childhood Australia.

13: The theoretical foundations of *Te Whāriki* and the *Early Years Learning Framework*: Enduring and living or capturing fossilised practices?

Hedges, H. (2010). Blurring the boundaries: Connecting research, practice and professional learning. *Cambridge Journal of Education, 40*(3), 299–314.

Hedges, H. (2011). Connecting 'snippets of knowledge': Teachers' understandings of the concept of working theories. *Early Years, 31*(3), 271–284. doi: 10.1080/09575146.2011.606206

Hedges, H. (2014). Young children's 'working theories': Building and connecting understandings. *Journal of Early Childhood Research, 12*(35), 35–49. doi: 10.1177/1476718X13515417

Hedges, H. & Cooper, M. (2018). Relational play-based pedagogy: theorising a core practice in early childhood education. *Teachers and Teaching, 24*(4), 369–383. doi: 10.1080/13540602.2018.1430564

Hedges, H., & Cullen, J. (2005). Subject knowledge in early childhood curriculum and pedagogy. *Contemporary Issues in Early Childhood, 6*(1), 66–79.

Hedges, H., Peterson, S., & Wajskop, G. (2018). Modes of play in early childhood curricular documents in Brazil, New Zealand and Ontario, *International Journal of Play, 7*(1), 11–26. doi: 10.1080/21594937.2018.1437379

Keesing-Styles, L. (2002). A critical pedagogy of early childhood education: The Aotearoa/New Zealand context. *New Zealand Research in Early Childhood Education, 5*, 109–122.

McLachlan, C. (2011). An analysis of New Zealand's changing history, policies and approaches to early childhood education. *Australasian Journal of Early Childhood, 36*(3), 36–44.

McLachlan, C., Fleer, M., & Edwards, S. (2018). *Early childhood curriculum: Planning, assessment and implementation* (3rd ed.). New York, NY: Cambridge University Press.

Meade, A. (2007). *Cresting the waves: Innovation in early childhood education.* Wellington: NZCER Press.

Millei, Z., & Sumsion, J. (2011). The 'work' of community in belonging, being and becoming: The early years learning framework for Australia. *Contemporary Issues in Early Childhood, 12*(1), 71–85.

Ministry of Education. (1993). *Te whāriki: Draft guidelines for developmentally appropriate programmes in early childhood services: He whāriki matauranga mo nga mokopuna o Aotearoa.* Wellington: Learning Media.

Ministry of Education. (1996). *Te whāriki: He whāriki mātauranga mō ngā mokopuna o Aotearoa: Early childhood curriculum.* Wellington: Learning Media.

Ministry of Education (2017). *Te whāriki: He whāriki mātauranga mō ngā mokopuna o Aotearoa: Early childhood curriculum.* Wellington: Author.

Mitchell, L. (2011). Enquiring teachers and democratic politics: Transformations in New Zealand's early childhood education landscape. *Early Years: An International Journal of Research and Development, 31*(3), 217–228.

Nuttall, J. (2003). *Influences on the co-construction of teacher role in early childhood curriculum: Some examples from a New Zealand childcare centre.* Unpublished paper.

Ortlipp, M., Arthur, L., & Woodrow, C. (2011). Discourses of the *Early years learning framework*: Constructing the early childhood professional. *Contemporary Issues in Early Childhood, 12*(1), 56–70.

Paley, V. (1990). *The boy who would be a helicopter.* Cambridge, MA: Harvard University Press.

Peers, C. (2011). *Contemporary theories in child development.* Melbourne, VIC: Monash University Professional Learning Program.

Piaget, J., & Inhelder, B. (1969). *The psychology of the child.* New York, NY: Basic Books.

Rameka, L. K. (2011). Being Māori: Culturally relevant assessment in early childhood education. *Early Years, 31*(3), 245–256. doi: 10.1080/09575146.2011.614222

Ritchie, J. (2002). Bicultural development: Innovation in implementation of *Te whaariki*. *Australian Journal of Early Childhood*, 27(2), 23–41.

Ritchie, J. (2008). Honouring Māori subjectivities within early childhood education in Aotearoa. *Contemporary Issues in Early Childhood*, 9(3), 202–210.

Ritchie, J. (2011). Ma wai he kapu ti?: Being, knowing and doing otherwise in early childhood education in Aotearoa. *International Critical Childhood Policy Studies*, 4(1), 86–106.

Ritchie, J. R., & Buzzelli, C. A. (2012). *Te whariki*: The early childhood curriculum of Aotearoa New Zealand. In N. File, J. J. Mueller, & D. B. Wisneski (Eds.), *Curriculum in early childhood education: Re-examined, rediscovered, renewed* (pp. 146–159). New York, NY: Routledge.

Salamon, A. (2011). How the *Early years learning framework* can help shift pervasive beliefs of the social and emotional capabilities of infants and toddlers. *Contemporary Issues in Early Childhood*, 12(1), 4–10.

Schweinhart, L. J., Barnes, H. V., & Weikart, D. P. (1993). *Significant benefits: The High Scope Perry pre-school study through age 27*. Ypsilanti, MI: High Scope Press.

Sumsion, J., Barnes, S., Cheeseman, S., Harrison, L., Kennedy, A. M., & Stonehouse, A. (2009). Insider perspectives on developing *Belonging, being and becoming: The early years learning framework for Australia*. *Australasian Journal of Early Childhood*, 34(4), 4–13.

Sumsion, J., & Wong, S. (2011). Interrogating 'belonging' in *Belonging, being and becoming: The early years learning framework for Australia*. *Contemporary Issues in Early Childhood*, 12(1), 28–45.

Tizard, B. (1986). *The care of young children: Implications of recent research*. Thomas Coram Research Unit working and occasional paper. London, UK: Thomas Coram Research Unit.

Vygotsky, L. S. (1978). *Mind in society*. Cambridge, MA: Harvard University Press.

Vygotsky, L .S. (1987). Thinking and speech. In R. W. Rieber & A. S. Carton (Eds., trans. N. Minick), *The collected works of L. S. Vygotsky, vol. 1* (pp. 39–285). New York, NY: Plenum Press.

Vygotsky, L. S. (1998). Child psychology. In R. W. Rieber (Ed., English translation, trans. M. J. Hall), *The collected works of L. S. Vygotsky, vol. 5*. New York, NY: Kluwer Academic and Plenum Publishers.

Wells, G. (1987). *The meaning makers: Children learning language and using language to learn*. London, UK: Hodder and Stoughton.

Wertsch, J. V. (1995a). The need for action in sociocultural research. In J. Wertsch, P. Del Rio, & A. Alvarez (Eds.), *Sociocultural studies of the mind*. (pp. 56–74). New York, NY: Cambridge University Press.

Wertsch, J. V. (1995b). *Vygotsky and the social formation of mind*. Cambridge, MA: Harvard University Press.

White, J. E. (2011). Dust under the whāriki: Embracing the messiness of curriculum. *Early Childhood Folio*, 15(1), 2–6.

White, J., O'Malley, A., Toso, M., Rockel, J., Stover, S., & Ellis, F. (2007). A contemporary glimpse of play and learning in Aotearoa New Zealand. *International Journal of Early Childhood*, 39, 93–105.

Wilks, A., Nyland, B., Chancellor, B., & Elliott, S. (2008). *An analysis of curriculum/learning frameworks for the early years (birth to age 8)*. East Melbourne, VIC: State of Victoria Department of Education and Early Childhood Development and Victorian Curriculum and Assessment Authority. Retrieved from http://www.dewr.gov.au/EarlyChildhood/OfficeOfEarlyChildhood/sqs/Docuemnts/AnalysisofCurriclum_LearningFrameworksfortheEarly.pdf

CHAPTER 14

Te Whāriki and the Nordic model
Comments on *Te Whāriki* from a Norwegian and Danish perspective

Stig Broström

Introduction

This chapter presents some central dimensions from the Nordic educational model, with special reference to Norwegian and Danish curricula, and relates these to *Te Whāriki* in order to put central educational ideas into perspective. The chapter has three parts. An introduction is provided about the educational roots of the so-called Nordic model of education, with a short outline of the model itself. The second part elaborates the Nordic model with Denmark and Norway as illustrative examples, and reflects on questions about democracy, children's active influence, children's perspectives, and the concept of 'Bildung'. The third part discusses *Te Whāriki* from the Nordic educational perspective.

During the last decades, we have seen a shift internationally in early childhood education towards a more learning-oriented educational tradition. Until the middle of the 1990s, early childhood education and life in preschool in most countries were characterised by a child-centred and play-oriented approach. This approach allows children to make choices about what they will do, explore, and learn, while teachers create a supporting environment. This approach is rooted in a tradition that reaches back to Rousseau, Pestalozzi, and Froebel, and was reformulated by a critical progressive wave early in the 20th century. Together, these approaches emphasise play, self-governed activity, self-development, and comprehensive development. These concepts draw on developmental psychology, which has formed the base for the development of early childhood education in the Nordic countries for almost a century. Based on humanistic psychology in general, pedagogues embrace the idea that a combination of a rich environment and the child's own activity provides the best opportunities for the child's comprehensive development, understood as an externalisation of the child's self (Kragh-Müller, 2017).

However, the child also has to interact with adults who are able to understand the child, interpret their needs and, in accordance with these, create an environment through which the child can act and develop themself; that is to say, a recognisable adult to whom the child has a secure attachment (Stern, 1985; Howes & Hamilton, 1992; Cassidy, Jones, & Shaver, P.R., 2013). The pedagogue or kindergarten teacher[1] expresses care defined through an equal relationship, a subject–subject relation and both parties must contribute "[a] connection in which each party feels something towards the other" (Noddings, 1992, p. 15). The teacher expresses a caring attitude and the recipient accepts the care. In order to obtain a subject-subject relation, or I–thou relation (Buber, 1958), the caretaker has to express a specific emotional and appreciative relationship to the recipient (Noddings, 1984) and also create spacious interactional patterns (Bae, 2012).

With reference to the OECD (2001, 2006) *Starting Strong* papers, this Nordic orientation is called "the social pedagogy approach" or "the Nordic model", characterised by concepts such as care, relation, activity, and development, which are local, child-centred, and holistic (Greve & Hansen, 2017; Ringsmose & Kragh-Müller, 2016; Wagner 2006; Wagner & Einarsdóttir, 2008). This contradicts a more recent "early education approach" with its centralising and academic strategy towards curriculum, teaching, learning, content, and methodology.

This longstanding Nordic tradition, as well as its actual practice, was criticised in the Nordic countries during the 1990s for moving towards an exaggeratedly self-governed approach, where teachers only interact in small-scale ways with the children in order to support their learning and development (Vejleskov, 1997). Because it was considered that this Nordic child-oriented approach might compromise children's learning, this model was discussed and reformed during the last decades of the 20th century.

Implementation of Nordic curricula for early years education and care

Consequently, the Nordic countries, like most European countries, have devised and implemented published preschool curricula (Broström & Wagner, 2003). The Danish curriculum was implemented in 2004 (Socialministeriet, 2004), the Norwegian curriculum in 1995 (Barne og familiedepartementet, 1995), the Swedish

---

[1] In Denmark, we use the word pedagogue instead of preschool teacher, and in Norway the word preschool teacher is replaced by the word kindergarten teacher [barnehagelærer]. This wording signals that education in preschool is different from what happens in school and also reflects an official stand against schoolification. However, because the other Nordic countries use the word preschool teacher, I here use the word "teacher" for the Nordic preschool teachers as well as for kaiako, the professionals in New Zealand.

curriculum in 1998 (Ministry of Education [Sweden], 1996), and likewise *Te Whāriki* (Ministry of Education, 1996). The Nordic curricula express the same understanding of "wholeness" where democracy, play, care, and learning are integrated. Such an approach, where care and education are balanced and integrated, is named educare (Broström, 2006a). In addition, an analysis of these curricula shows that democracy, caring, and education (learning and competences) are embedded and expressed as value fields in the educational policies of all the Nordic countries (Einarsdottir, Purola, Johansson, Broström, & Emilson, 2014). Thus, the policies call for an environment based on democratic principles that is caring *and* facilitates children's learning.

The implementation of curriculum in preschool at that time (the end of the 1990s) was a big change, marked by a decrease of the dominance of psychological perspectives in favour of an educational approach; one might talk about a "didactical turn", as questions about the educational goals, objectives, and content related to children's learning became central.

In the Nordic countries, this first wave of curriculum operated with rather open and wide goals, which the teachers themselves could define in relation to specific children. The Swedish curriculum emphasises that the goals should mark a direction for the child and point out something to *strive* for. The educational content too had an open character in the form of a number of themes to incorporate in the daily life of the preschool (more details in Roth, 2014). In Denmark, for example, the curriculum required all preschools to implement six dimensions of content, expressed as general themes:

1. personal competences
2. social competences
3. language
4. body and movement
5. nature and natural phenomena, and
6. cultural forms of expression and values.

The teachers and parents at the individual preschool were expected to discuss and interpret these themes, and once a year to create their own curriculum based on their own specific needs and circumstances. The teachers would become inspired by these themes and, together with the children, plan a variety of activities. However, they also observed children's actual interests and motivations, which they would support and analyse in order to relate to the themes of the curriculum. Simultaneously, they observed both the process and the children in order to document and evaluate educational quality.

According to the OECD (2012) this can be categorised as an input-based and multifaceted approach, which is typical for the Nordic countries when compared with Anglo-Saxon countries, which tend to take an outcome-based and academic approach (Bennett, 2010, 2013; Roth, 2014).

A movement towards measuring and testing

Although the Nordic model emphasises the educare dimension (play, democracy, and children's participation) and tones down an evaluation of the outcome (the learning results), during the last decade the governments have introduced different forms of testing as well as a certain skills orientation (described as key competences). As an example, in Denmark 3-year-old children must meet a language test. Similarly, in Sweden teachers have to carry out a systematic documentation of every child's development and learning. In Norway, language tests are carried out in some municipalities and, elsewhere, mapping over time and systematic observations are used.

Besides the language test, in Denmark an increasing number of tools for management have been implemented, including so-called educational standards and quality reports. Since 2011 local municipalities have had to evaluate the quality of educational activities in their region every second year. Using these quality reports, the municipalities construct cross-municipality assessments, so that we have seen a reformulation of early childhood education and care in terms of *efficiency*. Furthermore, the Danish Ministry of Finance and Education (Finansministeriet, 2009) has produced guidance on the skills and knowledge children have to achieve by 3 and 5 years of age. In relation to the six dimensions of aims and content mentioned above, teachers in some (but not all) municipalities also have to test children's learning using not less than 80 learning indicators.

Thus, in the Nordic countries, we have seen a tendency to narrow educational practice and reduce preschool to an introductory course for school, with a strong emphasis on literacy and mathematics. This corresponds with the fact that many countries have introduced structured learning areas to young children from the ages of 4 to 6 years with a focus on nature and the environment, emergent literacy, and numeracy (OECD, 2006, p. 135). In this way, early childhood education and care is under pressure, as expressed through documents such as The Treaty of Lisbon (2000).

Although documents such as *Starting Strong 2* (OECD, 2006) warn against a narrowing of the notion of early childhood education and care, we see an emerging tendency to focus on readiness for school, learning standards, and the use of narrow goals and objectives, followed by tests. Accordingly there is a clear risk of a dominating influence from school, which can lead to the implementation of methods based on particular forms of evidence, known as the 'what works' approach. The growing political control of the preschool can also result in adult-initiated activities focused on preparation for school, with less space for children's self-generated activities such as play and other spontaneous creative activities. A further consequence of this 'efficiency' is a limitation of both children's and preschool teachers' influence, which Biesta (2007) calls a "democratic deficit"(p. 20).

14: *Te Whāriki* and the Nordic Model: Comments on *Te Whāriki* from a Norwegian and Danish perspective

In Denmark, as well as in Norway, practitioners and researchers have argued against a 'schoolification' in preschool marked by use of formal and didactical teaching methods. As an example, Øksnes and Sundsdal (2016) from Norway and Sommer (2015) from Denmark argue, in accordance with Gopnik (2011), that early learning is best stimulated via play and moderate involvement of adults. This criticism has had an influence on upcoming change in early childhood education in both Norway and Denmark.

A democratic turn in Nordic preschool Act and curriculum

This period of a strong focus on a goal-directed and learning-oriented practice now seems to be being replaced by the Nordic model, with its social pedagogy approach emphasising democracy, children's views, play, and care, but without entirely dispensing with the learning dimension.

This optimistic development is based upon new Nordic educational Acts and revised curricula. For example, the revised Norwegian curriculum from 2017 (Forskrift om rammeplan for barnehagens innhold og opgaver, 2017) expresses clear, soft, humanistic, and Christian values such as respect for human life and values, spiritual liberty, democracy, Bildung, joy, humour, care, creativity, wonder, and desire for exploration. In addition to these traditional Nordic educational values, it is also mentioned that preschool must contribute to learning. The Act §1 states that "preschool must be aware of and secure children's need for care and play and promote learning and Bildung as fundament for a comprehensive development" (Barnehageloven, 2005, p. 1). Learning is promoted by play, curiosity, and children's own exploration. In addition, the content of education is expressed via seven themes, which do not represent specific learning subjects but areas, which "bear an interest and value in itself for children in preschool age, and are able to contribute to well-being, comprehensive development and health" (Forskrift om rammeplan for barnehagens innhold og opgaver, 2017, p. 13).

A parallel change has been undertaken in Danish early childhood education, expressed through a revised Act and curriculum (Elbæk, Meibom, Krogkjær, & Nielsen, 2016; Børne- og Socialministeriet, 2018a, 2018b). As with the Norwegian Act, the Danish Act also emphasises play, learning, and Bildung. The first paragraph states: "Preschool should promote children's well-being, learning, development and Bildung through secure learning environments in which play is fundamental, and with child perspective as point of departure" (Børne- og Socialministeriet (2018a, p. 7). The fourth paragraph deals with the democratic perspective: "Preschool should give children co-determination, joint responsibility, understanding and experience with democracy. Furthermore, preschool should contribute to the development of children's autonomy and abilities to participate in binding social communities" (p. 7).

Both the Norwegian and the Danish Acts and curricula bring important concepts and understandings to the surface, which can influence the development of a future Nordic early childhood education, namely Bildung, children's perspectives, and learning environments. These are explored in turn in the following section.

Bildung, child perspectives, and dynamic learning environments

The democratic dimension of education has been inscribed in legislation in all the Nordic countries since 1992 (Einarsdottir et al., 2014), and a democratic everyday life has been a central part of practice in educational institutions.

The overall aims emphasise participation, action, and democracy, and provide a distinction between ongoing adjustment and providing a foundation to legitimate political transformative education. Moreover, the aims describe children as thoughtful, active participants in a democratic process and not only as well-adjusted onlookers. In practice, preschool teachers listen to children and challenge them to reflect and express their thoughts and actions and to take initiatives themselves. This is exactly what is mentioned in the United Nations Conventions on the Rights of the Child (United Nations, 1989). First and foremost, democracy is characterised by people's possibility to participate in social actions.

Dewey focused on this democratic perspective in education, emphasising the importance of the social dimension for the democratic subject (Dewey, 1916); the democratic subject emerges via active participation in democratic life. Democracy is a conjoint mode of living, and subjectivity is socially mediated (see also Honneth, 1995). Thus, in early childhood education, the practitioner creates conditions for children's participation in playful social practices in which the educator assumes the child's perspective and maintains a state of emotional presence or closeness (Bae, 2009; Emilson & Johansson, 2009).

Bildung

According to Klafki (1998), working within a curriculum (and teaching in general), should be grounded on the concept of Bildung (which is a German word that translates into comprehensive personal development or formative development). In the Danish Act, Bildung is characterised by a "deeper form of learning in which the child as active participant appropriates values and knowledge in its own personality in order to act in a global world as a thoughtful and critical person" (Elbæk et al., 2016, p. 12).

Inspired by continental Bildung-philosophy with roots in the new humanism from the end of the 18th century, the concept dates back to Immanuel Kant and Wilhelm von Humboldt. On this basis, Klafki develops his own version of Bildung, which includes a significant element of societal critique. This reflects the way Klafki drew his inspiration from critical theory (Habermas 1987; Horkheimer, Adorno, & Noeri, 2002).

Bildung denotes an overarching educational purpose, and thus an ideal to strive for with a focus on qualities such as being authoritative and competent (German: *Mündigkeit*), courageous, with an ability to listen and argue, as well as participate actively in social life in order to have influence. According to Klafki (1996, 1998), Bildung involves the development of self- and co-determination, as well as solidarity; special, value-laden abilities that form the core of personal development. Self-determination provides the potential for the 'carry-through' of activities the child is able to do. Co-determination means children have a voice, are involved in shared decisions, and can influence their daily life. Children express solidarity when they strive to give other children the same rights and possibilities they have themselves; for example, by making room for children who are excluded from play. These values are visible in the Norwegian curriculum in the wording, "Freedom of spirit, forgiveness, equivalence and solidarity" (p. 4).

Undoubtedly, the concept of Bildung can be interpreted in several ways. While the abovementioned German understanding shares its origins with Denmark, the concept has several variations in Norway. In Norwegian philosophy and education, the concept of Bildung refers to its classic German roots and thus has a focus on democracy. On the other hand, to a wide extent the concept of Bildung (Norwegian: *dannelse*) is replaced by the Norwegian concept *danning*, which can be translated as the individual's formative development and cultural formation. In other words, *danning* is defined as the process of developing into an integrated cultural personality, as articulated by Hellesnes. Hellesnes (1976) sees *danning* as an antithesis to adaptation or adjustment and outlines a reflective socialisation in which "the rules of the games" will be uncovered—hence the child achieves a higher level of consciousness.

Nevertheless, the concept of *danning* has a critical dimension focused on democracy; first, it deals with the individual's personal process and competence related to reflection on one's own being and actions (Schei & Kvistad, 2012:99). Researchers such as Løkken and Søbstad (2011), Steinholt and Øksnes (2013), and Ødegaard (2012) understand the preschool as an arena for cultural formation (*danning*) in which children can create meaning and identity.

A child perspective

The Nordic countries, and thus the Norwegian Curriculum (Forskrift om rammeplan for barnehagens innhold og opgaver 2017) and the new Danish Act (Børne- og Socialministeriet, 2018a), also call for the *child's perspective*. The Norwegian Act states that the "kindergarten teacher must observe, acknowledge and follow children's perspectives and actions" (p. 21). The Danish curriculum states that "preschool is obliged to give children co-determination and create learning environments based in children's perspectives" (p. 12). Such formulations acknowledge that children have a perspective, which may differ decidedly from adults' perspectives, and that individual children may have differing perspectives from each other. A child's perspective also opens up the possibility of situations in which children themselves take a more active role as participants in education, and also in research (Broström, 2006b; Sommer, Pramling Samuelsson, & Hundeide, 2010).

The fundamental concept underlying the 'children's perspective' orientation is that children are competent, have rights, and are viewed as contributing members of a democratic society. Children are not preparing to be competent, or to earn rights or to contribute. They are already capable of active participation and competent use of their rights and agency.

This statement is based in research in the field of childhood psychology (Sommer, 2012), which does not view newborn children either as isolated from the surrounding world or born relatively unskilled. On the contrary, children are born with internal communicative competences and an interdependent mind (i.e., they have an awareness of being dependent on others and of others being dependent upon them). Thus, the phrase 'the competent child' has gained wide acceptance and cachet. For example, Trevarthen presents this perspective:

> The image of the biological newborn needing 'socialization' to become a person does not apply when attention turns to evidence for complex psychological expressions in the response of contented healthy newborns to people who take them as persons with intentions and feelings of companionship, and who feel pleasure when the infant responds. (Trevarthen, 1998, p. 16)

The "children's perspective" concept incorporates general societal views on children and on child-related policies, as well as teachers' and researchers' views on children and childhood and, most importantly, children's own views.

A dynamic learning environment

A third element that can contribute to a more democratic perspective is a Danish movement away from educational practice with use of narrow educational objectives, to a focus on the development and identification of *dynamic learning environments*. This means that large numbers of narrow learning objects, and general testing of children's individual learning, have been replaced by goals for the learning environment. At the homepage of Danish Ministry of Child and Social Affairs, the concept of learning environment is defined as: "All kinds of possibilities which can contribute to children's development, well-being and learning; among other things how the daily life and the activities are framed, organised and planned."

14: *Te Whāriki* and the Nordic Model: Comments on *Te Whāriki* from a Norwegian and Danish perspective

A learning environment of good quality consists of interactions between processes and structures (Bjørnestad, Baustad, & Alvestad, 2019; Drugli, Moser, Lekhal, Solheim, & Zachrisson, 2016; Christoffersen, Højen-Sørensen, & Laugesen, 2014; Sheridan, 2001). Structural quality deals with staffing and education of the staff, child group size (Sheridan, Williams, & Pramling Samuelsson, 2014), physical conditions, digital devices, and aesthetic framing. Process quality includes didactical reflections, empathic interactions between teachers and children (Bae, 2012; Tomasello & Carpenter, 2007), co-operation between teachers, structuring of the day, and a great number of creative play and being-together environments (Greve & Hansen, 2017). Furthermore, the educational content is a part of the learning environment, so that we can use the concept of content quality or didactical quality. Staffing and empathic relations between teacher and child are important, but a crucial point is the fact that children are presented with challenging and interesting content that has a formative character.

A critical-democratic content

Thus, it is necessary to formulate topics, problems, and categories, which on the one hand give children the necessary knowledge and, on the other hand, teach them to handle the here and now of everyday life and society in the long term. For this purpose, Klafki's approach, known as 'category Bildung', is useful as a starting point (Klafki, 1998). In this approach, the preschool teacher and the children select knowledge and categories through which the world will be available for the child and, at the same time, the child will be available for the world. For this reason, Klafki (1998) uses the term 'double opening' when describing the process of category development (i.e., identification of critical themes in the curriculum content). The preschool teacher's selection of such categories is the pivot, which also is expressed in Paulo Freire's (1972) concept of 'themes of generative character'. Through this process, children in preschool should encounter content that points ahead and helps to make the world transparent to them. When the children have grown up, they will live in a future world and should be able to solve the problems of *that* world. In order to achieve this, the children have to experience and learn to respond to some fundamental problems of their *present time*. This is the nature of educational 'content' within the 'category Bildung' approach.

The future can be viewed from a dual perspective. On the one hand, it can be described through the threatening tendencies of a high-risk society; on the other hand, it can be understood in the light of new visionary possibilities in a global world. Giddens (1990) describes the threatening tendencies as a mutual relation between growth in the totality of power, conflict over nuclear power, global war, ecological breakdown, and a collapse of the mechanisms of economic development and the relation between people—the I–You (Buber, 1958). Correspondingly, Klafki (1996) discusses the relationship between society and decisions about educational content. He outlines a number of core 'epoch-typical' problems, such as question about war and peace, the North–South conflict (rich in the global North, poor in the global South), the problem of nationalism, the ecological problem, global warming and sustainability, socially-produced disparity, and finally the danger and possibility of new management and communications media.

The Danish and Norwegian Acts and curricula are in accordance with this critical thinking. Thus the Danish curriculum calls for the development of "a critical democratic human being" (Elbæk et al, 2016, s. 12), who will express "critical thinking, ethical action and solidarity" as well as "a striving for equal status and equality" (Barnehageloven, 2005, p. 3). Both the Norwegian and Danish curricula hold a number of related educational themes, such as: comprehensive personal development; communication and language; social competencies and solidarity; body, senses and motion; nature, outdoor life and science; culture and aesthetics.

This educational frame opens up possibilities for children's active study of so-called epoch-typical problems. Every day such core problems are visible in the preschool and we can observe how children cope with these in their own way of doing. For example, children play and ask questions based on watching television about nature and climate problems, war in Afghanistan, the Palestinian conflict, or a specific terrorism event, which influence their thinking and feelings, so that they need adults helping them to come to terms with these questions (Broström, 2012).

Preschool teachers can define and select such problems and perspectives as the educational content of the preschool. For instance, in a Danish preschool some children talked about how their friends told them that the drinking water was poisoned and dangerous to drink. The truth behind the story was that, in the neighbouring municipality, there had been problems with the drinking water, and this had led to educational activities focused on pollution. In another preschool two 5-year-old boys had a dialogue during lunch. When 5-year-old Oskar started to eat his bread with sausage, a boy with an ethnic background other than Danish burst out, "Ugh this food is unclean, why do you eat such food? My father says this is really unappetising." Oskar replied quickly, "Don't speak about my food", and turned to a boy on his left side saying, "I like this, and me and my father eat this at home with roasted onion, uhm!" In this situation, the preschool teacher could *choose* to ask the boys not to speak slightingly about each other's food, and with that avoid a possible conflict. However, she gave the boys the possibility of exploring each other's norms and values. In this way, the boys entered into the themes of nationalism, the East–West conflict of values, etc. They have their own experiences and, during the following days, the preschool teacher can support the children's appropriation and construction of knowledge and norms.Thus, during recent years we have seen a numbers of educational projects where young children work with such societal problems; projects in preschools with focus on the ecological crisis and different initiative concerning a sustainable development are common (Pramling Samuelsson & Park, 2017).

Another educational principle, with reference to the I–You relation, deals with equality and the effort to involve every child in the group of children, and to facilitate that each child can be acknowledged by other children. The following example illustrates how children welcomed a new boy in a manner of solidarity, which helped him be a member of the group and thus develop self-esteem:

> Most preschools succeed in realizing the recognition related to emotional relations to other persons and also to be a part of the group of children. However, now and then children also experience recognition in the sphere of solidarity. This happened for a small group of five-year-old children during a session in their project group. The teacher informed them about a refugee child from Syria who would be starting in their group the following week. The children were informed about the new boy's traumatic background and were invited to suggest ideas for welcoming him. They proposed packing a little suitcase with informative items including a welcome letter, snapshots of interesting activities in preschool, drawings they made for him, and photos of themselves—his new friends. The teacher was very excited and encouraged the children to start work on the suitcase immediately. (Jensen & Broström, 2018, p. 49)

These children encountered an important societal theme which they handled in collaborative way and, through the practitioner's quick response, they experienced recognition within the sphere of solidarity. These examples illustrate the fact that it is not difficult for preschool teachers to identify and mobilise a number of epoch-typical core problems that help children to deal with current *and* future problems through appropriate preschool activity.

The Norwegian and Danish curricula are open to educational practice aimed at children's well-being, learning, development, and Bildung, and based in play-oriented activities. Children's wonder, creativity, and active experiments are starting points for teachers' and children's work with societally important academic subjects and problems described in the curricula. It is promising that the Nordic preschool is more than a learning area; it is also a democratic meeting place, where children, step by step, will have democratic experiences in order to achieve a form of Bildung.

Te Whāriki seen in the light of a Nordic educational perspective

Seen from an outside, and especially from a Nordic perspective, the revision of *Te Whāriki* contains several interesting and fruitful dimensions. The revision has succeeded in avoiding the international movement towards more narrow learning and school-oriented preschool. The didactical approach still avoids the hierarchic rational/objective model characteristic of the work of Tyler (1949), for example, which claims the existence of a close relationship between goals and means/methods. Such a model gives no room for spontaneity and has a tendency to adjust to narrow goals. Contrary to this, *Te Whāriki* adopts a cyclical model (Nicholls & Nicholls, 1978), which begins with a situational analysis in order to formulate goals and objectives and to guide the selection of content. The four principles of *Te Whāriki*—empowerment, holistic development, family and community, and relationships—and the relatively soft presence of educational 'content', suggest this interpretation. *Te Whāriki* can also be understood in the light of a so-called 'dynamic' model (Print, 1993) or a 'practice-based model' (Skilbeck, 1976), which argues for the importance of reflecting the reality of curriculum development within the educational organisation. Stenhouse (1975), for example, creates a 'process–didaktik/curriculum', arguing that all factors in the prevailing educational situation have to be taken into consideration. Educational practice is a creative and unpredictable process characterised by time and place, and by children's backgrounds and current situation.

Seen from a German didaktik perspective, which the Nordic countries have applied, the educational content is still of importance (Klafki, 1998), especially future-oriented content with potential to communicate critical–democratic values and knowledge on how to deal with societal problems, so-called epoch-typical themes (Klafki, 1996). Such general themes are missing in *Te Whāriki*. Instead, a mix of four principles (empowerment, holistic development, family and community, and relationship) and five strands (wellbeing, belonging, contribution, communication, and exploration) are designed to inspire teachers to make up an interesting and challenging everyday life in centres. Such principles and strands have the potential to direct children towards a critical–democratic perspective, and—integrated in the text—one can find 'critical' phrases; for example, "children are critical thinkers, problem solvers and explorers", and they are "able to connect with and care for their own and wider world" (p. 48). In addition, the curriculum also points out some learning subjects such as science and art. Nevertheless, from a Nordic didactic perspective, the content of *Te Whāriki* seems to be loose and lacking in obligation with respect to an explicit formulation of the content.

Learning and learning outcomes

The revised *Te Whāriki* has maintained the four principles, five strands, and numbers of educational goals without essential changes. The concept of learning is mentioned throughout the document, but without a depth and exact definition. However, *Te Whāriki* gives a clear definition of children's expected learning, in the form of learning outcomes.

It is interesting to observe that the revised *Te Whāriki* has reduced the previous large number of learning outcomes, from 118 to only 20. These learning outcomes signal what all children should achieve. Such a dimming of learning outcomes is in accordance with the new Danish curricula, which expresses a clear shift from exact learning goals and objectives (or in *Te Whāriki*'s terms, learning outcomes) to goals for the learning environment. Instead of testing children's learning, there is a focus on and evaluation of the quality of the learning environment. Therefore, the teachers create exciting, creative, and stimulating physical, mental, aesthetic, and didactic learning environments in order to challenge children's wondering, experiments, and explorations.

Maybe such changes can be understood as a sign of a general tendency in early childhood education to move away from narrow learning and goal-oriented practice. However, this does not indicate a retreat from giving children the possibility of being involved in active learning processes supported by the teachers. As mentioned in *Te Whāriki* (Ministry of Education, 2017, p. 59), the teachers need to be "knowledgeable about children's learning and development and able to identify their varied abilities, strengths, interest and learning trajectories" in order to organise an effective and play-based pedagogy.

Conclusion

This chapter identifies some democratic turning points in Nordic early childhood education and argues for a critical–democratic preschool education reflecting a sense of the serious problems of our time, aimed at Bildung and liberation. The revised *Te Whāriki* also holds some critical–democratic visions. However, the formulations are rather vague. *Te Whāriki* is not a fixed curriculum; it expresses an openness, which allows each preschool to draw its own educational conclusions. This is a positive dimension but, seen from a democratic point of view, a society has to express its overall values; this is a prerequisite for having a democratic debate. Although *Te Whāriki* does not foreground the concept of democracy, there is an indirect call for critical–democratic citizens, namely "competent and confident learners and communicators, healthy in mind, body and spirit, secure in their sense of belonging and in the knowledge that they make a valued contribution to society" (p. 6), and the wording "critical informed and responsible citizens" (p. 56), provides the potential (and legitimation) for critical democratic practice. However, because the critical–democratic message is soft, to be formulated by the teachers themselves, the teachers too need to have a strong political–democratic and educational schooling.

References

Bae, B. (2009). Children's right to participate—challenges in everyday interactions. *European Early Childhood Education Research Journal, 17*(3), 391–406.

Bae, B. (2012). Children and teachers as partners in communication: Focus on spacious and narrow interactional patterns. *International Journal of Early Childhood, 44*(1), 53–69. https://doi:10.1007/s13158-012-0052-3

Barne- og familiedepartementet. (1995). *Rammeplan for barnehagen*, 1995, Q-0903B. [Curriculum for prescholl]. Oslo: Author.

Barnehageloven (2005). *Lov 17. juni 2005 nr. 64 om barnehager.* Revised 01.08.2018. Retrieved from https://www.regjeringen.no/no/dokumenter/barnehageloven/id115281/

Bennett, J. (2010). Pedagogy in early childhood services with special reference to Nordic approaches. *Psychological Science and Education, 3*, 16–21.

Bennett, J. (2013). A response from the co-author of 'strong and equal relationship'. In Peter Moss (Ed.), *Early Childhood and Compulsory Education: Reconceptualising the relationship* (pp. 52–71). London and New York: Routledge.

Biesta, G. J. J. (2007). Why "what works" won't work. *Educational Theory, 57*(1), 1–22. https://doi.org/10.1111/j.1741-5446.2006.00241.x

Bjørnestad., E, Baustad, A. G., & Alvestad, M. (2019). To what extent does ITERS-R address pedagogical quality as described in the Norwegian framework plan? In S. Phillipson & S. Garvis (Eds.), *Teachers and families perspectives in early childhood education and care: Early childhood education and care in the 21st Century*, Vol II. London and New York: Routledge.

Børne- og Socialministeriet (2018a). *Bekendtgørelse om mål og indhold i de seks læreplanstemaer.* BEK nr. 853 af 22/06/2018. [Act on educational curricula]. Copenhagen, Denmark: Author.

Børne- og Socialministeriet. (2018b). *Den styrkede pædagogiske læreplan, Rammer og indhold.* Copenhagen, Denmark: Author. Retrieved from https://www.emu.dk/omraade/dagtilbud.

Broström, S. (2006a). Care and education: towards a new paradigm in early childhood education. *Child & Youth Care Forum*, 35, nr. 5-6, 391-409. https://doi.org/10.1007/s10566-006-9024-9

Broström, S. (2006b). Children's perspectives on their childhood experiences. In Einarsdóttir, J. & Wagner, J.T. (Eds.), *Nordic childhoods and early education. Philosophy, research, policy and practice in Denmark, Finland, Iceland, Norway and Sweden* (pp. 223–255). Greenwich, CT: Information Age Publishing.

Broström, S. (2012). Curriculum in preschool. Adjustment or a possible liberation? *Nordisk Barnehageforskning. 5*(7), 1–14.

Broström, S., & Wagner, J. T. (Eds.) (2003). *Early childhood education in five Nordic countries: Perspectives on the transition from preschool to school.* Aarhus, Denmark: Systime Academic.

Buber, M. (1958). *I and thou*. New York, NY: Schribner's.

Cassidy, J., D. Jones, J., & Shaver, P.R. (2013). Contributions of attachment theory and research: A framework for future research, translation, and policy. *Development and Psychopathology, 25*(4), 1415–1434. https://doi.org/10.1017/S0954579413000692

Christoffersen, M., Højen-Sørensen, A-K., & Laugesen, L. (2014). *Daginstitutionens betydning for børns udvikling. En forskningsoversigt.* [The influence of daycare on children's development]. Copenhagen, Denmark: SFI. Det Nationale Forskningscenter for Velfærd.

Dewey, J. (1916). *Democracy and education: An introduction to the philosophy of education.* New York, NY: MacMillan.

14: *Te Whāriki* and the Nordic Model: Comments on *Te Whāriki* from a Norwegian and Danish perspective

Drugli, M.B, Moser, T, Lekhal, R., Solheim, E. & Zachrisson, H.D. (2016). *Det ved vi om betydningen af kvalitet i daginstitutionen*. [This is what we know about quality in preschool]. Copenhagen, Denmark: Dafolo.

Einarsdottir, J.; Purola, A-M.; Johansson, E.M.; Broström, S., & Emilson, A. (2014). Democracy, caring and competence: Values perspectives in ECEC curricula in the Nordic countries. *International Journal of Early Years Education*, 23(1), 94–114. https://doi.org/10.1080/09669760.2014.970521

Elbæk, I., Meibom, C., Krogkjær, S.B, & Nielsen, H.S. (Eds.). (2016). *Master for en styrket pædagogisk læreplan. Pædagogisk grundlag og ramme for det videre arbejde med læreplanstemaer og få brede pædagogisk mål*. [Master for a strengthened curriculum]. Copenhagen, Denmark: Ministeriet for Børn, Undervisning og Ligestilling.

Emilson, A., & Johansson, E. (2009). Communicated values in teacher and toddler interactions in preschool. In D. Berthelsen, J. Brownlee, & E. Johansson (Eds.), *Participatory earning and the Early Years. Research and pedagogy* (pp. 61–77). New York & London: Routledge, Taylor & Frances Group.

Finansministeriet. (2009). *Om projekt Faglige Kvalitetsoplysninger på dagtilbudsområdet*. [On project quality information in the day-care sector]. Retrieved from https://www.kl.dk/ImageVaultFiles/id_45580/cf_202/Faglige_Kvalitetsoplysninger_i_dagtilbud_redskabsk.PDF/

Forskrift om rammeplan for barnehagens innhold og opgaver. (2017). *Forskrift om rammeplan for barnehagens innhold og opgaver av 24 April 2017 nr. 487*. (*Framevork plan for the content and tasks of kindergartens*). Retrieved from https://lovdata.no/dokument/LTI/forskrift/2017-04-24-487

Freire, P. (1972). *Pedagogy of the oppressed*. Harmondsworth, UK: Penguin Books.

Giddens, A. (1990). *The consequences of modernity*. Cambridge, UK: Polity.

Gopnik, A. (2011). Why pre-school shouldn't be like school. *Slate.com*, 16 March, 2011. Retrieved from https://slate.com/human-interest/2011/03/preschool-lessons-new-research-shows-that-teaching-kids-more-and-more-at-ever-younger-ages-may-backfire.html

Greve, A., & Hansen, O. H. (2017). Toddlers in Nordic early childhood education and care. In M. Fleer & B. van Oers (Eds.), *International Handbook of Early Childhood Education* (pp. 907–927). Dordrecht, The Netherlands: Springer. https://doi.org/10.1007/978-94-024-0927-7_47

Habermas, J. (1987). *Theory of communicative action, Volume two: Lifeworld and system: A critique of functionalist reason*. Boston, MA: Beacon Press.

Hellesnes (1976). *Socialisering og teknokrati*. [Socialization and technocracy]. Copenhagen, Denmark: Gyldendal.

Horkheimer, M., Adorno, T.W., & Noeri, G. (2002). *Dialectic of enlightenment*. Stanford, CA: Stanford University Press.

Honneth, A. (1995). *The struggle for recognition. The moral grammar of social conflicts*. Cambridge, UK: Polity Press.

Howes, C., & Hamilton, C. E. (1992). Children's relationships with caregivers: Mothers and child care teachers. *Child Development*, 63, 895–866.

Jensen, A.S., & Broström, S. (2018). Values education in practice in preschool. In E. Johansson & J. Einarsdottir (Eds.), *Values in early childhood education. Citizenship for tomorrow*. New York, NY: Routledge.

Klafki, W. (1996). Core problems of the modern world and the tasks of education. A vision of international education. *Education*, 53, 7–18.

Klafki, W. (1998). Characteristics of critical-constructive didaktik. In B. B. Gundem & S. Hopmann (Eds.), *Didaktik and/or curriculum. An international dialogue* (pp. 307–330). New York, NY: Peter Lang.

Kragh-Müller, G. (2017). The key characteristics of Danish/Nordic child care culture. In C. Ringsmose & G. Kragh-Müller (Eds.). *Nordic social pedagogical approach to early years* (pp. 3–23). Cham, Switzerland: Springer.

Kragh-Müller, G. & Ringsmose, C. (Eds.). (2016). *The Nordic social pedagogical approach to early years learning*. Switzerland: Springer.

Løkken, G. & Søbstad, F. (2018). Danning. [Cultural formation]. In V. Glasser, K. H. Moen, S. Mørreaunet, & F. Søbstad (Eds.). *Barnehagens grunnsteiner* (pp. 111–119). Oslo, Norway: Universitetsforlaget.

Ministry of Education. (1996). *Te whāriki: He whāriki mātauranga mō ngā mokopuna o Aotearoa: Early childhood curriculum*. Wellington: Learning Media.

Ministry of Education. (2017). *Te whāriki: He whāriki mātauranga mō ngā mokopuna o Aotearoa: Early childhood curriculum*. Wellington: Author.

Ministry of Education [Sweden]. (1996). *Curriculum for the preschool, lpfö 98*. Stockholm, Sweden: Fritzes kundeservice.

Nicholls, A., & Nicholls, A.H. (1978). *Developing a curriculum: A practical guide.* (2nd ed.). London, UK: George Allen & Unwin.

Noddings, N. (1984). *Caring: A feminine approach to ethics and moral education*. Berkeley, CA: University of California Press.

Noddings, N. (1992). *The challenge to care in school: An alternative approach to education*. New York, NY & London, UK: Teachers College Press.

Ødegaard, E.E. (2012). *Barnehagen som danningsarena*. [Preschool as arena for cultural formation]. Bergen, Norway: Fagbokforlaget.

OECD (2001). *Starting strong. Early childhood education and care*. Paris, France: OECD Publishing.

OECD. (2006). *Starting strong 2: Early childhood education and care*. Paris, France: OECD Publishing.

OECD. (2012). *Starting strong 3. A quality toolbox for early childhood education and care*. Paris, France: OECD Publishing.

Øksnes, M & Sundsdal, E. (2016). "Æ ha lært mæ det sjøl!" Læring i barnehagen. ["I have learned myself". Learning in kindergarten]. In M. Øksnes & E. Sundsdal (Eds.). *Læring* (pp. 11–26). Oslo, Norway: Cappelen Damm Akademisk.

Pramling Samuelsson, I., & Park, E. (2017). How to educate children for sustainable learning and for a sustainable world. *International Journal of Early Childhood, 49*(3), 273–285.

Print, M. (1993). *Curriculum development and design*. Sydney, Australia: Allen & Unwin.

Roth, V. A-C. (2014). Nordic comparative analysis of guidelines for quality and content in early childhood education. *Nordic Early Childhood Education Research Journal, 8*(1), 1–35.

Schei, S.H., & Kvistad, K. (2012). *Kompetenceløft. Langsiktige tiltak i barnehagen*. [Loft of competence in preschool]. Oslo, Norway: Universitetsforlaget.

Sheridan, S. (2001). Pedagogical quality in preschool. An issue of perspectives. Unpublished doctoral thesis, ACTA Universitatis Gothoburgensis.

Sheridan, S., Williams, P., & Pramling Samuelsson, I. (2014). Group size and organizational conditions for children's learning in preschool: A teacher perspective. *Educational Research, 56*(4), 379–397.

Skilbeck, M. (1976). *School-based curriculum development and teacher education*. Mimeograph. OECD Publishing.

Socialministeriet. (2004). *Lov om ændring af lov om social service: Pædagogiske læreplaner for børn i dagtilbud til børn* [Act on educational curricula]. Copenhagen, Denmark: Author.

Sommer, D. (2012). *A childhood psychology. Young children in changing times*. London, UK: Palgrave Macmillan.

Sommer, D. (2015). Tidligt i skole eller legende læring? Evidensen om langtidsholdbar læring og udvikling i daginstitutionen. [Early schhool start or playful learning?]. In J. Klitmøller & D. Sommer (Eds.), *Læring, dannelse og udvikling: Kvalificering til fremtiden i daginstitution og skole* (pp. 61–81). Copenhagen, Denmark: Hans Reitzel.

Sommer, D., Pramling Samuelsson, I., &, Hundeide, K. (2010). *Child perspectives and children's perspectives in theory and practice*. Cham, Switzerland: Springer.

Steinsholt, K. & Øksnes, M. (Eds.). (2013). *Danning i barnehagen. Perspektiver og udfodringer*. [Formation in preschool]. Oslo, Norway: Cappelen Damm.

Stenhouse, L. (1975). *An introduction to curriculum research and development*. London, UK: Heinemann Educational Books.

Stern, D. (1985). *The interpersonal world of the infant: A view from psychoanalysis and developmental psychology*. London, UK: Karnac Books.

The Treaty of Lisbon (2000). The Lisbon Special European Council: *Towards a Europe of Innovation and Knowledge*. Retrieved from: http://www.europarl.europa.eu/summits/lis1_en.htm

Tomasello, M., & Carpenter, M. (2007). Shared Intentionality. *Developmental Science, 10*(1), 121-125.

Trevarthen, C. (1998). The concept and foundations of infant intersubjectivity. In S. Bråten (Ed.), *Studies in emotion and social interaction, 2nd series. Intersubjective communication and emotion in early ontogeny* (pp. 15-46). New York, NY, US: Cambridge University Press.

Tyler, R. W. (1949). *Basic principles of curriculum and instruction*. Chicago, IL: University of Chicago Press.

United Nations (1989). United Nations Conventions of the Rights of the Child. Retrieved from https://www.ohchr.org/en/professionalinterest/pages/crc.aspx

Vejleskov, H. (Ed.). (1997). *Den danske børnehave. Studier om myter, meninger og muligheder*. [The Danish Kindergarten. Studies on myths, meanings and possibilities]. Copenhagen, Denmark: Danmarks Lærerhøjskole.

Wagner, J. T. (2006). "An outsider's perspective: childhoods and early education in the nordic countries." In J. Einarsdottir & J. T. Wagner (Eds), *Nordic childhoods and early education* (pp. 280–306). Greenwich, CT: Information Age Publishing.

Wagner, J. T., & Einarsdóttir, J. (2008). The good childhood: Nordic ideals and educational practice. *International Journal of Educational Research, 47*(5), 265–269.

CHAPTER 15

Early childhood curriculum policy texts in England and Aotearoa New Zealand: A rhetorical analysis

Elizabeth Wood and Joce Nuttall

Many of the chapters in this volume discuss *Te whāriki: He whāriki mātauranga mō ngā mokopuna o Aotearoa: Early childhood curriculum* (Ministry of Education, 2017) as a stimulus for practice in early childhood services in Aotearoa New Zealand. This chapter, instead, examines the nature of early childhood curriculum frameworks as *policy texts*, and the connections between global policy discourses and how these touch down at national levels. Following on from Wood's (2013) chapter in the second edition of *Weaving Te Whāriki* (Nuttall, 2013), we report here a parallel examination of England's *Early Years Foundation Stage* (*EYFS*) (Department for Education, 2017) and *Te Whāriki* (Ministry of Education, 2017). Both frameworks developed over a similar time period and have drawn to varying degrees on global discourses emanating from supra-national bodies such as the OECD and the United Nations Convention on the Rights of the Child.

The conceptual resources we bring to this analysis are drawn from the scholarship of rhetoric (Edwards, Nicoll, Solomon, & Usher, 2004). A focus on rhetoric assumes that policy texts are designed not only to communicate institutional intentions but also to persuade the reader that this intention is consistent with their interests. In our analysis of *Te Whāriki* and the *EYFS*, we ask: "What is the nature of the problem constructed within these texts?", "Who do these texts seek to persuade?", and "What solutions are proposed within the texts?"

We begin by outlining some basic principles of rhetorical analysis and the questions we employed in our analysis, derived from the scholarship of rhetoric. In the main part of the chapter we present first our analysis of the *EYFS*, then a parallel analysis of

Te Whāriki. We conclude by comparing our findings across the two national settings, based on these analyses, and by speculating on how such different curriculum policy texts came to be constructed out of the same political milieu, broadly described as "new public management" (Pollitt & Bouckaert, 2011). The coupling of supranational discourses and new public management has produced common discourses that focus on quality, human capital, and national competitiveness expressed as measures of educational outcomes and the ability to compete in global markets. Early childhood education (ECE) has to demonstrate economic and educational effectiveness, with outcomes closely tied to standards and concepts of school readiness.

Rhetorical analysis

Rhetorical analysis involves identification and examination of specific rhetorical devices designed to persuade intended audiences. As Winton (2013) explains, "It provides a method for identifying how arguments are constructed to persuade audiences to accept and support particular constructions of reality, truth, and courses of action" (p. 161). Historically, the scholarship rhetoric (which dates from Ancient Greece) was divided into five branches: invention, disposition, style, memory, and delivery. This chapter concentrates on the use of invention as a rhetorical approach, since invention is fundamentally about careful selection of appeals to an audience in constructing a persuasive argument. In early (Aristotelian) rhetoric, these arguments were categorised as *logos* (reasoned argument, such as drawing on scientific evidence), *pathos* (an argument that tugs at the emotions of an audience), or *ethos* (an appeal to the credibility of the speaker).

Although rhetorical analysis is analogous to critical discourse analysis in many ways, it differs in its consideration of the *rhetorical situation* in which particular discourses are employed. Bitzer's (1968) seminal definition of the rhetorical situation argued that:

> … a work is rhetorical because it is a response to a situation of a certain kind. In order to clarify rhetoric-as-essentially-related-to-situation, we should acknowledge a viewpoint that is commonplace but fundamental: a work of rhetoric is pragmatic; it comes into existence for the sake of something beyond itself; it functions ultimately to produce action or change in the world; it performs some task. (pp. 3–4)

This understanding of rhetoric as "essentially-related-to-situation" provides policy analysts with an important lens through which to make sense of the persuasive intent of policy texts. This is particularly so in the case of *Te Whāriki*, since only its principles and strands are legislated as mandatory, not the framework as a whole. As a policy text, *Te Whāriki* must seek to persuade, since it cannot rely entirely on a need for compliance to legislation.

15: Early childhood curriculum policy texts in England and Aotearoa New Zealand: A rhetorical analysis

As Bitzer (1968) goes on to argue, the persuasive function of rhetoric is about change; specifically, it seeks to convince an audience to engage in actions that will result in change:

> In short, rhetoric is a mode of altering reality, not by the direct application of energy to objects, but by the creation of discourse which changes reality through the mediation of thought and action. The rhetor alters reality by bringing into existence a discourse of such a character that the audience, in thought and action, is so engaged that it becomes mediator of change. In this sense rhetoric is always persuasive. (p. 4)

At the heart of the rhetorical situation is the most human of characteristics, the impulse for change: something is objectively wrong in the world, it is capable of change, and people can act to overcome the inevitable constraints on human action to achieve this change. Fostering these actions is the core activity of policy makers.

For Bitzer (1968), the impulse for change must be founded on "publicly observable historic facts in the world we experience, [which] are therefore available for scrutiny by an observer or critic" (p. 11). Yet we live in a time when 'facts' are also publicly contested, and differing constructions and explanations of 'reality' are supported by groups with widely diverging values and proposed solutions (Winton, 2013). In a political environment where there is no one clear or best way to address the impulse for change, the use of rhetoric takes on special significance in persuading audiences to act in one way or another. Policy texts both bring discourses into existence (in Bitzer's term) as well as seeking to persuade their audience to enact the solution envisaged by their sponsors and writers.

With these purposes of policy texts in mind, and informed by principles of rhetorical analysis, we identified three questions to drive our analysis of the *EYFS* and *Te Whāriki*: "What is the nature of the problem constructed within these texts?", "Who do these texts seek to persuade?", and "What solutions are proposed within the texts?". It is beyond the scope of this chapter to offer a comprehensive rhetorical analysis of both documents; instead, we illustrate the relationship between policy and rhetoric through some examples purposively selected from the texts.

Rhetorical features of the *Early Years Foundation Stage*

What is the nature of the problem constructed within the text?

The *Statutory Framework for the Early Years Foundation Stage* (Department for Education, 2017) sets the standards for learning, development, and care for children from birth to 5 years of age, and the requirements for their safeguarding and welfare. The final *EYFS* year (age 4–5) is known as the Reception year, when most children are in primary schools. The framework is premised on the pathos that "Every child deserves the best possible start in life and the support that enables them to fulfil their potential" (Department for Education, 2017, p. 5). This statement links directly to the logos and ethos of four key policy aspirations: to provide quality and consistency; establishing a secure foundation; partnership working; and equality of opportunity. In terms of their rhetorical power, such aspirations would appeal to the ethos of all stakeholders within ECE, and to the professional and moral agency of practitioners. However, an underlying intention is to ensure that government investment is justified (economic effectiveness), and that quality, standards, and outcomes improve (educational effectiveness). Thus, the rhetorical power of the *EYFS* is not just persuasive but authoritative and is reinforced through the work of the government's inspection body: the Office for Standards in Education (Ofsted).

Underpinning this rhetorical power are concerns, expressed in official reports, about lack of high-quality provision for disadvantaged children (Ofsted, 2016), the insecure foundation for pedagogy and curriculum in ECE (Ofsted, 2017), variable effects and outcomes of partnerships and interventions with families (Asmussen, Feinstein, Martin, & Chowdry, 2016), and quantitative evidence that indicates lower than average achievement amongst children from disadvantaged families (as measured in the 2016 *Early Years Foundation Stage Profile*) (Department for Education, 2016)). The wider policy rhetoric reinforces these 'problems' and creates an additional impetus for action: that improving children's outcomes in the early years is crucial to their educational success and subsequent life chances, which will be secured through effective practitioners, high-quality provision, and the *EYFS* learning and development requirements. The *EYFS* is thus a policy response to a number of 'problems' that need to be solved, and it is not just rhetoric but also a developed policy architecture that reinforces constructions of reality, truth, and course of action (Winton, 2013, p. 161).

Who does the text seek to persuade?

The four policy aspirations noted above inevitably appeal to the principal stakeholders—practitioners and families—who are enmeshed in how the *EYFS* must be delivered and experienced. With reference to assessment, practitioners are required to endorse particular constructions of reality because they must enable "parents, carers and practitioners to recognise children's progress, understand their needs, and to plan activities and support practitioners" (Department for Education, 2017, p. 12). Parents and caregivers are thus persuaded that their children can be understood in terms of their development and outcomes as measured by the Early Learning Goals (ELGs) of the *EYFS*. The ELGs define the expected level of development by the end of the Reception year ("good"), evidenced by a child's score across three categories: "emerging" (1), "expected" (2), and "exceeding" (3). In order to receive a "Good Level of Development" a score of at least 2 is required in all areas. The score also connotes a 'school-ready' child. The three categories underscore the normative, development leading learning ontology of the *EYFS*, and construct children who are, variously, showing typical development for their age, or who may be at risk of delay, or are ahead for their age. The category of 'emerging' connotes being 'at risk' and 'in need' on the basis of 'low development'. Application of the category signifies the need for interventions for children and families. Thus, the *EYFS* persuasive discourse about partnership working also potentially constructs a deficit discourse, because its assessment requirements are a means of developmental categorisation that normalise/ab-normalise children.

In relation to the economic/educational effectiveness discourse, ECE provision for children from birth to 5 is not compulsory, which means that the public has to be persuaded of the value of the significant financial investment in the field that has been made in the past 20 years. This exigence is consistent with wider global discourses, which argue that investment must be justified in terms of the immediate gains for children *and* longer-term benefits of society and the economy. Thus, it is not just the rhetoric of the *EYFS* that is significant but what that rhetoric produces as solutions to the 'problems' it identifies.

What solutions are proposed within the text?

The *EYFS* sets out learning and development requirements, which are constructed to serve different purposes: to structure the educational programme; to assess children's progress and achievements; to assess practitioners' effectiveness; and to evaluate the quality of the setting. The *EYFS* (Department for Education, 2017) and *Te Whāriki* were informed by child development theories and particular interpretations of sociocultural theories (Wood & Hedges, 2016), again reflecting global discourses. However, the *EYFS* espouses a 'development leading learning' onto-epistemology. Development is expressed through normative and hierarchical sequencing of the 17 ELGs, which are "the knowledge, skills and understanding all young children should have gained by the end of the Reception year" (Department for Education, 2017, p. 7). The ELGs are organised around three Prime Areas and four Specific Areas of learning and development, and "must involve activities and experiences for children":

Prime Areas
Personal, Social and Emotional Development
Communication and Language
Physical Development

Specific Areas
Literacy
Mathematics
Understanding the World
Expressive Arts and Design (Department for Education, 2017, p. 7)

The learning and development requirements in each of these areas constitute the educational programme and define:

> ... what providers must do, working in partnership with parents and/or carers, to promote the learning and development of all children in their care, and to ensure they are ready for school. The learning and development requirements are informed by the best available evidence on how children learn and reflect a broad range of skills, knowledge and attitudes children need as foundations for good future progress. Early years providers must guide the development of children's capabilities, with a view to ensuring that children in their care complete the EYFS ready to benefit fully from the opportunities ahead of them. (Department for Education, 2017, p. 7)

The rhetorical appeal of the phrase "best available evidence" positions the ethos of the authors of this text as higher authorities, justifying their right to define what practitioners must do. In fact, closer analysis of policy texts indicates a circular discourse in which government-funded research and commissioned reports typically form the basis for this evidence (Wood, 2019).

It is therefore difficult to isolate what constitutes the curriculum, as such, because the *EYFS* (Department for Education, 2017) uses the term 'educational programme', and its logos constructs a close linkage between this programme and the assessment of the ELGs and recommended pedagogical approaches. The absence of the word 'curriculum' is puzzling because the *EYFS Profile 2017 Handbook* (Standards and Testing Agency, 2016) does refer to the planned curriculum. Rather, in evaluating the effectiveness of their assessment processes, practitioners should consider "Planning which ensures a relevant, motivating, flexible and interesting curriculum ... [and] ... Organisational aspects of provision, resources, curriculum and people" (Standards and Testing Agency, 2016, pp. 11–12).

One strategy for linking the educational programme to assessment is a developmental progress check at age 2, which is carried out by health visitors, followed by practitioner assessment of the ELGs via the *EYFS Profile* (*EYFSP*). At the same time, the ELGs were revised in the 2017 version of the *EYFS* to align the Reception year more closely with Key Stage 1 of the National Curriculum (age 5–7). However, the three categories of "emerging", "expected", and "exceeding" are problematic because it is not clear whether practitioners are assessing children's observable *behaviours*, their *levels of development*, or their *achievement of the early*

15: Early childhood curriculum policy texts in England and Aotearoa New Zealand: A rhetorical analysis

learning goals. Furthermore, an Ofsted report focuses on the Reception Curriculum as what children are taught (Ofsted, 2017, p. 8) and, although this includes activities and experiences beyond the ELGs, an emphasis on school readiness is foregrounded.

The persuasive/authoritative rhetoric of the *EYFS* endorses approved pedagogical approaches that are responsive to children's needs, interests, and natural developmental pathways, and include observation, adult–child interactions, and flexibility between adult-led and child-initiated play. However, play must be planned and purposeful, and serve age-related developmental purposes. Although there appears to be some appeal to familiar professional discourses in ECE, Kay (2018) has shown that an Ofsted report on school readiness constructs a dominant narrative of the importance of teaching Mathematics and Literacy in the Reception year, alongside a direct assertion that notions of "free play" are "too rosy" and create an "unrealistic view of childhood" (Ofsted, 2017, p. 16). Furthermore, the *EYFS* constructs pedagogic progression as the transition from informal play to formal learning during the Reception year (age 4–5) thus reinforcing a logos of school readiness: "As children grow older, and as their development allows, it is expected that the balance will gradually shift towards more activities led by adults, to help children prepare for more formal learning, ready for Year 1" (Department for Education, 2017, p. 9).

The *EYFS* conveys an authoritative discourse that goes beyond persuasion to reinforce the statutory requirements and produce the actions that will result in change. The words 'must' and 'should' appear 246 and 40 times respectively, attached to all areas of practitioners' roles. Consistent with Bitzer's definition of rhetoric-as-essentially-related-to-situation (1968, pp. 3–4), the *EYFS* is performative, in that it creates the conditions for regulation and conformity in which practitioners, children, and families are enmeshed. Regulation and conformity are reinforced by the direct intervention of Ofsted in matters of play, curriculum, and pedagogy (Ofsted, 2015) and in constructing school readiness (Ofsted, 2017). As Wood (2019) has argued, from its original remit as a government inspection body, Ofsted has acquired a mandate to become the sole arbiter of quality. Ofsted acts as a mediator of change by producing the 'knowledge' (via reports, surveys, and reviews) that reinforces its authoritative discourse and the actions that will result in change, and influences how practitioners go about their work. Thus, in the exigencies presented in the *EYFS* and related documents, the policy rhetoric constitutes both problems and preferred solutions, in order to produce the desired outcomes.

In the next section of this chapter we turn to a rhetorical analysis of *Te Whāriki* (Ministry of Education, 2017) before concluding with our reflection on the similarities and differences between the two curriculum policy texts.

Rhetorical features of *Te Whāriki*

What is the nature of the problem constructed within the text?

The Foreword to the revised *Te Whāriki* (Ministry of Education, 2017) opens with a list of assertions:

> *[1]* All children are born with immense potential. *[2]* Quality early learning helps our children begin to realise that potential and *[3]* build a strong foundation for later learning and for life. *[4]* New Zealand's early learning standards are amongst the highest in the world and *[5]* almost all of our children are participating and *[6]* benefitting from a rich array of relationships and experiences in our early learning settings. (p. 2, enumeration added)

The rhetorical power of this dense sequence of claims is considerable. First, there is the emotional appeal (pathos) to the image of newborn children, closely followed by an invocation of evidence (logos) for the effects of early learning (provided it is "quality" provision). And the claim to authority (ethos) of the writer is high: the Foreword is attributed to the then Minister of Education, Hon Hekia Parata.

A second feature of the document, particularly in its opening pages, is its use of te reo Māori (the Māori language), including a whakataukī (proverb) about a child being a "treasure" at the beginning of the Foreword (p. 2). The Foreword is followed on the next page with a description of the significance of Te Tiriti o Waitangi (Aotearoa New Zealand's founding treaty document between Māori and the Crown, signed in 1840) and each page of the document is edged with an image of a stylised woven mat, reflecting the metaphor of a whāriki (woven mat) which underpins the document's principles of curriculum design. The commentary on Te Tiriti includes the text:

> Te Tiriti | the Treaty has implications for our education system, particularly in terms of achieving equitable outcomes for Māori and ensuring that te reo Māori not only survives but thrives. Early childhood education has a crucial role to play here, by providing mokopuna [young children] with culturally responsive environments that support their learning and by ensuring that they are provided with equitable opportunities to learn. (p. 3)

These features of *Te Whāriki* powerfully reflect the rhetorical situation in which the document was both written and revised. *Te Whāriki* conforms to the legal requirement (established under the Treaty) for all actions by the Crown to recognise and uphold the sovereignty of Māori as Aotearoa New Zealand's first inhabitants. However, a rhetorical situation is not history-dependent; it is constituted from *present* exigencies (Bitzer, 1968) that demand change. In Aotearoa New Zealand, as in many other post-colonial nations where first peoples have been historically marginalised, a present exigence is the ongoing project of Māori achieving the same outcomes in education, health, employment, and the justice system as their Pākehā peers (New Zealanders of European descent). The development of curriculum policy to address the ongoing effects of historical marginalisation is a positive strategy for governments but it is not the only construction of reality signalled in the Minister's Foreword to *Te Whāriki*. The invocation of "realising potential", building the "foundation for later learning and for life", and "New Zealand's early learning standards [being] amongst the highest in the world" each point to contemporary neo-liberal anxieties about national competitiveness, and a desire to minimise present and future burdens on the state (and therefore taxpayers), informed by human capital theory (Sidorkin, 2007).

A third important rhetorical feature of *Te Whāriki* is the metaphor of the whāriki itself:

> Kaiako [educators] in ECE settings weave together the principles and strands, in collaboration with children, parents, whānau [family] and community, to create a local curriculum for their setting. Understood in this way, the curriculum or whāriki is a 'mat for all to stand on … The whāriki can also be understood as a metaphor for the developing child. Interpreted in this way, as in *Te Whāriki a te Kōhanga Reo* [the version of *Te Whāriki* used in Māori language immersion services or 'language nests'], the whāriki includes four dimensions of human development: tinana [bodily health], hinengaro [mind, consciousness], wairua [spirituality] and whatumanawa [the emotions]. (p. 10)

The concept of a woven matrix of curriculum strands and practice principles is not only a reflection of the inter-weaving of multiple cultural perspectives but a symbol of the holistic model of child development promulgated in the document. *Te Whāriki* not only reflects a move away from the long-dominant Cartesian separation of mind and body in ECE, inherited from developmental psychology, but, we would argue, has been a contributor to this trend internationally.

To summarise, the policy problem constructed in the opening sections of *Te Whāriki*, to which the remainder of the document responds, is a complex and demanding mix of cultural aspiration (particularly for Māori), risk minimisation for governments, and a theoretical re-calibration of the early childhood profession. So, who will do this work?

Who does this text seek to persuade?

Policy texts published by governments always and necessarily have a complex mix of intended audiences. In the case of curriculum frameworks, most rhetoric is outward-facing and overlapping (for educators, voters, diverse cultural communities, families) but some is inward-facing (for policy actors within government, Treasury officials, future governments). The need to address these multiple audiences with equal persuasive power can make for some curious grammatical features. The text of

Te Whāriki, for example, is dominated by the use of the *plural present continuous tense* (Kaiako *are aware* …; Toddlers *have opportunities* …; The *environment offers* …). This sentence construction is useful when a rhetor needs to convey both present actions and future plans as in the case of curriculum outcomes, which are typically both descriptive (present) and aspirational (future). Its limitation is that it is also commonly used to express annoyance when repeatedly frustrated (this *isn't getting* any better; email *always interrupts* me). This means that sections of *Te Whāriki* can be read as having a hectoring tone if its assertions are difficult to maintain or not yet realised; for example: "Kaiako and whānau *agree on expectations* regarding appropriate behaviour. Kaiako *are consistent, reliable and realistic* in their expectations and responses, and *they foster harmonious working relationships* with each other and with parents and whānau" (p. 35, emphasis added).

Given that the principal audience for any early childhood curriculum framework is early childhood teachers, it might be expected that the rhetorical grammar of the document's construction would be much less complex and address educators directly (for example, "You will provide …"). However, this would distance the document from other secondary (but crucial) audiences, particularly families. Curriculum frameworks not only have multiple audiences but multiple functions; a framework in ECE may not only guide practice and provide a common language for a field but also offer a professional lexicon for communication with families.

What solutions are proposed within the text?

The overarching solution to the problem of cultural aspiration, risk minimisation, and theoretical re-calibration is the rhetoric of 'quality' signalled in the Minister's Foreword. To enrich the quality *pathos* of the document, and in keeping with countless other curriculum frameworks, *Te Whāriki* uses the quasi-scientific logos of goals and learning outcomes. The document supplements these with sections headed:
- 'Evidence of learning and development' (aligned with the learning outcomes)
- 'Examples of practices that promote these learning outcomes' (with sub-sections for 'Infants', 'Toddlers', and 'Young children')
- 'Considerations for leadership, organisation and practice'
- 'Questions for reflection'.

This combination of outcomes and practices is also found in Australia's *Early Years Learning Framework* (Department of Education, Employment and Workplace Relations, 2009), and reflects two components of the policy solution for ECE.

The first is a solution to the problem, elaborated earlier in this chapter, of how to view development holistically. Historically, early childhood curricula have adopted an all-encompassing definition of curriculum as "all the experiences, activities and events, both direct and indirect, that occur within the ECE setting" (Ministry of Education, 2017, p. 7). This necessarily means that teaching practices are a component of the curriculum (Edwards & Nuttall, 2005), rather than processes that sit apart from the content of the curriculum; in other words, practices of relationships between educators and learners are acknowledged as the cornerstone of the early childhood curriculum. Secondly, and more pragmatically, the inclusion of practice examples within curriculum frameworks acknowledges the uneven qualifications base of the early childhood workforce. In the hands of experienced and well-qualified practitioners, the framework becomes a tool for developing and upskilling colleagues with minimal or no formal qualifications in early childhood practice.

Whether such an approach is a better return on investment than directly financing qualifications in the sector is a discussion for the future. Before then, it is critical that the early childhood field comes to terms with how policy makers are recontextualising the global policy flows that underpin both *Te Whāriki* and the *EYFS*. In other words, how could two such different documents emerge out of the same global policy context? This is the focus of the final section of this chapter.

Te Whāriki, the *EYFS*, and the rhetoric of early years reform

Te Whāriki and the *EYFS* have both been developed and mandated within significant global policy trends in ECE that have signalled a shift away from locally determined approaches to educational frameworks. The most notable of these trends is the political milieu of 'new public management' (Pollitt & Bouckaert, 2011).

One feature of this new public management is for governments to focus on drivers such as educational improvement, raising standards and quality, and defining curriculum goals as a means of extending economic reach and influence into education settings. It is therefore unsurprising that the logos of quality, potential, and strong foundations is common to both frameworks. Likewise, ways of understanding learning and development are conveyed through the interrelationship of curriculum, pedagogy, and assessment in both documents. We argue that such advice is the means by which policy influence on curriculum content, coherence, and control is exercised, in tandem with other regulatory frameworks for the professional preparation and development of the workforce. In moving from broad aims and aspirations to specific goals and outcomes, both documents aim to exert power in terms of what they displace or re-inscribe, the expectations they create, and which effects they aim to produce for practitioners, children, and families.

Although *Te Whāriki* and the *EYFS* share common policy levers and drivers, our rhetorical analysis has also identified important differences in relation to cultures, histories, and ways of constructing families, children, and childhoods. When reflecting on rhetoric-as-essentially-related-to-situation (Bitzer, 1968, pp. 3–4), it is inevitable that *Te Whāriki* positions Māori as Treaty partners with the Crown, not only because this is a legal requirement in Aotearoa New Zealand but also because it reflects the professional commitments of the ECE field. A second important distinction is in the way *Te Whāriki* understands children as embedded within family and community as a source of development, reflected in its holistic image of children and childhoods. The *EYFS*, by contrast, positions families and communities as a backdrop to development, evidenced in its decontextualised approach to assessment based on the quantifiable standards of the ELGs. As other chapters in this volume show, approaches to assessment in ECE in Aotearoa New Zealand have systematically resisted attempts to move to standards-based assessment in the years before school entry.

Finally, both texts seek to guide the work of early childhood professionals, yet the contrasting texts are also reflective of the professional differences in the early childhood workforce between Aotearoa New Zealand and England. In Aotearoa New Zealand, this workforce is largely (though not universally) degree-qualified, whilst the English workforce has a much more diverse qualifications base. Where policy developers can rely on a good standard of knowledge of curriculum, pedagogy, and assessment amongst professionals, the urge to over-specify learning outcomes is less compelling.

In an era when national economic competitiveness persists in tension with increasing calls for recognition of first nations peoples, children's rights, and the work of early years professionals, it is impossible to predict how future iterations of *Te Whāriki* and the *EYFS* will attempt to guide curriculum, pedagogy, and assessment in early years education. One claim we do feel assured in making, however, is that policy makers will continue to see ECE as a policy problem to be regulated and surveilled, irrespective of national context.

References

Asmussen, K., Feinstein, L., Martin, J., & Chowdry, H. (2016). *What works to support parent child interaction in the early years.* London, UK: The Early Intervention Foundation.

Bitzer, L. F. (1968). The rhetorical situation. *Philosophy & Rhetoric, 1*(1), 1–14.

Department for Education. (2017). *Statutory framework for the early years foundation stage. Setting the standards for learning, development and care for children from birth to five.* London, UK: Author.

Department for Education. (2016). Statistical First Release FR 2016 EYFSP 2015–2016. Retrieved from www.gov.uk/government/statistics/early-years-foundation-stage-profile-results-2015-to-2016

Department of Education, Employment and Workplace Relations. (2009). *Being, belonging, becoming — The early years learning framework for Australia.* Canberra, ACT: Author.

Edwards, R., Nicoll, K., Solomon, N., & Usher, R. (2004). *Rhetoric and educational discourse: Persuasive texts?* London, UK: RoutledgeFalmer.

Edwards, S., & Nuttall, J. (2005). Getting beyond the 'what' and the 'how': Problematising pedagogy in early childhood education. *Early Childhood Folio, 9*, 14–18.

Kay, L. (2018). *School readiness: A culture of compliance?* Unpublished doctoral thesis, University of Sheffield, Sheffield, UK.

Ministry of Education. (2017). *Te whāriki: He whāriki mātauranga mō ngā mokopuna o Aotearoa: Early childhood curriculum.* Wellington: Author.

Nuttall, J. (Ed.). (2013). *Weaving te whāriki: Aotearoa New Zealand's early childhood curriculum framework in theory and practice* (2nd ed.). Wellington: NZCER Press.

Office for Standards in Education, Children's Services and Skills [Ofsted]. (2015). *The report of Her Majesty's Chief Inspector of Education, Children's Services and Skills 2015: Early years.* London, UK: Author.

Office for Standards in Education, Children's Services and Skills [Ofsted]. (2016). *Unknown children—destined for disadvantage?* London, UK: Author.

Office for Standards in Education, Children's Services and Skills [Ofsted]. (2017). *Bold beginnings: The Reception curriculum in a sample of good and outstanding primary schools.* London, UK: Author.

Pollitt, C., & Bouckaert, G. (2011). *Public management reform: A comparative analysis—New public management, governance, and the neo-Weberian state* (3rd ed.). Oxford, UK: Oxford University Press.

Sidorkin, A. (2007). Human capital and the labor of learning: A case of mistaken identity. *Educational Theory, 57*(2), 159–170.

Standards and Testing Agency. (2016). *Early years foundation stage profile: 2017 handbook.* London, UK: Author.

Winton, S. (2013). Rhetorical analysis in critical policy research. *International Journal of Qualitative Studies in Education, 26*(2), 158–177.

Wood, E. (2013). Contested concepts in educational play: A comparative analysis of early childhood policy frameworks in New Zealand and England. In J. Nuttall (Ed.), *Weaving te whāriki: Aotearoa New Zealand's early childhood curriculum framework in theory and practice* (2nd ed., pp. 259–276). Wellington: NZCER Press.

Wood, E. (2019). Unbalanced and unbalancing acts in the Early Years Foundation Stage: A critical discourse analysis of policy-led evidence on teaching and play from the Office for Standards in Education in England. *Education 3–13, 47*(7), 784–795.

Wood, E., & Hedges, H. (2016). Curriculum in early childhood education: Critical questions about content, coherence and control. *The Curriculum Journal, 27*(3), 387–405.

Index

ableism   122, 124, 126, 129–31
   see also disabled learners
achievement aims (ngā taumata whakahirahira)   37–38
achievement standards   166, 173, 224–25
   and Communities of Learning | Kāhui Ako   174–75
   disadvantaged children and   9–10, 32, 234
   Early Learning Goals (ELGs)   234–35
   in Nordic curricula   216–18
   resisted in NZ ECE   242
activity theory (AT)   150–51
'additional learning support' labelling   126
Advisory Group on Early Learning (AGEL)   11, 14
   on *Te Whāriki* 1996   59
agency, children's (mana mokopuna)   12–13, 106
age-oriented approach   105, 187, 190, 206, 235
   paradox of   106–07, 112, 114–15
age-related play   237
āiga   93–94
   see also family and whānau
Alvestad, M.   197
'Anthropocene crisis', children and   83, 182–83, 190–91, 221–22
aroha   29–30
art and craft work   138, 236
assemblages   189, 191
assessment   174–75, 216, 242
   age-oriented   236–37
   Early Learning Goals (ELGs)   234–35
   kaupapa Māori and   49
   OECD proposal 'preschool PISA'   13
   teachers' work in   149–50, 150–52 (*see also* Learning Stories)

attachment theory   109
Australia, curriculum development in   197
   Te Whāriki and   195
   see also Early Years Learning Framework (EYLF)
Awareness and Confidence to Work with Te Whāriki (2017)   53–54

Bachmann, M.   16
Bakke, S.   152, 154
Barad, K.   186, 188, 189, 191
Barlow, C.   46
Baylis, S.   110
'becoming' as lifelong development stance   107, 111–14
behaviourism   207
'being' as developmental age-stage   107–11
Bell, Nancy   15, 16, 74
belonging (mana whenua)   38, 40, 94, 182–83, 187, 204
'belonging' concept   207–08
Bennett, J.   186, 189, 190
Berge, J.   197
Best Evidence Syntheses (Ministry of Education)   92–93
bicultural approach of *Te Whāriki*   15, 114, 188
bicultural practices   45, 53
Biesta, G.   112, 167, 216
Bildung   217–19, 223, 225
   'category Bildung'   121
biocultures   73–74, 83
biodiversity of planet   77–78, 83–84
bioecological model, theory   110, 196, 201
Bitzer, L. F.   232–33, 237
Blaise, M.   205
borders, borderlands in transitions   170–71
   see also 'meadows in between'

Bowlby, John   109
Braidotti, Rosi   83, 181, 186, 188–89
Bronfenbrenner, Urie   93, 110, 196, 199, 200, 201
Brown, Vera   135, 140–45

Carr, Margaret   7, 138–39
   Te Whāriki 1996   45, 48, 106, 199
   Te Whāriki 2017   15
case studies
   Gym, a physical activity project   155–56, 158
   Learning Stories assessment portfolio   139–46
   lunch preparation task   144–45
   Making Name Tags, a literacy project   154–55, 156–58
Ceder, S.   191
Centres of Innovation   64
   Roskill South Kindergarten as   137, 139
change, impulse for   233
Cherrington, S.   63, 64, 67
child, family and whānau (shared expertise)   168
child development theories   202, 235
child wellbeing. *See* wellbeing
child–adult relationships   109, 214, 237
child-centred approach   11, 213–14
childhood, concepts of   184, 185, 186–87
childhood studies   183–86
   see also posthumanism
'children,' generic terms for   51, 112–13
children as global citizens   84–85, 135, 139, 218, 222
children as taonga   188, 238
children with disabilities. *See* disabled learners
children's agency   184, 187, 190–91, 219–20
child's perspective in Nordic curricula   219–20
climate change   8, 73, 74, 77, 83
   see also Anthropocene crisis, children and
Code of Professional Responsibility and Standards for the Teaching Profession   98
collective and individual, disjunct between   204
colonisation and its impacts   32, 76–7, 79–80, 208, 238–39
commercialisation of ECE   120–21, 186

communication. *See* language(s); mana reo (communication)
Communities of Learning | Kāhui Ako   164–65, 171–75
Communities of Schools   164
   see also Communities of Learning | Kāhui Ako
community, child and   204
computer software platforms. *See* technology
constructivist theory   202–03
consultation, public on Te Whāriki 2017   15–16
continuity as curriculum concept   164, 169, 174
contribution (mana tangata)   204
Cooper, Maria   19
CORE Education   8, 63
corporatisation. *See* commercialisation of ECE
Craft, Anna   136, 138, 140, 142
critical theory(ies)   196, 201, 202, 206, 207, 208
critical–democratic content   21–23, 224, 225
Csikszentmihalyi, Mihalyi   136
Cubey, P.   64, 67
Cullen, J.   10, 58, 196, 200, 204
cultural competency (of kaiako)   96–97, 103
   and Pacific children   96, 98
cultural expectations of children's development   185
Cultural–historical activity theory (CHAT)   65–66, 67
cultural–historical theory(ies)   204, 205, 206, 207, 208
culturally responsive pedagogy   100–01
curiosity and exploration. *See* mana aotūroa
curricula, post-developmental concepts and   208
curricula and policy texts. *See* Danish ECE curriculum; *Early Years Foundation Stage*; *Early Years Learning Framework*; Te Whāriki 2017; Norwegian ECE curriculum; Nordic ECE
curriculum   12–13, 76–7, 80, 163–64
   biculturalism and   11, 53
   and Communities of Learning   171–74
   and Pasifika ECE   91–92
   spheres of control   199
   theorising of   166–67, 199–202

Index

curriculum design, development 12–14
   changing contexts of 77–79
curriculum documents and policy texts 10
   control and development of 198–99
   key competencies in 174, 235–36
   research methodology 197–98
curriculum longevity 199

Dalli, C. 10, 11
Danish ECE curriculum 214–15, 217, 219–20, 222
   see also Nordic curricula
data in Communities of Learning | Kāhui Ako 172–73
data in curriculum research 197–98
Deaf community 78, 82, 126, 128
Declaration of Independence 1835 (He Whakaputanga o te Rangatiratanga o Nu Tireni) 76
Delafield-Butt, J 109
Deleuze, G. 112
democracy, democratic perspective in Nordic curricula 215, 218, 219
demography 8, 11
   NZ as 'superdiverse' 78, 81
Denmark. *See* Danish ECE curriculum; Nordic curricula
developmental psychology 187, 203, 213–14, 239
developmental theories 205*(fig)*
'developmentally appropriate' concept 105, 106
   Developmentally Appropriate Practice in ECE 200
Dewey, J. 218
digital learning tools. *See* technology
dimensions of strength (ABCDE format) 139
disability, social model of 122–24
   see also ableism
Disability Studies in Education (DSE) 120, 123, 126
disabled learners 9, 10, 124–25, 126, 129–30
   barriers for 120–22
   and teacher agency 121–22
disadvantaged children, achievement of 234
discourse, concept 165
diversity, approaches to 125, 181

nationalism and 222–23
   see also demography
Donaldson, Margaret 108
Duhn, I. 186, 196, 203, 204, 207
Duncan, J. 197
'dunning' (cultural formation) concept 219
Durie, Edward Taihakurei 81
dynamic learning environments 220–21

early childhood care and education (ECCE) 119–22
Early Childhood Convention 1995 25
Early Childhood Education Taskforce 11, 59
Early Learning Goals (ELGs) 235–36
Early Years Foundation Stage (EYFS) 231, 233–37, 242
Early Years Learning Framework (EYLF) 112, 113–14, 197, 203–04
   and longevity 199
   theoretical plurality in 205–06, 205–08
ecological theory approaches 199–201
economic effectiveness 234–35
educare (holistic, wholeness) approach 215
education as socio-political construct 130
Education Conversation 19
Education Hub, The 63
Education Review Office (ERO) 11, 14, 53–54, 59–60
   and Communities of Learning | Kāhui Ako 171–72, 172–73
   and PLD 60, 65
educational achievement. *See* achievement
educational effectiveness 234–35
Egan, K. 166–67
Elkind, D. 106–07
emerging research and theory 202
emotional (whatumanawa) dimension of learning 36–37, 42, 239
engagement, enthusiasm, and élan 139, 143, 145
EYFS goals 235
empowerment (whakamana) 200
English curriculum 236
   see also Early Learning Goals (ELGs); *Early Years Foundation Stage (EYFS)*
'epoch–typical' themes 222–23, 224
   see also Anthropocene crisis; global relationships

equality as policy aspiration *(EYES)* 234
ethnicities, multiple 96–97
   see also demography
exploration. *See* mana aotūroa (curiosity and exploration)

Facebook 8
family and community (whānau tangata) 200, 242
   see also whānau
Fanon, F. 80
Ferris, Miles 84
Fleer, Marilyn 207
'flow' 136
Foucault, M. 165
Freire, Paulo 221
funding 9
   for disabled learners 120–21
   professional learning communities (PLCs) 64–65

Gaztambide-Fernández, R. A. 79
gene activation research 202
Giddens, A. 221
Gilbert, R. 14
Giugni, M. 203, 205
global relationships 191, 221–22
global warming. *See* Anthropocene crisis
Goodfellow, J. 98
group learning environment 109
Grove, G. 49
Gunn, Alexandra (Alex) C. 150–51, 153–58

harakeke (flax) 31, 46
He taonga te tamaiti. Every child a taonga: The strategic plan for early learning 2019–2029 18
He Whakaputanga o te Rangatiratanga o Nu Tireni–Declaration of Independence 76
Hedges, Helen 15, 17, 58, 200, 203, 204
Hellesnes (1976) 219
Heretaunga Kindergarten Association study 92, 97–102
hermeneutics 165–66
Hernandez-Sheets typology 100–01
hinengaro (mental) dimension of learning 36, 41*(fig)*, 239
Hipkins, R. 169

holistic development (kotahitanga) 200, 240–41
home-based ECE 93
human development, knowledge of 114

Immordino-Yang, Mary Helen 139
Indigenous knowledge 74, 79–80
   see also te ao Māori
infant and toddler pedagogy 110–11, 114–15, 187–88
   Western development theory and 61–62
infants and toddlers 105, 112–13
Initial Teacher Education (ITE) programmes 54–55
Inter-relationality 191
intersectionality, concept of 185
intra-action 189, 191
invention as rhetorical approach 232
Investing in Education Success initiative 164

Joy, Mike 83–84

Kāhui Ako. *See* Communities of Learning | Kāhui Ako
kaiako (teachers), role of 202, 204, 214
   agency and disabled learners 121–22, 130–31
   te ao Māori 51–54, 85–86
   kaupapa Māori assessment 49
   assessment practice 151–53
   see also Learning Stories
   in 'category Bilding' 21–22
   and curriculum 164, 167, 196
   whānau partnerships 52–55, 121, 152, 202, 239–40
kaiako, skills and training 13
   engagement with theory 204, 208–09
   funding 10, 62–63
   infant and toddler pedagogy 114–15
   politicisation of 113–14
   professional knowledge shortfalls 58–59, 60
   professional learning and development (PLD) 57–59, 60–62
   qualifications of 62, 85–86, 102–03, 151, 241
   te reo Māori recommendations 85–86

Index

teacher-as-pedagogue 167, 169, 171
teacher-as-technician 167
kaitiaki, kaitiakitanga 15, 46, 85
karakia 36, 46
kaupapa Māori 12, 200
   theory 48–49, 62, 196, 201*ig*
Kehoe, John 37
key competencies 136, 168–69, 174
Klafki, W. 121–22, 218–19
knotworking 57–58, 65–66
   principles of 67
Kōhanga Reo. *See* Te Kōhanga Reo
Kumar, A. 100–02
Kupa, Lealofi 15ft
Kura Kaupapa Māori 8, 35

land. *See* mana whenua
language identity and culture 38, 76–7, 103, 125
   biocultural diversity, demography 8, 74, 81–82
   racism and 80
   see also mana reo
language(s) and communication 50–51, 129, 142
   communication and ableism 126, 127–29
   pedagogical assessment 101–02, 216, 235
   tense (plural present continuous) in *Te Whāriki* 2017 240
   see also New Zealand Sign Language (NZSL)
Latour, B. 183, 191
learner's portfolio 136
   see also Learning Stories
learning, concept of 224
learning, dimensions of 36–37, 139
learning, lifelong (learning how to learn) 136–37
learning environments in Nordic curricula 220–21
learning outcomes in curricula 240
   diminished 224–25
Learning Stories 136–38, 150, 151–52
   case studies 140–45, 154–55, 155–56, 156–58
Learning Stories: Constructing Learner Identities in Early Education 138–39
Lee, Wendy 138–39

Lemke, Jay 136
'linguafaction' 79, 80
literacy 10, 235, 236, 237
lullaby (oriori) Po! Po! 28–29

Mac Naughton, G. 165
Malone, K. 183, 185
mana 46, 47, 127, 188
   of whāriki 46
mana aotūroa (curiosity and exploration) 38, 40, 85, 204
mana atua. *See* wellbeing
mana reo 38, 40, 52, 204
   and ableism 127–29
   literacy and 142
   see also te reo Māori
mana tangata 37–38, 40, 127, 204
mana whenua 182–83
   See also belonging (mana whenua)
Māori, tangata whenua status of 81
Māori children 9, 39, 50, 188, 238
   and bicultural curriculum 53–54
   socioeconomically disadvantaged 10
   (statistics) 33
Māori concepts. *See* te ao Māori
Māori Education Framework 80
Māori immersion education 8, 35, 76, 77, 239
   see also Kura Kaupapa Māori; Te Kōhanga Reo
Māori land, colonisation and 79
Māori school principals' association (Te Akatea) 84
Māori whānau. *See* whānau
Māori worldviews and ECE 54–55
   see also te ao Māori
Mara, Diane 100–02
marae as cultural setting 35
marketisation. *See* commercialisation of ECE
mathematics, numeracy 10, 216, 236, 237
mauri 37, 41, 46
May, Helen 10, 15, 45, 48, 199
McDowell, S. 169
McDowell Clark, R 110
McLachlan, Claire 14–15, 17
Mead, H. 49, 52
Meade, A. 62
'meadows in between' 204, 208, 209

measuring and testing achievement. *See* achievement
mental (hinengaro) dimension of learning 36, 41, 239
metaphors, visual 168
Ministry of Education 8, 60–61, 62–63, 79
  Best Evidence Syntheses 92–93
  and Communities of Learning 172–73
  and United Nations SDGs 85–86
Mitchell, Linda 64, 67, 106, 187
'mokopuna' as generic term 51, 113
multiculturalism and tangata whenua status 81

National Standards 10
National Te Kōhanga Reo Trust 74
nationalism and diversity 222–23
nautilus metaphor 168, 172
neoliberalism 186
Netherlands, The, infant and toddler curriculum in 111
neurological science, neuroscience 61, 108, 139, 182, 202
'new public management' 232, 241
New Zealand Curriculum, The 14, 163–64, 166, 167–69
  see also Te Aho Mātua, Te Marautanga o Aotearoa
New Zealand Planning Council reports 32
New Zealand Sign Language (NZSL) 82, 126, 127–28
ngā hononga (relationships) 190, 200, 201
Ngata, Āpirana (poroporoaki) 28
Ngāti Porou 26–27, 29
Ngāti Raukawa ki te Tonga university 35
Nordic ECE 214–15
Nordic curricula 215, 218, 219
'Nordic model' (social pedagogy approach) 213–14, 217–18
Norwegian ECE curriculum 214, 217, 219–20, 222
numeracy. *See* mathematics, numeracy
Nuttall, Joce 108, 202–03, 207

OECD reports 12–14, 214
Office for Standards in Education (Ofsted) 234
  as arbiter of English ECE 237

'oral language,' concept of 128
oriori (lullaby) Po! Po! 28–29
Our Code, Our Standards 86, 96

Pacific children 9, 10, 93, 98, 102
  culturally responsive pedagogy 97–100
Pacific families and communities 93, 94–95, 96
  see also Pasifika approaches
Papatūānuku 29, 37, 188
paradox of age. *See* age-oriented approach
Parata, Hekia 78, 238
Paratene, Rawiri (poem) 33–35
partnership as policy aspiration *(EYES)* 234
Partnership with Whānau Māori in Early Childhood Services (2012) 53
Pasifika approaches 196, 201, 202
  Heretaunga Kindergarten Association study 97–100
Pasifika concept and terminology 94–95
  'Pasifika umbrella' 92–93
Pasifika ECE 12, 91–103
  barriers to quality 102–03
Pasifika Education Plan 2013–2017 91, 98
Pasifika Education Research Guidelines 98
people, places and things, conceptions of 109, 114, 129, 149, 159, 182, 183, 186–91
Peters, Sally 15, 170
Pewhairangi, Keri 15
photography 152–54, 156
  as assessment tool 159
  children's 137, 140–41
phylogenesis 109
physical (tinana) dimension of learning 36, 40, 40, 239
  EYFS goals 235
Piaget, Jean 108, 203, 207
Play-oriented approach 225, 237
Po! Po! lullaby (oriori) 28–29
poems 31–32, 33–35
  see also oriori; waiata
policy aspirations in *EYFS* 234
policy texts, curricula as 233
possibility thinking 138, 142
post–colonial theory 208
postdevelopmental theory in *EYLF* 205
posthumanism 181–83, 188–89
poststructuralist theory(ies) 206, 207, 208
'preschool PISA' 13

problem finding, problem solving   138–39, 142
professional learning and development (PLD)   62–65, 103, 151
   Eight principles of   64
   ECE organisations, engagement with   60–61
   funding   62–63
   and knotworking culture   66–68
   see also kaiako; professional learning and development (PLD)
professional learning communities (PLCs)   64–65
   and negotiated knotworking   67
progress   135–36
   dimensions of   139
   Learning Stories as progress tracking tool   137
   case study   140–45

quality and consistency as policy aspiration (EYES)   234

racism   35, 80, 84, 86
Rameka, Lesley   15, 62
readiness for school. See school readiness
Reception year (in EYES)   233, 234, 235, 236–37
   see also school readiness
reciprocity (concept)   46
Reedy, Moehau   30, 43
Reedy, Riripeti   27
Reedy, Tamati Muturangi   32, 45, 47, 48, 50–51, 52
Reedy, Tilly Te Koingo   15, 25, 45, 47, 48
   pepeha and heritage   26–28
Reeves, Danneille   150–52, 153–58
reference lists in Te Whāriki   17, 78, 110, 195–96, 197–98, 199–200
refugee children   9, 223
relationships (ngā hononga)   190, 201
research and theory, emerging   201
research studies   140–45
   activity theory and Learning Stories   150–52, 153–58
   see also Heretaunga Kindergarten Association study
rhetorical analysis   231–33
   of Early Years Foundation Stage (EYFS)   233–37
   of Te Whāriki   238–241
Ricoeur, P   165–66
Ritchie, Jennie   11, 200, 202, 205, 207, 208
rites of passage. See transitions
Roskill South Kindergarten   137–38
   case studies (Learning Stories assessment portfolio)   139–46
Royal Commission on Social Policy 1987   32

Samoa and 'Pasifika'   95
Samoan language   81, 94, 142
Sandberg, G.   170
school readiness   232, 235
   and Office for Standards in Education (Ofsted)   237
   'schoolification'   216–17
   see also Reception year; transitions
Scotland, infant and toddler curriculum in   111
security of foundation as policy aspiration (EYES)   234
self-esteem. See mana tangata (contribution, self–esteem)
shared expertise (child, family, and whānau)   169
sign language. See New Zealand Sign Language (NZSL)
Skelton, T.   185
Skutnabb-Kangas, T   74
Smith, A.   14, 18, 184
Smith, G.   48
social media   8
social pedagogy approach. See 'Nordic model'
socio-behaviourist theories   206, 207
sociocultural approaches   93, 149, 186–87
   to curricula   199–201, 235
   to disability and diversity   122
sociocultural theory(ies)   110, 201, 206–07, 206, 207
   and constructivist theory   202–03
   and developmental psychology   203
Soutar, Brenda   15, 106
'special needs'   93, 126
   as barrier to learning   121–22
   see also ableism; disabled learners

spiritual (wairua) dimension of learning 36–37
Starting Strong; Starting Strong 2 (OECD reports) 214, 216
Stenhouse, L. 224
Stewart, G. 188
stories, dictating, and making books (case study) 140–43
  see also Learning Stories
Sumsion, J. 112, 113–14, 197, 207–08
sustainability, ecological 8, 85, 86, 182–83, 223
  see also United Nations Sustainable Development Goals 2030
Swedish ECE curriculum 214–15
  see also Nordic curricula

Tagata Pasefika, Pasifika 81, 93–95
  Tangata Pasifika in *Te Whāriki* 1993 93
  see also Pasifika approaches
Tagata Pasefika: Pacific Islands early childhood centres 93
Talanoa framework, process 91–92, 98–99, 100
tamariki as generic term 113
tangata whenua status of Māori 81
taonga 15, 80
  children as 39, 188, 238
Tapasā: Cultural competencies for teachers of Pacific students 91, 95–97
tapu 46
Tau Mai te Reo Māori language strategy 79
Taylor, A 185
Te Aho Mātua 8, 12
  see also New Zealand Curriculum, The; Te Marautanga o Aotearoa
Te Akatea (Māori school principals' association) 84
te ao Māori 7, 46–47, 84
  Māori children in 28–32, 50
  and *Te Whāriki* 2017 40–42
Te Kete Ipurangi (website) 61, 63
Te Kōhanga Reo 35, 239
  Te Whāriki a te Kōhanga Reo 47, 76
Te Marautanga o Aotearoa 8, 12, 14
  and *Te Whāriki* 12, 14
  see also New Zealand Curriculum, The; Te Aho Mātua
Te Matapuna 29–30

te reo Māori 38, 50–52, 73–74, 80
  competence in 78, 85–86
  'linguafaction' of 79–80
  and New Zealand Sign Language (NZSL) 82
  Tau Mai te Reo strategy 79
  and *Te Whāriki* 2017 45, 47–48, 76–77, 238
Te Rita Maioha Early Childhood New Zealand 97
Te Tiriti o Waitangi 79–80
  differs from The Treaty of Waitangi 74–77
  and reality of bicultural practices 11, 12, 53
  Teaching Council commitments to 85–86
  and tino rangatiratanga 74–75
  and *Te Whāriki* 1996 75
  and *Te Whāriki* 2017 15, 45, 47–48, 74–77, 238
Te Whāriki a te Kōhanga Reo 47, 74, 239
Te Whāriki: Draft Guidelines for Developmentally Appropriate Programmes in Early Childhood Services (*Te Whāriki* 1993) 93, 195–96
Te Whāriki: He Whāriki Mātauranga mō ngā Mokopuna o Aotearoa: Early Childhood Curriculum (*Te Whāriki* 1996) 186, 196
  critiques, reports 10–13, 17–19, 58, 60
  differences 75, 93–94, 198
  refresh 8, 9–10, 14–17
  theoretical framework of 199–200, 202–03
  see also reference lists
Te Whāriki: He Whāriki Mātauranga mō ngā Mokopuna o Aotearoa: Early Childhood Curriculum (*Te Whāriki* 2017) 45, 98, 166, 197, 232, 242
  ableism, disabled learners 121–22, 124–25
  and te ao Māori 39, 40–42(*fig*), 51–53
  bicultural approach 76–7, 188
  childhood, concepts of 105, 108, 186
  critiques and reviews 60, 86, 191, 195, 238–241
  and *Early Years* (EYFS) 242
  differences from earlier versions 110, 198
  and *The New Zealand Curriculum* 163–64, 167–69

a Nordic perspective   223–25
positioning of Māori text   45
process   16–17, 78–79
roles of   196–97, 239–40
and Tagata Pasefika   94–95
tense (plural present continuous) in   240
theory and pedagogy   61–62, 196, 200–01, 203–04
and Te Tiriti o Waitangi   74–77, 238–39
Te Whatu Pōkeka   53
Teacher–Led Innovation Funded projects (TLIFs)   65
teachers. *See* kaiako
Teaching and Learning Resource Initiatives (TLRI)   65
Teaching Council of Aotearoa New Zealand   60, 65
and United Nations SDGs   85–86
technology(ies)   8, 63, 140–41, 150, 159
assistive communication   128–29
computer software platforms   151–54
see also photography
Tesar, Marek   19, 184
Teu Le Va   91–92, 98, 99, 100
theories, diversity, plurality of   201–02*fig*, 202–04
Thornton, K.   64, 67
tikanga Māori   45, 52–53
tinana. *See* physical (tinana) dimension of learning
tino rangatiratanga   76
tīpuna   46, 49
Tivaevae as pedagogical model   96
transitions   110, 170–71
see also borders; meadows in between; school readiness
Treaty of Waitangi   32, 74–77
see also Te Tiriti o Waitangi
Trevarthen, C.   109, 220
Tuck, E.   79
tūrangawaewae   27, 29
Tyler, R. W.   223–24

understanding the world (ELG)   236
United Nations Convention on the Rights of Persons with Disabilities (UNCRPD)   123–24, 130
United Nations Convention on the Rights of the Child   110, 218

United Nations Sustainable Development Goals 2030 (SDGs)   13, 74, 83–84, 85–86
'Unuhia te rito ō te harakeke' (poem)   31–32

'vergesellschaftung'   111
video. *See* photography
Vygotsky, Lev   65, 110, 200

waiata   28–29, 30, 31
see also poems
wairua dimension of learning   36–37, 41, 239
Waitangi Tribunal 1983 ruling on Te Tiriti o Waitangi   76
weaver, weaving metaphor   46–47, 67
see also knotworking; whāriki   46–47
Weaving Te Whāriki (2012)   231
wellbeing (mana atua)   37, 40, 125, 146
in te ao Māori   50, 53, 84
falling standards of   9–10, 18
Pasifika approaches to   100, 102
as *Te Whāriki* strand   93, 94, 204, 224
Wenmoth, D.   14
Wendt Samu, T.   92-93
Western development theory   61–62
whakamana   127
whakapapa   46
whakataukī in *Te Whāriki*   36, 46, 49, 51, 67, 188, 238
function of   49–50
whānau   48–49, 53, 119
Learning Stories and portfolios   142, 145, 155
partnerships and relationships   11, 53, 95, 131
and technologies   152
see also kaiako; whānau partnerships
whāriki   7, 46–47
as metaphor   168, 238, 239
whatumanawa. *See* emotional (whatumanawa) dimension of learning
whenua, concept. *See* mana whenua
'Whiringa Wairua' (waiata)   30
White, E. Jayne   115, 119, 204
Winton, S.   232
Wong, S.   207–08
Wood, Elizabeth   231, 237
Working with Te Whāriki (2013)   53

www.ingramcontent.com/pod-product-compliance
Lightning Source LLC
Chambersburg PA
CBHW080802300426
44114CB00020B/2799